Don't wait

p108 - 112

Love vs attachment p111

p17 o roles

p128   helping, fixing or serving

p137   as we mature access to a less reactive more
         discerning wisdom

p168   correcting statements

p175   when compassion is truly present in a room
         a great deal of pain + suffering is likely to show up
         in response. Pain wants to expose itself to
         the healing agent of lovingkindness

p200   breathing is a microcosm of life itself

p215   when fear speaks, courage is the heart's answer

p252   a good teacher doesn't tell you what to know,
         he or she shows you how to see

p255   a willingness to not know is at times our
         greatest asset

p270   Dying happens on two levels simultaneously ...
         physical + spiritual. The body is closing down while
         consciousness is opening up

"Frank Ostaseski is a pioneer in mindful care at the end of life. He embodies the wisdom and compassion he shares in these magical and compelling pages. You feel it instantly, because it is real, and it is really about you and your life."

—**Jon Kabat-Zinn**, founder of MBSR and author of
Full Catastrophe Living and *Coming to Our Senses*

"These moving teachings can open your heart and change your life. For decades, Frank Ostaseski has been a compassionate guide to thousands of people facing death. In *The Five Invitations,* he shares his timeless wisdom, beautifully, as a blessing to all."

—**Jack Kornfield**, international Buddhist teacher and
author of *A Path with Heart*

"As a physician, I often work with people who view death as the ultimate isolating experience, solitary confinement for eternity—the ultimate dark terror. In this extraordinary, eloquent, and powerful book, Frank Ostaseski reveals how we can transform this darkness into a bright light (brilliant in every way), a return to the source, the ultimate in intimacy, healing, and meaning—the essence of love. What could be better than that?"

—**Dean Ornish, M.D.**, *New York Times* bestselling
author of *The Spectrum*

"When I set out to produce my PBS series on death and dying—*On Our Own Terms*—I called Frank Ostaseski. As cofounder of the Zen Hospice Project, he was known far and wide as a wise and tender shepherd of the dying, and I considered him the one person without whose counsel the series would have been incomplete. Frank was cautious; filming the death of another human being while protecting the sacredness of the moment and the dignity of the individual could, he knew, violate the intimacy of hospice care. He finally agreed, and the experiences he shared on camera are among the most moving and instructive of the series. In one of those inexplicable convergences of fate, we were actually in the middle of the interview when word came of my mother's death on the far side of the continent. I have never forgotten his incredible compassion and comfort, as you, dear reader, will never forget this book."

—**Bill Moyers**, American journalist, social commentator, and producer of
On Our Own Terms: Moyers on Death and Dying

"Exquisitely profound and gut-wrenchingly real, I'm not sure a wiser book has been written in the digital age. Frank Ostaseski's storytelling helped me to see that to step fully into life we need to embrace death as an adventure rather than as an adversary."

—**Chip Conley**, author of the *New York Times* bestseller *Emotional Equations*
and head of Global Hospitality and Strategy at AirBnB

"Our capacity to live and love fully awakens as we open our hearts to death. Frank Ostaseski guides us in this opening with a luminous wisdom derived from his own full immersion in the journey. Please give yourself to *The Five Invitations*; these teachings reveal the mystery and beauty of our essential Being."

—**Tara Brach, Ph.D,** author of *Radical Acceptance* and *True Refuge*

"Frank Ostaseski is a very dear friend. I have worked in the field of death and dying close to him and this book represents the distillation of many years of his efforts. He shows us that if you are to die consciously, there's no time like the present to prepare. This book is a loving, compassionate reminder that the best preparation for death is a life fully lived."

—**Ram Dass**, international spiritual teacher and author of *Be Here
Now* and *Still Here: Embracing Aging, Changing, and Dying*

"This book is an inspiring, comforting, and accessible gift."

—**Sogyal Rinpoche**, spiritual master and author
of the international bestseller *The Tibetan Book
of Living and Dying*

"A powerful book by my good friend Frank Ostaseski, who has brought together wisdom and compassion in his life and his long years of work with the dying. We will all be enriched, inspired, and edified by his extraordinary book on how facing death can enrich our life."

—**Roshi Joan Halifax, Ph.D.**, founder and abbot at the Upaya
Zen Center and author of *Being with Dying: Cultivating
Compassion and Fearlessness in the Presence of Death*

"This book is deep, right and rare. The compelling lessons shared in *The Five Invitations* are valuable to people at any phase of life. Whether facing your own imminent death or that of a loved one, navigating a crisis, or looking to embrace and enjoy living your life more fully, you will find the wisdom lovingly offered in these pages inspiring and enlightening."

—**SARK,** artist and coauthor of *Succulent Wild Love*

"Frank Ostaseski is one of the great contemporary teachers of ancient Buddhist wisdom and practice. Over the years, his teachings have informed both my meditative and clinical practices. Now, through *The Five Invitations* a broader audience can benefit from Frank's insights, soulful perspectives, and practical guidance. What a gift!"

—**Ira Byock M.D.**, international leader in palliative care,
Chief Medical Officer for the Institute for Human Caring of
Providence Health and Services, author of *The Best Care Possible:
A Physician's Quest to Transform Care Through the End of Life*

"Stephen always had great trust in Frank Ostaseski's good heart. As his teacher and longtime friend he encouraged Frank to write and share his wisdom on conscious living and conscious dying. Finally, we have this gift to the world. This book is a beautiful, loving gift and a manifestation of a lifetime of selfless service and compassionate care."

—**Ondrea Levine**, coauthor with Stephen Levine
of *Who Dies?: An Investigation of Conscious
Living and Conscious Dying*

"As a physician and neurosurgeon, I have learned that those who have truly lived are those that understand death as an integral part of life. In Frank Ostaseski's profound book, *The Five Invitations*, he shares this reality, giving us insights and wisdom on the nature of dying but, more importantly, on how to truly live."

—**James R. Doty, M.D.**, professor of neurosurgery, founder and director of the Center for Compassion and Altruism Research and Education, Stanford University School of Medicine, and *New York Times* bestselling author of *Into the Magic Shop: A Neurosurgeon's Quest to Discover the Mysteries of the Brain and the Secrets of the Heart*

"*The Five Invitations* is a remarkable book, one that is deeply needed by all of us. Five invitations to live our lives fully, in the present, all the way through. Frank Ostaseski, whose journey spans more than three decades of creating and participating in the hospice movement, imparts timeless wisdom that should inform our every day: how to embrace uncertainty and live with joy, peace, and acceptance. This is not a book about death, it's a book about life and living. Buy it, share it, live it—I know I will."

—**Henry S. Lodge, M.D.**, Robert Burch Family Professor of Medicine, and coauthor of the Younger Next Year series

"How to die and how to be with the dying are questions everyone faces. Here are sharp, insightful answers from one of the great end-of-life counselors."

—**Stewart Brand**, creator of the *Whole Earth Catalog*

"[Frank Ostaseski] has found the space where awareness of death is revealed as a powerful elixir for living more abundantly, and he shares that secret brilliantly in this landmark book. If you want to live fully and free from fear, read it and give yourself and those who love you a rare gift!"

—**Robert A. F. Thurman**, professor of religion, Columbia University, and author of *Infinite Life*

"Frank Ostaseski inspires us to live with joy by fully embracing all facets of life, including our dying. With heartfelt compassion and wisdom gathered over thirty years as a Buddhist teacher and hospice founder he helps us understand that love matters most."

—**Chade-Meng Tan**, Google's "Jolly Good Fellow" and author of *Joy on Demand* and *Search Inside Yourself*

"This is a gem of a book! With a lifetime of inspiring service and deep spiritual wisdom to draw from, Frank Ostaseski has given us all a gift straight from the heart."

—**James Baraz**, author of *Awakening Joy: 10 Steps to Happiness* and cofounding teacher at Spirit Rock Meditation Center

"Frank Ostaseski speaks with clear wisdom and deep compassion. Sharing stories and insights from his decades of working with people at the very end of their lives, his ultimate revelation has to do with how meaningful, in both our living and our dying, is the capacity to be open to and present in grace. His words offer much worthy of contemplation and his service to all of us is worthy of deep respect."

—**Kathleen Dowling Singh**, author of *The Grace in Dying: How We Are Transformed Spiritually As We Die* and *The Grace in Aging: Awaken As You Grow Older*

THE FIVE

INVITATIONS

*Discovering What Death
Can Teach Us About Living Fully*

FRANK OSTASESKI

Foreword by Rachel Naomi Remen, M.D.

FLATIRON
BOOKS
NEW YORK

This book is dedicated to the men, women, and children
who gave me the blessing of being with their dying.
My true teachers.

And
to Stephen Levine, heart friend.

THE FIVE INVITATIONS. Copyright © 2017 by Frank Ostaseski. Foreword
copyright © 2017 by Rachel Naomi Remen. All rights reserved.
Printed in the United States of America. For information, address
Flatiron Books, 175 Fifth Avenue, New York, N.Y. 10010.

www.flatironbooks.com

The Library of Congress Cataloging-in-Publication Data is available upon request.

ISBN 978-1-250-07465-2 (hardcover)
ISBN 978-1-250-07466-9 (e-book)

Our books may be purchased in bulk for promotional, educational, or business use.
Please contact your local bookseller or the Macmillan Corporate and Premium
Sales Department at 1-800-221-7945, extension 5442, or by e-mail at
MacmillanSpecialMarkets@macmillan.com.

First Edition: March 2017

10 9 8 7 6 5 4 3 2 1

CONTENTS

FOREWORD

All tempest has, like a navel, a hole in its middle,
through which a gull can fly in silence.
—HAROLD WITTER BYNNER

As a physician, I was taught that death was life's opposite, a physical event marked by specific physiological changes. I was trained to "manage the dying," to prolong life whenever possible, and to control pain and suffering when it was not. The pain of survivors was hardest to manage, but in time, most people took comfort in the thought of an afterlife and found a way to move on. Despite a great many experiences with those who were dying or who died, I and my fellow professionals had little or no emotional reaction to death and certainly no curiosity about it. Such curiosity would have been seen as morbid. The idea that death might offer the living something vitally important would have been perceived as simply bizarre. In a less extreme form, our professional stance was a reflection of a culture-wide attitude toward death and the dying.

This is the environment in which Frank Ostaseski began his courageous and pioneering work, and first offered his genius of seeing each death as unique and meaningful, as an opportunity for wisdom and healing—not only for the dying, but also for those who live on. The great depth of experience he brings to this book can only be accumulated by those who are fearless, who have found their way to stillness and presence, who possess an ability to connect to the heart and soul of others, and who are blessed with the gift of story for sharing the road traveled. *The Five Invitations* is filled with stories so profound that they function as a compass, a way to travel an unknown road to a desired destination. Many of the true stories in this book can be read as parables, wisdom stories that enable us all to live more purposefully and wisely in many diverse circumstances.

I first encountered death at the time I was born. I weighed 2.1 pounds and spent the first six months of my life between worlds, in an incubator, untouched by human hands. I encountered death again at fifteen, when my chronic illness declared itself in the night and I was rushed unconscious to a hospital in New York City, where I spent almost a year in a coma. Most of the people I know well I have met on the edge between life and death, magnetized there as I have been by the deep wish to glimpse what is most real. Frank Ostaseski is one of these people—my colleague, my fellow traveler, my teacher. In *The Five Invitations*, he has written a beautiful book about life on the edge—about all of life, really—and invited us to join him in the space between the worlds. To sit at the table of unknowing. To wonder together. To become wise.

My grandfather was a Kabbalist and by nature a mystic. For him, life was a constant dialogue with the soul of the world. All events were doorways, and the world revealed itself constantly. He was able to see the most profound of realizations in the most ordinary of occurrences. Most of us do not have this gift. We need something larger, something that stops us in our habits of seeing and hearing with more authority, something that challenges our habitual perceptions and ways of thinking in order to recognize the true nature of things. Death is one such doorway. Awareness is the great gift of death. For many people, authentic life starts at the time of death—not our own death, but someone else's.

Simply put, the nature of life itself is holy. We are always on holy ground. Yet this is rarely a part of our daily experience. For most of us, the sacred shows up like a flash of lightning, a sharp inhalation between one unnoticed breath and the next. The daily fabric that covers what is most real is commonly mistaken for what is most real until something tears a hole in it and reveals the true nature of the world. Yet the invitation to become aware is commonplace. In his brilliant book *Small Is Beautiful*, E. F. Schumacher suggests that we can see only what we have grown an eye to see. He proposes that the endless debate about the nature of the world is not about differences but simply about the differing capacity of our eyes.

The book that you are holding offers simple, powerful practices to enable you to see what is most real in the midst of what is most familiar. It is an opportunity to see beyond the ordinary. Unlike many books about death and dying presently available, this book is not about a theory or a cosmology—either traditional or personal. It is not someone's ideas or beliefs about what the experience of dying is and means. This book is a sharing of deep experience by a superbly aware observer. It invites you to grow your eyes.

My grandfather taught me that a teacher is not a wise man, but a pointing finger directing our attention to the reality that surrounds us. Frank Ostaseski is such a teacher. This book will remind you of many things. It has reminded me of how few things really matter and how much they matter. How often we go spiritually hungry in the midst of plenty, and how many, many teachers surround us, patiently offering all that we need in order to live wisely and well. I am reminded that death, like love, is intimate, and that intimacy is the condition of the deepest learning. I am reminded, too, of the simplicity of the true teacher, and the power of story to include us in a web of connection far more profound than the superficial things that divide us. Lastly, I am reminded that we are all invited to the dance. I feel a deep gratitude for the invitation to participate fully in life, which is so graciously offered here. So will you.

Ultimately, death is a close and personal encounter with the unknown. Many of those who have died and been revived by the skills of science tell us that the experience has revealed to them the purpose of life. This is not to become wealthy or famous or powerful. The purpose of every life is to grow in wisdom and learn to love better. If this is your purpose, then *The Five Invitations* is the book for you.

RACHEL NAOMI REMEN, M.D.
Author of *Kitchen Table Wisdom* and *My Grandfather's Blessings*

THE TRANSFORMATIVE POWER OF DEATH

Love and death are the great gifts that are given to us;
mostly, they are passed on unopened.

—RAINER MARIA RILKE

Life and death are a package deal. You cannot pull them apart.

In Japanese Zen, the term *shoji* translates as "birth-death." There is no separation between life and death other than a small hyphen, a thin line that connects the two.

We cannot be truly alive without maintaining an awareness of death.

Death is not waiting for us at the end of a long road. Death is always with us, in the marrow of every passing moment. She is the secret teacher hiding in plain sight. She helps us to discover what matters most. And the good news is we don't have to wait until the end of our lives to realize the wisdom that death has to offer.

Over the past thirty years, I have sat on the precipice of death with a few thousand people. Some came to their deaths full of disappointment. Others blossomed and stepped through that door full of wonder. What made the difference was the willingness to gradually live into the deeper dimensions of what it means to be human.

To imagine that at the time of our dying we will have the physical strength, emotional stability, and mental clarity to do the work of a lifetime is a ridiculous gamble. This book is an invitation—five invita-tions, actually—to sit down with death, to have a cup of tea with her, to let her guide you toward living a more meaningful and loving life.

Reflecting on death can have a profound and positive impact not just on how we die, but on how we live. In the light of dying, it's easy to dis-tinguish between the tendencies that lead us toward wholeness, and those that incline us toward separation and suffering. The word *wholeness* is related to "holy" and "health," but it is not a vague, homogenous one-ness. It is better expressed as interconnectedness. Each cell in our bodies is a part of an organic, interdependent whole that must work in harmony to maintain good health. Similarly, everybody and everything exists in a constant interplay of relationships that reverberates throughout the entire system, affecting all the other parts. When we take action that ignores this basic truth, we suffer and create suffering. When we live mindfully of it, we support and are supported by the wholeness of life.

The habits of our lives have a powerful momentum that propels us toward the moment of our death. The obvious question arises: What habits do we want to create? Our thoughts are not harmless. Thoughts manifest as actions, which in turn develop into habits, and our habits ul-timately harden into character. Our unconscious relationship to thoughts can shape our perceptions, trigger reactions, and predetermine our rela-tionship to the events of our lives. We can overcome the inertia of these patterns by becoming mindful of our views and beliefs, and by doing so, we make a conscious choice to question those habitual tendencies. Fixed views and habits silence our minds and incline us toward life on automatic pilot. Questions open our minds and express the dynamism of being human. A good question has heart, arising from a deep love to discover what is true. We will never know who we are and why we are here if we do not ask the uncomfortable questions.

Without a reminder of death, we tend to take life for granted, often becoming lost in endless pursuits of self-gratification. When we keep death at our fingertips, it reminds us not to hold on to life too tightly. Maybe we take ourselves and our ideas a little less seriously. We let go a little more easily. When we recognize that death comes to everyone, we appreciate that we are all in the same boat, together. This helps us to become a bit kinder and gentler with one another.

We can harness the awareness of death to appreciate the fact that we are alive, to encourage self-exploration, to clarify our values, to find meaning, and to generate positive action. It is the impermanence of life that gives us perspective. As we come in contact with life's precarious nature, we also come to appreciate its preciousness. Then we don't want to waste a minute. We want to enter our lives fully and use them in a responsible way. Death is a good companion on the road to living well and dying without regret.

The wisdom of death has relevance not only for those who are dying and their caregivers. It can also help you deal with loss, or a situation in which you feel caught in small-mindedness or are feeling out of control—whether you are going through a breakup or divorce, coping with an illness, a layoff, the shattering of a dream, a car accident, or even a fight with a child or colleague.

Shortly after the famous psychologist Abraham Maslow suffered a near-fatal heart attack, he wrote in a letter: "The confrontation with death—and the reprieve from it—makes everything look so precious, so sacred, so beautiful that I feel more strongly than ever the impulse to love it, to embrace it, and to let myself be overwhelmed by it. My river has never looked so beautiful . . . Death, and its ever-present possibility, makes love, passionate love, more possible."

I am not romantic about dying. It is hard work. Maybe the hardest work we will ever do in this life. It doesn't always turn out well. It can be sad, cruel, messy, beautiful, and mysterious. Most of all it is normal. We all go through it.

None of us get out of here alive.

As a companion to people who are dying, a teacher of compassionate care, and the co-founder of the Zen Hospice Project, most of the folks I have worked with were ordinary people. Individuals coming face-to-face with what they imagined was impossible or unbearable, walking toward their own deaths or caring for someone they loved who was now dying. Yet most found within themselves and the experience of dying the resources, insight, strength, courage, and compassion to meet the impossible in extraordinary ways.

Some of the people I worked with lived in terrible conditions—in rat-infested hotels or on park benches behind city hall. They were alcoholics, prostitutes, and homeless folks who barely survived on the margins of society. Often they wore the face of resignation or were angry about their loss of control. Many had lost all trust in humanity.

Some were from cultures I did not know, speaking languages I could not understand. Some had a deep faith that carried them through difficult times, while others had sworn off religion. Nguyen feared ghosts. Isaiah was comforted by "visits" from his dead mother. There was a hemophiliac father who had contracted the HIV virus from a blood transfusion. Years before his illness, he had disowned his gay son. But at the end of life, father and son were both dying of AIDS, lying next to one another in twin beds in a shared bedroom, being cared for by Agnes, the father's wife and the son's mother.

Many people I worked with died in their early twenties, having hardly begun their lives. But there was also a woman I cared for named Elizabeth, who, at ninety-three, asked, "Why has death come for me so soon?" Some were clear as bells, whereas others couldn't recall their own names. Some were surrounded by the love of family and friends. Others were entirely alone. Alex, without the support of loved ones, became so confused from his AIDS dementia that he climbed out onto the fire escape one night and froze to death.

We cared for cops and firefighters who had saved numerous lives; nurses who had tended to the pain and breathlessness of others; doctors who had pronounced patients dead of the same illnesses that now were ravaging their own bodies. People with political power, acquired wealth, and good health insurance. And refugees with little more than the shirts on their backs. They died of AIDS, cancer, lung disease, kidney failure, and Alzheimer's.

For some, dying was a great gift. They made reconciliations with their long-lost families, they freely expressed their love and forgiveness, or they found the kindness and acceptance they had been looking for their whole lives. Still others turned toward the wall in withdrawal and hopelessness and never came back again.

All of them were my teachers.

These people invited me into their most vulnerable moments and made it possible for me to get up close and personal with death. In the process, they taught me how to live.

No one alive really understands death. But as one woman who was close to death once told me, "I see the exit signs much clearer than you do." In a way, nothing can prepare you for death. Yet everything that you have done in your life, everything that has been done to you, and what you have learned from it all can help.

In a beautiful short story, the Nobel laureate Rabindranath Tagore describes the meandering paths between villages in India. Skipping along, guided by their imaginations or a winding stream, a detour to a beautiful overlook, or stepping around a sharp rock, barefoot children wove zigzag trails through the countryside. When they grew older, got sandals, and began carrying heavy loads, the routes became narrow, straight, and purposeful.

I walked barefoot for years. I didn't follow a linear path to this work; I meandered. It was a journey of continuous discovery. I had little training and no degrees save a Red Cross lifesaving certificate that is surely now expired. I followed the Braille method, feeling my way along. Staying close to my intuition, trusting that listening is the most powerful way to connect, bringing forward the refuge of silence, and letting my heart be broken open. These are the ways I discovered what really helps.

Death and I have been longtime companions. My mother died when

I was a teenager and my father just a few years later. But I had lost them years before the events of their deaths. They were both alcoholics, and so my childhood was characterized by years of chaos, neglect, violence, misguided loyalty, guilt, and shame. I became adept at walking on eggshells, being my mother's confidant, finding hidden liquor bottles, clashing with my father, keeping secrets, and growing up too quickly. So in a way, their deaths came as a relief. My suffering was a sword that cut two ways. I grew up feeling ashamed, frightened, lonely, and unlovable. Yet that same suffering helped me to empathetically connect with others' pain, and that became part of my calling to move toward situations that many others tend to avoid.

Buddhist practice, with its emphasis on impermanence, the moment-to-moment arising and passing of every conceivable experience, was an early and important influence for me. Facing death is considered fundamental in the Buddhist tradition. It can mature wisdom and compassion, and strengthen our commitment to awakening. Death is seen as a final stage of growth. Our daily practices of mindfulness and compassion cultivate the wholesome mental, emotional, and physical qualities that prepare us to meet the inevitable. Through the application of these skillful means, I learned not to be incapacitated by the suffering of my earlier life, but rather to allow it to form the ground of compassion within me.

When my son Gabe was about to be born, I wanted to understand how to bring his soul into the world. So I signed up for a workshop with Elisabeth Kübler-Ross, the renowned psychiatrist from Switzerland who was best known for her groundbreaking work on death and dying. She had helped many leave this life; I figured she might teach me how to invite my son into his.

Elisabeth was fascinated with the idea and took me under her wing. She invited me to attend more programs over the years, although she didn't give me much instruction. I'd sit quietly in the back of the room and learn by watching the way she worked with people who were facing death or grieving tragic losses. This fundamentally shaped the way I later accompanied people in hospice care. Elisabeth was skillful, intuitive, and often opinionated, but above all, she demonstrated how to love those she served, without reservation or attachment. Sometimes the anguish in the room was so overwhelming that I would meditate in order to calm myself or do compassion practices, imagining that I could transform the pain I was witnessing.

One rainy night after a particularly difficult day, I was so shaken as I walked back to my room that I collapsed to my knees in a mud puddle and started to weep. My attempts at taking away the participants' heartache were just a self-defense strategy, a way of trying to protect myself from suffering.

Just then, Elisabeth came along and picked me up. She brought me back to her room for a coffee and a cigarette. "You have to open yourself up and let the pain move through you," Elisabeth said. "It's not yours to hold." Without this lesson, I don't think I could have stayed present, in a healthy way, with the suffering I would witness in the decades to come.

Stephen Levine, a poet and Buddhist teacher, was another influential figure in my life. My primary teacher and good friend for thirty years, he was a compassionate rebel as well as an intuitive and authentic guide who embraced multiple spiritual traditions while skillfully avoiding the dogma of any one approach. Stephen and his wife, Ondrea, were true pioneers, leading a gentle revolution in the way we care for those who are dying. Much of what we created at Zen Hospice Project was an expression of their teachings.

Stephen showed me that it was possible to gather up the suffering in my life, use it as *grist for the mill*, and alchemically change it into the fuel for selfless service—all without making a big deal about it. In the beginning, I modeled my work and sometimes my behavior on his example, as devout students tend to do. He was very kind and generously lent me his voice until I could find my own.

How do we come to be where we find ourselves? Life accumulates, exposes us to opportunities for learning, and if we are lucky, we pay attention.

While traveling in Mexico and Guatemala in my early thirties, I volunteered to serve Central American refugees who had suffered enormous hardships, and I witnessed horrible deaths. Back in San Francisco in the 1980s, the AIDS crisis hit hard. Nearly thirty thousand local residents were diagnosed with HIV. I worked on the front lines as a home health aide and cared for too many friends who died of this devastating virus.

It quickly became clear that my individual response wasn't enough. So in 1987, working together with my dear friend Martha deBarros and a handful of others, we started the Zen Hospice Project. It was, in fact, Martha's idea to create the hospice, and a brilliant one at that. She was the mother who gave birth to the program through the auspices of the San Francisco Zen Center.

The Zen Hospice Project was the first Buddhist hospice in America, a fusion of spiritual insight and practical social action. We believed there was a natural match between the Zen practitioners who were cultivating a "listening heart" through meditation practice, and those who needed to be heard—people who were dying. We had no agenda and few plans, but ultimately we did train a thousand volunteers. While the stories I share are primarily about my own encounters, no one person created Zen Hospice. We all did it together. A community of great hearts committed to a shared purpose responding to a call to service.

While we wanted to draw on the wisdom of the 2,500-year-old Zen tradition, we had no interest in pushing any dogma or promoting a strictly Buddhist way of dying. My slogan was "Meet 'em where they're at." I encouraged our caregivers to support the patients in discovering what they needed. We rarely taught people to meditate. Nor did we impose our ideas about death or dying. We figured the individuals we served would show us how they needed to die. We created a beautiful and receptive environment in which the residents felt loved and supported, and where they were free to explore who they were and what they believed.

I learned that the activities of caregiving are themselves quite ordinary. You make soup, give a back rub, change soiled sheets, help with medications, listen to a lifetime of stories lived and now ending, show up as a calm and loving presence. Nothing special. Just simple human kindness, really.

Yet I soon discovered that these everyday activities, when taken as a practice of awareness, can help awaken us from our fixed views and habits of avoidance. Whether we are the ones making the beds or the ones confined to them, we have to confront the uncertain nature of this life. We become aware of the fundamental truth that everything comes and goes: every thought, every lovemaking, every life. We see that dying is in the life of everything. Resisting this truth leads to pain.

Other pivotal experiences shaped the way I meet suffering and informed my understanding of what death can teach us about life. I joined other spiritual leaders and took a deep plunge into human suffering by helping to facilitate a unique retreat at Auschwitz-Birkenau. I led grief groups, counseled countless people through terminal illnesses, guided retreats for people with life-threatening illness, and facilitated many— perhaps too many—memorial services.

In the midst of it all, I was a father to four children, helping them grow into remarkable adults who now have children of their own. I can tell you that raising four teenagers at the same time was often a lot tougher than taking care of dying patients.

In 2004, I founded the Metta Institute to foster mindful and compassionate end-of-life care. I gathered up great teachers, including Ram Dass, Norman Fischer, Rachel Naomi Remen, M.D., and others, to form a world-class faculty. Ours was a legacy project aimed at reclaiming the soul in caregiving and restoring a life-affirming relationship to dying.

We have trained hundreds of health care professionals and also created a national support network of clinicians, educators, and advocates for those facing life-threatening illness.

Finally, several years ago, I faced my own personal health crisis—a heart attack that brought me face-to-face with mortality. The experience showed me how different the view was from the other side of the sheets. It made me even more empathetic to the struggles I have witnessed my students, clients, friends, and family members face.

So often in life, we move beyond what we imagined we were capable of, and breaking through that boundary propels us toward transformation. Someone once said, "Death comes not to you, but to someone else whom the gods make ready." This sentiment feels true to me. The person I am today, living in this story, is not exactly the same person as the one who will die. Life and death will change me. I will be different in some very fundamental ways. For something new to emerge within us, we must be open to change.

In general, as a society we are more open to a discussion of death than we were in years past. There are more books on the subject; hospice care is well integrated on the continuum of health care; we have advance directives and do-not-resuscitate orders. Physician-assisted death is now legal in several states and countries.

However, the predominant view is still that dying is a medical event and that the most we can hope for is to make the best of a bad situation. I have witnessed the pain of people going to their deaths feeling themselves to be victims of circumstance, suffering ill consequences because of factors that were beyond their control, or worse yet, believing that they were the sole cause of their problems. As a result, too many people die in distress, guilt, and fear. We can do something about that.

When you live a life illuminated by the fact of your death, it informs your choices. Most of us have images of dying at home surrounded by those we love and those who love us, comforted by the familiar. Yet that is rarely how it goes. While seven out of ten Americans say they would prefer to die at home, 70 percent of Americans die in a hospital, nursing home, or long-term-care facility.

The cliché says, "We die as we live." In my experience, that is not entirely true. But suppose we lived a life that turned toward what death had to teach, rather than trying only to avoid the inevitable? We can learn a lot about living fully when we get comfortable sitting with death.

Suppose we stopped compartmentalizing death, cutting it off from life. Imagine if we regarded dying as a final stage of growth that held an unprecedented opportunity for transformation. Could we turn toward death like a master teacher and ask, "How, then, shall I live?"

The language we use plays an important role in our relationship with death and dying. I do not like to use the phrase *the dying*. Dying is an experience that people go through, but it is not their identity. Like other generalizations, when we group all the people living through a particular experience into a single batch, we miss out on the uniqueness the experience—and what each individual going through it—has to offer.

Dying is inevitable and intimate. I have seen ordinary people at the end of their lives develop profound insights and engage in a powerful process of transformation that helped them to emerge as someone larger, more expansive, and much more real than the small, separate selves they had previously taken themselves to be. This is not a fairy-tale happy ending that contradicts the suffering that came before, but rather a transcendence of tragedy. The discovery of this capacity regularly occurs for many people in the final months, days, or sometimes even minutes of life.

"Too late," you might say. And I might agree. However, the value is not in how long they enjoyed the experience, but the possibility that such transformation exists.

Lessons from death are available to all those who choose to move toward it. I have witnessed a heart-opening occurring in not only people near death, but also their caregivers. They found a depth of love within themselves that they didn't know they had access to. They discovered a profound trust in the universe and the reliable goodness of humanity that never abandoned them, regardless of the suffering they encountered.

If that possibility exists at the time of dying, it exists here and now.

The exploration of that potential is what we will dive into together here: the innate capacity for love, trust, forgiveness, and peace that lives in each of us. This book is about reminding us what we already know, something the great religions try to exemplify, but which often gets lost in translation. Death is much more than a medical event. It is a time of growth, a process of transformation. Death opens us to the deepest dimensions of our humanity. Death awakens *presence,* an intimacy with ourselves and all that is alive.

The great spiritual and religious traditions have any number of names for the unnamable: the Absolute, God, Buddha Nature, True Self. All these names are too small. In fact, all names are too small. They are fingers pointing at the moon. I invite you to translate the terms I use in whatever way helps you connect with what you know and trust most in your heart of hearts.

I will use the simple term *Being* to point at that which is deeper and more expansive than our personalities. At the heart of all spiritual teachings is the understanding that this *Being* is our most fundamental and benevolent nature. Our normal sense of self, our usual way of experiencing life, is learned. The conditioning that occurs as we grow and develop can obscure our innate goodness.

Being has certain attributes or essential qualities that live as potentials within each of us. These qualities help us to mature, to become more functional and productive. They fill out our humanity and add a richness, beauty, and capacity to our lives. These pure qualities include love, compassion, strength, peace, clarity, contentment, humility, and equanimity, to name a few. Through practices such as contemplation and meditation, we can quiet our minds, hearts, and bodies, and as a result, our ability to sense our experience becomes subtler and more penetrating. In the discovered stillness, we are able to perceive the presence of these innate qualities. They are more than emotional states, though we may feel them at first as emotions. It might be more helpful to think of them as our inner guidance system, which can lead us to a greater sense of well-being.

These aspects of our essential nature are as inseparable from *Being* as wetness is from water. Said another way, we already have everything we need for this journey. It all exists within us. We don't need to be someone special to access our innate qualities and utilize them in the service of greater freedom and transformation.

I first wrote the five invitations down on the back of a cocktail napkin at thirty thousand feet somewhere over Kansas. I was traveling to join other critical thinkers on the campus of Princeton University to contribute to a six-hour documentary about dying in America called *On Our Own Terms*. The room would be filled with the country's leading health care experts, advocates for physician-assisted death, proponents for Medicare policy changes, and a group of hard-nosed journalists. There would be no desire for Buddhist rhetoric. Bill Moyers, the producer of the documentary, pulled me aside and asked if I could speak to the heart of companioning the dying.

When the time came for me to speak, I pulled out the cocktail napkin on which I had scribbled during the flight.

1. Don't wait.
2. Welcome everything, push away nothing.
3. Bring your whole self to the experience.
4. Find a place of rest in the middle of things.
5. Cultivate don't know mind.

The five invitations are my attempt to honor the lessons I have learned sitting bedside with so many dying patients. They are five mutually supportive principles, permeated with love. They have served me as reliable guides for coping with death. And, as it turns out, they are equally relevant guides to living a life of integrity. They can be applied just as aptly to people dealing with all sorts of transitions and crises—from a move to a new city, to the forming or releasing of an intimate relationship, to getting used to living without your children at home.

I think of these as five bottomless practices that can be continually explored and deepened. They have little value as theories. To be understood, they have to be lived into and realized through action.

An invitation is a request to participate in or attend a particular event. The event is your life, and this book is an invitation for you to be fully present for every aspect of it.

THE FIRST INVITATION

Don't Wait

Whatever we have done with our lives makes us what we are when we die.
And everything, absolutely everything, counts.

—SOGYAL RINPOCHE

Jack had been a heroin addict for fifteen years, living out of his car. Thinking he had a chest cold one day, he went to the emergency room at San Francisco General Hospital. He was diagnosed with lung cancer. Three days later, he moved into Zen Hospice Project. He never went back to his car.

Jack kept a journal, which he occasionally shared with me and other volunteers. He wrote:

> *Over the years, I've put things off. I figured there was always plenty of time later on. At least I've managed to do one major project: I finished that training to be a motorcycle mechanic. Now, they tell me I got less than six months. I'm gonna fool them. I'm gonna make it longer than that . . .*
>
> *Ah, who am I kidding? To tell the truth, I'm scared, angry, tired, and confused. I'm only 45 years old and I feel like I'm 145. I have so much that I want to do, and now there isn't even time to sleep.*

When people are dying, it is easy for them to recognize that every minute, every breath counts. But the truth is, death is always with us, integral to life itself. Everything is constantly changing. Nothing is permanent. This idea can both frighten and inspire us. Yet if we listen closely, the message we hear is: *Don't wait*.

"The problem with the word *patience*," said Zen master Suzuki Roshi, "is that it implies we are waiting for something to get better, we are waiting for something good that will come. A more accurate word for this quality is *constancy*, a capacity to be with what is true moment after moment."

Embracing the truth that all things inevitably must end encourages us not to wait in order to begin living each moment in a manner that is deeply engaged. We stop wasting our lives on meaningless activities. We learn to not hold our opinions, our desires, and even our own identities so tightly. Instead of pinning our hopes on a better future, we focus on the present and being grateful for what we have in front of us right now. We say "I love you" more often because we realize the importance of human connection. We become kinder, more compassionate, and more forgiving.

Don't wait is a pathway to fulfillment and an antidote to regret.

1

THE DOORWAY TO POSSIBILITY

It is almost banal to say so, yet it needs to be stressed continually:
all is creation, all is change, all is flux, all is metamorphosis.

—HENRY MILLER

As I washed his back, Joe turned toward me, glanced over his shoulder, and said resignedly, "I never thought it would be like this."

"What?" I asked.

"Dying."

"What did you think it would be like?"

He sighed. "I guess I never really thought about it."

Joe's regret at never having reflected on his own mortality was a greater cause of suffering than his terminal lung cancer.

The great Korean Zen master Seung Sahn was famous for saying, "Soon dead." A wry wake-up call.

Death is the elephant in the room. A truth we all know but agree not to talk about. We try to keep it at arm's length. We project our worst fears onto it, joke about it, attempt to manage it with euphemisms, sidestep it when possible, or avoid the conversation altogether.

We can run, but we cannot hide.

There is an old Babylonian myth, "Appointment in Samarra," which W. Somerset Maugham retells in his play *Sheppey*. A merchant in

Baghdad sends his servant to the marketplace for supplies. But the man returns a short while later empty-handed, pale, and shuddering with fear. He tells his boss that a woman in the crowd bumped into him. When he looked at her more closely, he recognized her as Death.

"She looked at me and made a threatening gesture," the servant says. "Now, lend me your horse, and I will ride away from this city and avoid my fate. I will go to Samarra and there, Death will not find me."

So the merchant lends his servant his horse. The man rides off in a wild fury.

Later, the merchant goes to the marketplace to buy his own supplies. There, he sees Death and asks why she threatened his servant earlier that day.

"That was not a threatening gesture," Death replies. "It was only a start of surprise. I was astonished to see him in Baghdad, for I had an appointment with him tonight in Samarra."

Like Joe, when we turn a blind eye to the inevitability of death, it takes us by surprise. Yet even running in the other direction, we always arrive at her door. Death only sneaks up on us because we haven't noticed the clues she has hidden in plain sight.

Mostly, we imagine death will come later. No sense worrying about it too much now. "Later" creates the comfortable illusion of a safe distance. But constant change, impermanence, is not later. It is right now. Change is the norm.

We set ourselves up for great disappointment when we cling, hoping that things will never change. It is an unreasonable expectation of life. When I was a teenager, my father would remind me often to "enjoy every moment. It goes by in a blink." I didn't believe him. A few years later, my mother died. I didn't have a chance to say good-bye, to tell her I loved her as I would have liked. I had been living in a kind of dream. I lived within the confinement of that regret for many years.

George Harrison told the truth when he sang, "All things must pass." This moment gives way to the next. Everything is vanishing before our eyes. This is not a magic trick. It is a fact of life. Impermanence is an essential truth woven into the very fabric of existence. It is inescapable, perfectly natural, and our most constant companion.

A sound comes and then it is gone. A thought arises and then quickly passes away. Sights, tastes, smells, touch, feelings—they are all the same: impermanent, fleeting, ephemeral.

My blond hair is long gone. Gravity is having its way with me—my muscles are weaker, my skin has less elasticity, my bodily functions have slowed. This is not a mistake. It's part of the natural process of aging.

Where is my childhood? Where is last night's lovemaking? All that is here today will be only a memory tomorrow. Intellectually, we may understand that our mother's treasured vase will one day fall off the shelf, the car will break down, and those we love will die. Our work is to move this understanding from our intellect and to nestle it deep within our hearts.

Evolution shines a light on this immutable law when it reveals change on vastly different scales, from the micro to the macro. The magnification of an electron microscope reveals the miraculous structure of a human cell. The nucleus, the oscillating field, the waves of rhythm, protons, neutrons, even smaller particles in constant flux, living and dying, moment to moment.

Looking through the Hubble Telescope, we observe the same dynamic. Our ever-expanding universe is subject to the same processes. True, planets may live longer than human cells. The sun will likely continue on as it is now for many billions of years. But impermanence is a characteristic of even the vastest galaxies. They come into form from large clouds of gas, atoms bind together, and, at some point, stars are created. In time, some fade away and some explode. Much like us, galaxies are born, they live for a time, and then they die.

Years ago, a friend and I started a small preschool program. Occasionally, we would take the three- to five-year-olds into the nearby woods with the task of finding "dead things." The children loved this game.

They would happily collect fallen leaves, broken branches, a rusty old car part, and occasionally the bones of a crow or small animal. We would lay these discoveries out on a big blue tarp in a grove of fir trees and have a sort of show-and-tell.

At their young age, the children had no fear, only curiosity. They would examine each item carefully, rub it between their fingers, smell it—exploring the "dead things" in a close-up and personal way. Then they would share their thoughts.

Sometimes they would craft the most amazing stories about the history of an object. How a rusty car part had fallen from a star or spaceship as it passed above, or how a leaf was used as a blanket by a mouse until summer came and it was no longer needed.

I remember one child saying, "I think the leaves that fall from trees are very kind. They make room for little new ones to grow. It would be sad if trees couldn't grow new leaves."

While we mostly associate impermanence with sadness and endings, it is not all about loss. In Buddhism, impermanence is often referred to as the "Law of Change and Becoming." These two correlated principles provide balance and harmony. Just as there is constant "dissolving," there is also constant "becoming."

We rely on impermanence. The cold you have today won't last forever. This boring dinner party will come to an end. Evil dictatorships crumble, replaced by thriving democracies. Even ancient trees burn down so that new ones can be born. Without impermanence, life simply could not be. Without impermanence, your son couldn't take his first steps. Your daughter couldn't grow up and go to the prom.

Like the confluence of great rivers, our lives are a series of different moments, joining together to give the impression of one continuous flow. We move from cause to effect, event to event, one point to another, one state of existence to another—which gives an outward impression that our lives are one continuous and unified movement. In reality, they are not. The river of yesterday is not the same as the river of today. It is like the sages say: "We can't step into the same river twice."

Each moment is born and dies. And in a very real way, we are born and die with it. There is a beauty to all this impermanence. In Japan, people celebrate the brief but abundant blooming of the cherry blossoms each spring. In Idaho, outside the cabin where I teach, blue flax flowers live for a single day. Why do such flowers appear so much more magnificent than plastic ones? The fragility, the brevity, and the uncertainty of their lives captivate us, invite us into beauty, wonder, and gratitude.

Creation and destruction are two sides of the same coin.

In 1991, His Holiness the Dalai Lama visited San Francisco. In preparation for his arrival, Tibetan monks created a sand mandala at the Asian Art Museum in Golden Gate Park. Using tiny tools, they mindfully funneled finely colored crystals onto the floor in an intricate design. The sacred piece of art depicting the Kalachakra, or Wheel of Time, spanned six feet in diameter. It took many days of tireless work for the monks to complete.

But one day not long after the mandala was finished, a disturbed woman jumped the velvet rope surrounding the fragile creation. She stormed through it like a tornado, kicking the sand wildly and completely destroying the monks' meticulous craftsmanship.

Museum officials and security forces were shocked. They grabbed the woman, called the police, and had her arrested.

The monks, however, remained unperturbed. They assured the museum officials that they would be happy to make another mandala; this one had been scheduled to be taken apart in a dissolution ceremony in about a week's time, anyway. The monks calmly scattered the sands of the demolished mandala off the Golden Gate Bridge and began again.

Ven. Losang Samten, the leader of the sand-painting monks, told reporters, "We don't feel any negativity. We don't know how to judge her motivations. We pray for her with love and compassion."

To the monks, the mandala had served its purpose. Its creation and destruction were intended from the very outset to offer a lesson in the nature of life.

The museum staff viewed the mandala as an irreplaceable work of art, a precious object. To the monks, the mandala was a process whose value and beauty existed in its teaching on impermanence and non-attachment.

In an everyday sense, we have the same experience the monks did in making their mandala when we cook. I love baking bread—the measuring, the mixing, the juggling of pans, the kneading, the rising of the dough, the bread browning in the oven, the cutting of the loaf, and the buttering of it. Then the bread is gone. We partake in a mini-celebration of impermanence with every well-prepared meal consumed with enjoyment.

At first, the news of impermanence typically generates a great deal of anxiety. In response, we attempt to make things solid and secure. We try our best to arrange the conditions of our lives, to manipulate the circumstances so that we can be happy.

I love to lie in bed, particularly on a cold winter morning. The sheets are soft and warm. My body is well rested and enjoys taking refuge under the blankets. My mind is at peace and has yet to leap forward into the day's tasks. For a while, all is right with the world. A moment of perfection.

Then I have to pee.

After a moment of resistance, I run quickly to the bathroom. Upon attaining the temporary ease of release, I leap back under the blankets in the hope of re-creating perfection. But I can't get everything back the way it was just moments earlier. I can't create conditions that are capable of providing an enduring happiness that is resistant to change.

Like most of us, I appreciate good conditions. I am among the fortunate ones with enough food to eat; I have a supportive family and remarkable friends, a life of considerable joy and ease. I'm not advocating an ascetic lifestyle. I am talking about learning to live in a harmonious way with constant change.

Usually, we seek happiness through trying to arrange the world in such a way that we meet things that are pleasant and avoid what is unpleasant. That seems only natural, right?

We fool ourselves because sometimes we can manipulate the conditions of our lives to bring us temporary happiness. It feels good in the moment, but as soon as the moment passes, we are looking for the next satisfying experience or taste. We become like "hungry ghosts," those mythical characters with bulging stomachs, long, thin necks, and tiny mouths who can never be satisfied.

The truth of life is that its one constant is change. When we look closely, is there anything else?

Not living in harmony with this truth causes us no end of suffering. It strengthens our ignorance and sets up the habits of craving, defense, and regret. These habits harden into character and have a powerful momentum that frequently shows up as obstacles to peace at the time of dying.

One day, three large, formidable, middle-aged Jewish women came to see me in my tiny office at the Zen Hospice Project. They were sisters. One was a high-powered political consultant in the city. Their mother was dying, and her doctor, a brain cancer specialist, had told them to come see me.

I started to talk to them about our quality of care, what we did, how we respected everyone's beliefs. But I could tell they weren't buying it. They were taking in the sparse décor, the limited space in my office, where we could all barely fit.

Linda, the consultant, asked straight out, "Why should we bring our mother here? Let's put her up in a nice room at the Fairmont Hotel and hire caregivers to be with her round the clock. Why wouldn't we do that, when we can afford it?"

I replied, "Sure, you could do that. And I could suggest some people to help you out." Then I paused and picked up a booklet of photos of our hospice. "But can I ask you to just do this one thing? Show your mom these photos so she can see what it looks like here, and get her input."

When they left soon after, I thought I'd never see these three women again. But forty-five minutes later, the phone rang. I instantly recognized Linda's sharp, forceful voice. "Mother wants to see you," she said.

I had been summoned. I went to the mother's hospital room at one of the finest facilities in San Francisco. There, I found not only the three daughters, but also their rabbi, their mother's brain cancer specialist, and a psychiatrist. The pressure was on.

I introduced myself to the mother, Abigail. She sat calmly on the bed, flipping through the picture book and asking me all sorts of questions. "Can I bring my china?"

"Sure. You can bring some of it," I said.

"How about my rocking chair? I really love my rocking chair."

"Sure. You can bring your rocking chair."

Suddenly, Abigail froze. "Wait a minute. There's no private bathroom in my room? You want me to go down the hall to use the bathroom?"

I looked her in the eyes. "Tell me. Are you getting up and going to the bathroom a lot these days?"

Abigail sank back into her pillow. "No, I don't go to the bathroom. I can't walk anymore." Then she turned to her daughters and said, "I want to go with him."

I believe what Abigail liked was that I didn't rebel against her crabbiness or try to make her into someone else. She appreciated my honesty. She could trust that. She didn't have a clue how to go through this dying process, but she believed that I did. She knew she'd feel safe with us.

Abigail moved in the next day, stayed for a week, then passed away. All her daughters were there by her bedside when she died.

Abigail's attitude changed when she was willing to meet the truth that was right in front of her—to be honest, not balk at it or turn away. She recognized that she was impermanent and that all the conditions of her life were in flux. She stepped into alignment with the law of change and becoming.

That naming of what is going on in our present moment is so powerful. Instead of clinging to the past, we come into alignment with the truth of our present circumstances, and then we can let go of the fight.

Why wait until we are dying to be free of struggle?

Impermanence is humbling. It is absolutely certain, yet the way it will manifest is completely unpredictable. We have little control. We can either shrink in fear from this predicament or choose a different response.

The gift of impermanence is that it places us squarely in the here and now. We know that birth will end in death. Reflecting on this might cause us to savor the moment, to imbue our lives with more appreciation and gratitude. We know that the end of all accumulation is dispersion. Reflecting on this might help us to practice simplicity and discover what has real value. We know that all relationships will end in separation. Reflecting on this might keep us from being overwhelmed by grief and inspire us to distinguish love from attachment.

Attention to constant change can help prepare us for the fact that the body will one day die. However, a more immediate benefit of this reflection is that we learn to be more relaxed with impermanence now. When we embrace impermanence, a certain grace enters our lives. We can treasure experiences; we can feel deeply—all without clinging. We are free to savor life, to touch the texture of each passing moment completely, whether the moment is one of sadness or joy. When we understand on a deep level that impermanence is in the life of all things, we learn to tolerate change better. We become more appreciative and resilient.

In "Living and Dying: A Buddhist Perspective," Carol Hyman wrote, "If we learn to let go into uncertainty, to trust that our basic nature and that of the world are not different, then the fact that things are not solid and fixed becomes, rather than a threat, a liberating opportunity."

Everything will come apart. That is true of our bodies, our relationships, all of life. It is happening all the time, not just at the end when the curtain falls. Coming together inevitably means parting. Don't be troubled. This is the nature of life.

Our lives are not solid and fixed. Knowing this intimately is how we prepare for death, for loss of any kind, and how we come to fully embrace constant change. We are not just our past; we are becoming. We can release grudges. We can forgive. We can free ourselves of resentment and regret before we die.

Don't wait. Everything we need is right in front of us. Impermanence is the doorway to possibility. Embracing it is where true freedom lies.

2

AT ONCE HERE AND DISAPPEARING

Apprentice yourself to the curve of your own disappearance.
—DAVID WHYTE

The most common devices in hospitals for the measurement of death are TV-like monitors that signal the pace of respiration with an electronic beep and track the rhythmic beating of the heart on an up-and-down graph. Anyone who has watched a medical drama is familiar with the scene of an individual valiantly applying CPR or a doctor attempting to save a life by shocking a patient's heart that is not beating correctly with a defibrillator in the fruitless fight against the flatline. It is this dreaded flatline that families wait for in hospitals. The monitor announces with a steady high-pitched tone that there is an absence of activity in the body, that death has indeed occurred.

Sadly, we are so disconnected from the actual experience of death that I frequently have observed family members watching their loved ones' deaths on a TV screen, rather than looking into their beloveds' eyes or sensing the death viscerally in their own bodies.

But there are other, subtler signals of death's arrival than the beeping of a monitor. Ones that connect rather than disconnect us. Ones that have us participate rather than wait.

In Southeast Asia, it is quite common for young men, as part of their education, to enter the monastic life for a period of a year, which may turn into a whole lifetime. On entry into the community, their heads are ritually shaved, and they are given the bright saffron-colored robes of a novice. In certain forest hermitages, these young monks are told to go into the jungle, sit in meditation, and remain there until they know they belong.

This "belonging" the young monks are asked to seek represents more than a mere membership in a certain monastic community. The encouragement is to reflect on a more fundamental sense of belonging, which involves a falling away of differences.

This is similar to what happens naturally in the dying process. The ways we have defined our "self," the identities we have carried for so long—of mother or father, provider or caregiver, loner or people person, rich or poor, success or failure—all these descriptions gradually are stripped away by illness and old age, or they are gracefully surrendered. Then we discover something more elemental and connective, a fundamental truth of human nature.

Many spiritual traditions and cosmologies, including that of the ancient Greeks, have suggested that all life is composed of four basic elements: earth, water, fire, and air. The Zohar, a Jewish mystical text written in the thirteenth century, saw these four elements as the foundation of all substance. Other worldviews, including Indian thought and Chinese philosophy, speak similarly of five or six gross elements. Buddhism notes that each is an ever-changing process rather than a static thing. All of these components are said to dissolve when we die, through an interdependent process of body and mind. The four elements are more than physical form; they are emotional and mental states, creative processes. They have a spectrum of characteristics: Earth's hardness and softness, the fluidity and cohesiveness of water, the coolness and heat of the fire element, the stillness and motion of air.

Sometimes medical explanations of the signs and symptoms of approaching death are just too sterile and foreign. I often have felt the model of the four elements useful to call to mind as family members keep vigil through long days and nights of their loved ones' active dying. It is a way to understand how we release our identities and their component parts; the gross physical elements of the body, thoughts, perceptions, feelings, conditioning all dissolving.

Samantha was a wilderness guide in her mid-forties. I sat with her one endless night as her husband, Jeff, was dying. She asked me what she could do for him that might help.

I asked, "What do you do when your young children are sick?"

She said, "Well, I sit quietly right next to their bed, or sometimes I snuggle up with them. I speak less and listen more. I let them know I am right here with them. I retell them in words and in touch how much I love them."

"Beautiful," I said. "What else?"

I could see her remembering what she already knew.

She almost whispered, "I try to create a kind environment that is peaceful so they are not as afraid. I try to do simple things with great attention. I promise I won't leave them. I tell them it's okay that they are sick and that it won't be like this forever."

She began to cry and then weep. "But I've never done this dying thing before. I don't understand what's happening."

It's natural for us to fall apart in the face of loss. No need to stop it. Often our old coping mechanisms simply don't work in this new context. However, finding our ground or recalling what has been most meaningful can help us stay present with what we are experiencing. For some, that is the breath or the strength of relationships; for others, it is cultural traditions or religious faith. Samantha's church was the wilderness.

Knowing that she and Jeff had fallen in love on a backpacking trip, I asked Samantha what she loved most about the outdoors.

She said, "Being in the middle of it, all of it, everything—the rocks I climb, the rain that soaks me to the bones, the cold night sky, the winds that sweep across the mountains, carrying smells and sounds to my feet. It's my real home. It's where I most belong."

Samantha and Jeff had lived in nature; they knew its ways and language, and did not see it as something apart from themselves. I took a risk and suggested that Jeff, perhaps, was "in the middle of it, all of it." His body was in a very elemental way made up of earth, water, fire, and air. So in dying, he was returning to the nature they so loved.

Jeff's body had become very still. This happens as the earth element fades. In the early stages of dying, people might complain that their legs or feet have gone numb. They might become difficult to arouse, unresponsive.

"Can you see the earth element in Jeff? Was he a solid guy?" I asked.

Samantha held his hand and kissed his head. She laughed and then tenderly said, "He's always been so hardheaded and stubborn, but he has the softest skin." She spoke not only to his physical qualities, but also his personality characteristics, which she was watching fade away.

"Right," I said. "Solid, fixed form, that's losing its strength, being drained of energy, unable to support itself anymore." I thought to myself of a few lines from *Cat's Cradle* by Kurt Vonnegut:

> *And I was some of the mud that got to sit up and look around.*
> *Lucky me, lucky mud.*

As the earth element—form—dissolves, it gives way to water. The person who is dying may then experience an inability to swallow fluids, urinary or bowel incontinence, and the slowing of blood circulation.

In the days prior, Samantha had given Jeff sips of water, and later, ice chips. Now she would moisten his mouth with a sponge because he could no longer swallow. She talked about the free movement of creative thought that she and Jeff had enjoyed when planning a wilderness excursion. Samantha said that in the past days, she could see that Jeff's body and mind had begun to contract in fear. I reminded her of the water element and its characteristics of both fluidity and cohesiveness. We spoke of great rivers, how some dry up in certain seasons, and of the ice calving of Alaska's frozen glaciers, the way edges break off and slip beneath the water.

The Persian poet Ghalib wrote, "For the raindrop, joy is in entering the river."

Now the water element was dissolving, giving way to fire. When this happens, the body's temperature fluctuates. Infections may give rise to fever or a slowing metabolism may cause the skin to become cool and moist.

As Jeff came closer to death, his hands and feet became cooler, the heat gathered in the center of his body toward his big heart. Samantha reminisced about the passionate fire of their love, the heat of their arguments, and that awful feeling of turning away from each other in bed in cool indifference. She kissed him from his head to his toes and apologized for ever having argued with him.

Scientists theorize that somewhere in our galaxy long ago, a star exploded, throwing out masses of gas and dust. This supernova, over billions of years, eventually formed our solar system. The poets would say we were once bright stars now cooled, sunlight congealed into human form.

The fire element was dissolving, giving way to air. At this final stage of physical death, people frequently exhibit dramatic changes in breathing patterns—slow and fast breathing with long gaps between exhales and inhales. Sometimes the only thing left in the room is breath. Death is much like birth in that way, with everyone's attention naturally focused on the simplicity of breath.

There was no more struggle or agitation for Jeff. The anxiety, disorientation, and chaos that had shaped the last few days were gone. All that remained was the erratic rhythm of his breathing. Time slipped away, and Samantha sat quietly in an informal meditation, feeling the vitality, the miracle of life that was at once evident and ebbing.

T. S. Eliot wrote, "At the still point of the turning world. Neither flesh nor fleshless; Neither from nor towards; at the still point, there the dance is. . . . Except for the point, the still point, there would be no dance, and there is only the dance."

Shortly before Jeff's last breath, Samantha spoke to him, saying, "I am right here, and I want to go deep inside to meet you one last time." She closed her eyes and grew still. Jeff and Samantha seemed to meet in a profound, bottomless space. The past was gone, there was no future. There was only the present.

Jeff exhaled a few more times and didn't breathe in again.

A stillness and ease embraced us. I felt it as warmth and sensed a luminosity, a sort of brilliance. After some time, Samantha spoke out loud, as if talking to the space more than to me. "I thought I was losing him, but he is everywhere."

Earth dissolves into water. Water dissolves into fire. Fire dissolves into air. Air dissolves into space. Space dissolves into consciousness.

Dying, in many cases, does not happen all of a sudden. It is a gradual process of withdrawing from life in form. When I speak of the four elements dissolving, I am not speaking exactly of the physical form. Rather, I am pointing to the ineffable but observable animating qualities that are so apparently missing when we are left only with the heaviness of the corpse after death. There is something beyond the four elements—the spirit, soul, or animating presence. Our instruments and devices can certainly measure the physical disintegration, but the inner dissolution that happens simultaneously is subtle and still.

They are all dissolving—the elements and their associated states, and as a result, the self is dissolving, as well. This is happening all the time, we just see it at the surface at the time of dying.

Now who are you?

Even people like Samantha, who do not hold a belief in the afterlife or any kind of subtle consciousness, can perceive an increasingly radiant quality of being, which spiritual adepts have spoken of for centuries. They only need to open themselves to it. This light, subtle aspect of existence seems more accessible the closer someone comes to death.

While unexplainable, it can be felt, intuited, and easily known by regular, everyday people as the seeming solidity and density of the body is receding.

We don't have adequate language to describe this sort of incomprehensible experience, so we name it Mystery with a capital M. Over the years, I have found that what we can experience or know directly may be much more important than our ability to explain or measure it.

What becomes undeniable when we sit with people who are dying is that fragility and impermanence are in the nature of life. It's all always coming together and falling apart—not just the physical properties of life, and not just at the time of death.

And it is possible to hold it all in love and compassion.

It's funny—we all pretty much agree that life is in constant flux. Yet we prefer to cling to the illusion that we ourselves are solid things moving through a changing world. "Everything is changing except me," we tell ourselves.

But we are mistaken. We are not only the small solid selves we have taken ourselves to be.

We are not the accountant. Not the schoolteacher. Not the barista. Not the software engineer. Not the writer, nor the reader of this book. At least not exactly as we imagined. Not separate and apart. We are in flux. We are made up of dancing elements. We are, like everything else, at once here and disappearing.

We are like the windows in the hundred-year-old farmhouse where I used to live. The panes looked as solid as those of any window. I could knock on the glass and hear the bright sound of my knuckles making contact. But on closer inspection, it was apparent that the glass was thicker at the bottom of the frame than at the top. Glass is not entirely solid; it is a fluid, subject to the force of gravity. Over many decades, the window, which appeared so rigid, so permanent, had been moving and changing, the glass settling in a downward direction.

Our sense of self is as impermanent as that window glass. It has a purpose, but it is not solid. Don't get seduced by its enduring appearance.

While illness can contract us into an even smaller sense of self, many people who are sick or dying speak of no longer being limited by the previous boundaries of their old, familiar identities. They are exposed to a more expansive landscape. In a strange way, illness—like a powerful encounter with beauty—shakes us, ripens us, and opens us to deeper dimensions of being. It's not that life becomes perfectly sweet and neatly ordered. There is still plenty of madness, mayhem, and chaos. However, we come to embody much wider identities. The interior life and the external world permeate each other and commingle.

Charles was an elegant man. When he moved into the Zen Hospice Project, he brought with him his fine crystal champagne glasses and Spanish Provincial silver service. He proudly hosted small dinner parties for friends on Friday evenings. He dressed in Italian suits and silk ties each day . . . until he couldn't anymore. Gradually, he stopped dressing in anything other than his robe, and he called off the intimate suppers.

Over time, other elements of his self-image started to slip, as well. He started grabbing for women's breasts and swearing like a sailor. This was understandably upsetting to his friends, who were quite horrified by his improper behavior. "So out of character!" they muttered under their breaths. It's not easy or fun to be around such radical behavioral changes.

As Charles grew more tired and confused, he withdrew from his previous social circles, choosing only to invite in an old, trusted friend who once had been his lover. This was perhaps the only person who understood that Charles wasn't acting differently as a result of his AIDS-related dementia. It was that his unconscious world was intruding into his conscious, everyday life.

We learn pretty early on in life to keep the lid on unwanted material. We begin to shape ourselves in early infancy because we want our parents to love us, and we depend on them for our survival. Inevitably, we adopt their unconscious assumptions, biases, and prejudices—good and bad—along with those of our particular culture and religious upbringing. Or we rebel against them. In either case, we are conditioned from very early on in our lives to act in a certain way. The pattern of adaption—of seeking approval and avoiding disapproval—continues throughout our schooling, with our employers and friends, and serves as the template for our future intimate relationships.

In short, we push below the surface of our awareness what we fear will threaten our survival, and we present to the world whatever we believe will get us what we need. Over the years, patterns become deeply ingrained, forming and sustaining our self-image, which in turn gives birth to a sense of personal identity.

When we are seriously ill, like Charles, it can take all our energy just to stand, to get to the toilet, or to perform the simplest functions of daily life. Illness cracks our notions of control. We don't realize it, but the lifelong process of repression takes energy. When we simply don't have that energy available to us anymore, unconscious material begins slipping out. Frequently, it surprises us.

It can prove quite difficult to not recognize oneself or a friend when these repressed tendencies come bubbling up to the surface and identities shift. At the same time, there is a freedom in no longer pushing down what we have been ashamed of or felt unworthy about, often for our entire lives. The dualities and false boundaries that have been created can dissolve. When given room, the truth can be known, and it can be integrated into a more expanded sense of self.

Sometimes what we repress is not our raw sexual energy, our shame, or something we feel guilty about, but rather our innate goodness.

Sean came to Zen Hospice Project on compassionate release from prison, where he had been serving a term for manslaughter after fatally stabbing his older sister seventeen times. A lifelong convict, Sean was guarded, isolated, and tough.

At first, hospice was too challenging for Sean. It was too intimate. He pushed us away. He would get cranky and irritable when his demands for his favorite junk food weren't immediately met. He rarely talked about his life and instead criticized the volunteers for being nosy. We continued to treat him just like everyone else, with respect and love.

I liked to just hang out with Sean, gabbing and smoking cigarettes. Slowly, I learned that he had grown up in foster care and had gone to juvie at age thirteen. He had been incarcerated for most of his adult life. If he'd ever asked for help or shown kindness to anyone in those days, he would have been ridiculed or perhaps even killed.

One day, we were sitting in the backyard when Sean said, "Frank, I let them help me today."

"What did you let them do?" I asked.

"I let the nurses help me get in the shower." Get *in* the shower. Not *give* him a shower. Sean had let the nurses help him into the stall with all his clothes on so that he could get naked after they left the room. That was the first time he had let anyone help him in decades.

Gradually, as the kind and accepting environment of hospice relaxed his defenses, Sean was free to discover and reveal more of himself—parts of his identity that had long been hidden away for safekeeping. Qualities came forth like warmth and generosity.

During the almost twenty years I worked at the Zen Hospice Project, Sean was the only person who ever threw me a surprise birthday party. He insisted on using money from his meager government check. He wanted to hire a stripper to jump out of a fake cake, but the nurses talked him out of that idea. He settled for balloons and a real cake.

All the volunteers and nurses were assembled when they rolled the cake in, candles lit, and started singing "Happy Birthday" to me. I didn't know it was coming, and I didn't know until later that it had all been Sean's idea. I was deeply touched. This was the kindest thing he could have done for me.

Before he died, Sean made a video for his son—a son he had never known. He said, "You know I've never been there. You don't even know me. But I'm telling you now, I'm coming to the close of my life, and these

things are important to know." He went on to give his son fatherly instructions about kindness and forgiveness.

It was the most marvelous turnaround. As Sean set down his defenses
and allowed his heart to open, his innate compassion, love, and tenderness came forward. It wasn't because we tried to change him, enlighten
him, or convert him. It was just because we loved him. With love, Sean
finally was able to let go of his fiercely constructed, self-protective, yet
ultimately self-limiting identity: the idea that he was a convict, a bad guy,
with nothing good to offer the world.

My own sense of self was undone by my heart attack. One day, I was the
respected Buddhist teacher; the next, I was just another patient in a hospital gown with my butt hanging out. In the months that followed, I felt
stripped of psychological defenses and identities that had once defined
me. I was humbled and helpless. I gave over entire days to tears, longing, regret, panic, and clinging to familiar stories that gave me a temporary sense of control.

Losing touch with my self-image felt frightening at first. I had always
been the strong one, the one who cared for others. Now I was black and
blue, weaker than ever before, unable to shower or tie my shoes without help. I felt feeble and dependent, and I experienced an unreasonable
fear that I would never be able to work again or be of real service in the
world. Part of me thought that I could muscle my way through recovery. But what I needed to do was just the opposite—to surrender to the
process.

I was reminded of the old Sumerian myth of Queen Inanna's descent
to the underworld, the metaphorical image of the deep unconscious. It
is the story of an archetypal journey to wholeness, which involves her
embracing her dark, shadowy side and shedding the trappings of her former self and gaining essential insight into death in order to eventually
return with a fuller appreciation of the cycle of life. She begins dressed

in fine robes and wearing the crown of a heavenly god. On the way to the underworld, she passes through seven gates. At each gate, she is required to relinquish her symbols of power: a gold ring, her breast-plate, the lapis scepter. Until she is left bare.

I felt that naked.

We habitually string ourselves together with various shiny ornamentations to shape a positive self-image, sometimes inflating our capacities or importance. Conversely, we may add fuel to the fire of a negative self-concept and exaggerate flaws or weaknesses. We know intrinsically that this construction we carry around and project to the world is not substantial or real, and yet we invest in it and come to mistake it for reality.

Then something comes along and exposes what seemed so solid. We realize that we are constantly changing impressions and representations; that our story is held together by nothing more than spit and glue and habit. We see that identity is not a static state.

To identify is an inner action, a process we do to ourselves. We can identify with almost anything—a job, a nationality, a sexual preference, a relationship, our spiritual progress, or a passing thought. Just as importantly, we can begin to let go of our identities by getting curious. Right now, we can notice the attitudes and reactions, the preferences that lead to us becoming attached to what we are identified with. Once recognized, we can allow the identification to be without pushing it away. No need to fight it. Gradually, it will dissolve because it, too, is impermanent.

This is what the Zen master Suzuki Roshi was pointing to when he said, "What we call *I* is just a swinging door which moves when we inhale and when we exhale."

Softening around these identities, we will feel less constraint, more freedom, more immediacy and presence. But at first, we usually feel vulnerable.

At the entrance to most Zen meditation halls, there is a *han*: a large, solid wooden block that the monks strike with a mallet to call students to the *zendo* for meditation. Written across the block in black *sumi* ink is the teaching:

Be aware of the Great Matter of Birth and Death
Life passes swiftly,
Wake up, Wake up!
Do not waste this life.

Students and teachers pass the block each morning, reminding us of the fundamental truth of impermanence. Over the years, the mallet wears a hole where it hits the thick oak block, and what seemed so solid becomes thin, vulnerable.

The words disappear, and the block itself becomes the teaching.

It seems this is what comes of being vulnerable. When we relax the clinging to our treasured beliefs and ideas, soften our resistance to the blows of life, stop trying to manage the uncertainty and hold ourselves more lightly, then we become a less solid thing. Less of a fixed identity.

In the months following my heart attack, I realized that the more I allowed my vulnerability to emerge, the less wedded I felt to being somebody. I became less occupied with the full-time job of self-generation. I could feel the exhaustion of propping up my personality. At times, my personality seemed like a giant balloon that I had become breathless constantly trying to inflate. As I accepted the fragility of my life, it opened me. I felt myself to be a porous thing, more transparent, more permeable.

One of the very few memories I have from my high school biology class is the teaching of osmosis—the process by which molecules move in and out of our cells across a semi-permeable membrane. I think of our consciousness like this semi-permeable membrane. And I think our deepest nature can permeate us through a process much like osmosis.

Thanks to our vulnerability, the possibility of knowing our most essential identity is always present. We need not wait for some other time or for perfect conditions or for our death to realize it. In fact, the recognition of our own impermanence often appears when we least expect it, stimulated by the very conditions we seek to avoid.

During my recovery, I felt permeable to everything. The sublime beauty and the horror of the world could enter my consciousness without resistance. I was receptive to it all. I welcomed it. There were no filters between me and any part of myself or the world. I was just *Being*.

I recalled holding the hand of Sid, an elderly patient at hospice who had arrived to us crusty and curt. "Good morning!" a volunteer would say.

"I'm dying of cancer. What's good about that?" Sid would bark back.

But in her final days, Sid moved from being this tough, badass gal to being increasingly translucent. Her skin became almost see-through, and her whole being followed suit. She lost so much weight it seemed like the wind could blow right through her. Her bravado faded away, replaced by a calm, loving demeanor. It was as if this evolution allowed her more essential nature to show itself, because she was no longer occupied with attempting to maintain the worn-out narrative of her life.

The more permeable I became, the more I realized that we humans are just bundles of ever-changing conditions. We ought to hold ourselves more lightly. Taking ourselves too seriously is the cause of much suffering. We tell ourselves that we are in charge: "Buckle up! Get this done!" When in reality, we are quite helpless, subject to the events taking place around us. But that helplessness brings us into contact with our vulnerability, which can be a doorway to awakening, to a deeper intimacy with reality.

My sense of self didn't completely disappear after my heart attack. I was still Frank, but my personality was no longer the dominant force it had once been. During those months of recovery, I spent much of my time sitting in an old leather chair with a beautiful view of the sea. I usually kept the front door unlocked so that if people came to visit, I could shout out a welcome and they could let themselves in without my having to get up, which was difficult for me.

Then one day, about six months after the surgery, I heard the doorbell ring. I instinctively jumped up to answer it. As I was walking across the living room, I felt my sense of self return to my body. It was like a scene from *Invasion of the Body Snatchers*. My self was reasserting itself with a vengeance.

"I'm back. Don't worry. I'm in charge again," it said.

Strange as it may sound, I wasn't elated when this happened. It actually felt like a loss. I was afraid that I might slip back into my old habitual ways and lose touch with my newfound sense of my fundamentally limitless nature.

Thankfully, that is not what transpired.

Instead, I discovered that I was able to function as Frank, my personality who gets things done in the world, but I also had access to the greater sense of *Being* that I had discovered during recovery. I realized the possibility for an inner peace. No matter the conditions of my life, I could let go. I could change. I could find contentment.

Luckily, we don't have to wait until we are sick or dying to embrace our own impermanence. Any major life-changing event provides us with this opportunity. Think of how new parents expand their views of themselves to include their role as father or mother. Take, for example, the corporate executive who loses her high-powered job. She may flounder for months, years even, after such a blow if she is too attached to her identity as a career woman. Only when she is able to let go and embrace herself as a person who is bigger than the job she performed, as a human being with passions, interests, fears, and hurts that grow and evolve over time, can she begin to recover and forge a new path for herself.

When our sense of ourselves shifts toward *Being*, we move beyond our reactivity to impermanence. Not only that, but just as I did after my heart attack, we become aware of something beyond impermanence: the permanent source from which life springs. Suzuki Roshi wrote, "To live . . . means to die as a small being moment after moment." What he meant is the self is not a separate static thing but a process, or actually a network of interconnected processes. When we realize this, we see that there is always an opportunity to respond to a situation creatively. Nothing is holding us back from change and transformation—and nothing ever was.

Embracing our own impermanence is a journey, taking us deeper and deeper into contact with the true nature of things. First we accept that things around us change. Then we realize that we, ourselves, are ever changing: our thoughts and feelings, our attitudes and beliefs, even our identities.

The beauty is that our impermanence binds us to every other human being. Empathy arises through an appreciation of our transience and an understanding of our interconnectedness. We are not separate, as we once thought we were. We are, in fact, deeply connected to everyone and everything.

3

THE MATURATION OF HOPE

Hope inspires the good to reveal itself.
—ANONYMOUS (OR ATTRIBUTED TO EMILY DICKINSON)

Briskly walking down the wide corridor of a massive steel-and-glass medical center in the Midwest, I was musing to myself about the impersonal nature of today's health care system. Just then, the sound of Brahms's "Lullaby" began to play through the hospital's PA system.

I asked the head of nursing, who was escorting me to my grand rounds talk, about this charming music.

She said with a smile, "A baby was just born."

Amazed by her response, I asked her to tell me more.

She explained that whenever a baby was born in that medical center, the maternity department would play Brahms's "Lullaby." The music was pumped into every room.

"Even the patient rooms?" I asked incredulously.

"Yes, and all of the departments: orthopedics, cardiac intensive care, the ER, the operating rooms, the administrative offices, the cafeteria, even the security command center," she said proudly.

"Is it played for all births, even the difficult ones?" I asked in astonishment.

She replied, "Yes, it's played for all births: natural births, preemie babies, and cesarean sections."

As I looked around, I saw people who had been rushing to their next meetings pause for a breath. Conversations stopped and gave way to subtle grins. For a few moments, where there had been tension and stress, there was delight and ease.

Hospitals are magnets for suffering. They're environments filled with a great deal of physical pain, fear, anxiety, and other discomforts. Staff tend to get swept up in the technical details of care, overwhelmed by patients' suffering and their inability to respond to it.

Brahms's "Lullaby" was a salve, a joyful reminder of the potential for new life that exists in any moment, an uplifting encouragement to go on even in the face of adversity. The music served as more than an announcement of feel-good optimism. For a short while, hope filled the air.

Hope is a subtle, sometimes unconscious attitude of heart and mind that is an essential resource in this human life. It is the ingredient that supplies the motivation for us to get up in the morning and look forward to the possibilities of a new day. It is an anticipation of a future that is good. Desmond Tutu, South Africa's moral conscience and the outspoken critic of apartheid, once said, "Hope is being able to see that there is light despite all of the darkness."

Experts differ on whether hope is an emotion, a belief, a conscious choice, or all three. Václav Havel, the philosopher and first president of the Czech Republic, suggested that hope is "an orientation of the spirit." I think of hope as an innate quality of being, an open, active trust in life that refuses to quit.

What we know for certain is that hope takes us beyond the rational. At times, this can be invaluable to our survival. Yet at other times, when hope is misunderstood, it can plunge us into delusion and become a hindrance to facing the facts of life.

To discern the real value of hope, we must draw a line between hope and expectation. Hope is an optimizing force that moves us and all of life toward harmony. It doesn't arrive from outside; rather it is an abiding state of being, a hidden wellspring within us. When the mind is still and awake, we can see reality more clearly and recognize it as a living, dynamic process. Hope that is active has an imaginative daring to it, which helps us to realize our unity with all life and find the resourcefulness required to act on its behalf. We can sense the lightness, the buoyancy of this kind of hope, the enthusiasm and positivity it engenders. It energizes us to engage in activities that we imagine will enrich our future. This version of hope is a basic human need.

Yet our usual kind of hope is little more than wishful thinking. It's frequently tied to an almost childlike belief, sometimes even blind faith, that an external agency or authority will bring about what we desire. Driven by our preference for a different set of conditions, this conventional view of hope is a rejection of what is present for us in the here and now. It is the flipside of fear.

Ordinary hope disguised as expectation is fixated on a specific outcome. This hope gets conflated with the desire for a certain future result. It becomes object-focused. It takes us outside of ourselves. The quandary is that when the outcome isn't achieved, the object isn't grasped, then our hopes are dashed.

Attaching our happiness to a specific outcome causes us all sorts of suffering. To manage that distress, we attempt to control everything that is happening around us. But we have no control over the weather on our wedding day, the moods of others, winning the lottery, or even receiving a cancer diagnosis. As we have seen, the law of impermanence trumps our best-laid plans.

In the ever-changing landscape of our lives, attachment to outcome posing as hope only generates anxiety and interferes with our ability to be present to our experience of life as it is unfolding in this very moment. My friend the late anthropologist Angeles Arrien advised that we be "open to outcome, not attached to outcome." She wrote, "Openness and non-attachment help us recover the human resources of wisdom and objectivity."

I watched as Fred visited his wife, Rachel, at Zen Hospice Project. She was dying of colon cancer, and Fred came every day to feed her watermelon. Not just a little bit, but what appeared to be an entire melon each time.

"Wow, you must really love watermelon!" I remarked to Rachel one day.

"Actually, I don't care for it much," she replied. "Fred read on the Internet that it would help me fight this cancer, so I eat it to keep him happy."

Watermelon. I know, it sounds absurd. It's not uncommon for desperate people to reach for all manner of cures. On occasion, some even work.

Fred loved Rachel and wasn't able to accept the reality that his wife was dying. Clinging to the fantasy that he had discovered a secret cancer cure was a blind hope.

Late one night, I asked Fred to show me the website that claimed the watermelon cure. With enthusiasm, he read me the material out loud. Then suddenly, he became despondent, covering his face in his hands. He realized that earlier on, he had misread the website. It was suggesting not that watermelon was some miracle cure, but rather that consuming the fruit could help with hydration, and that hydration was an important part of healing.

After allowing time for him to feel the loss of his watermelon dreams, I asked Fred what he hoped for in what were likely his last days with Rachel.

He didn't hesitate for one moment. "I hope to love her with my whole heart," he said. "To love every part of her without reservation. To make sure she knows how blessed my life has been to be married to her."

During the remaining week of Rachel's life, I don't think Fred once left her side.

Like Fred, those who are very ill and their loved ones frequently begin the journey toward death with an egoic hope for a miracle—for example, a full recovery from their cancer or the return of all their physical and mental capacities. What we are calling hope in these circumstances is really just an expression of our fear. We do not generate reliable solutions in this state because they emerge from our confusion.

Hope is an innate human quality that can positively contribute to a sense of wellness. Tossing hope away doesn't seem helpful. Maybe we need to rework our understanding and application of hope.

I have found that with compassionate support, this hope can shift. It stops being about managing the symptoms we did not choose and cannot avoid, and instead turns toward discovering the value in living fully given our current conditions. Often it transforms into what I have come to call *mature hope*, a hope that takes us inside ourselves and toward finding the good in the experience.

Mature hope requires both a clear intention and a simultaneous letting go. This hope is not dependent upon outcome. In fact, hope is tied to uncertainty because we never know what is going to happen next. The hope is in the potential for our awakened response, not in things turning out a particular way. It is an orientation of the heart, grounded in value and trust in our basic human goodness, not in what we might achieve. That fundamental trust guides our actions and allows us to cooperate with others and to persevere, without attachment to a specific result. In illness, mature hope helps us come to a place of wholeness, even if a cure is unavailable.

When we relax our single-minded vision of the future—the idea that "this is the only way for things to happen"—we are no longer trapped by our conventional view of hope. We leave room for surprise. As Fred found, with flexibility and kindness, we can re-imagine hope even in a situation that appears hopeless. The energizing quality of mature hope helps us to remain open to the possibility that while life may not turn out the way we first thought, opportunities we never imagined may also arise.

Natural disasters, earthquakes, fires, and floods offer clear examples of devastating circumstances that dramatically disrupt everyday life. Homes are lost, people die. The unanticipated chaos impacts us in vastly different ways. Yet time and again, we have seen people come together in positive ways, feeding each other, acting bravely, befriending strangers, and bringing their best selves forward. Perhaps this is in part because we are thrust into the immediacy of life in an intense way, not unlike the blow of receiving a life-threatening diagnosis. Stories of people meeting impossible conditions with grace uplift us and inspire hope in the basic goodness and altruism of human beings.

Most of us choose comfort over truth. But when you think about it, we don't grow and transform in our comfort zones. We grow when we realize we are no longer able to control all the conditions of our lives, and are therefore challenged to change ourselves. When we release our clinging to what *used to be* and our craving for what we think *should be*, we are free to embrace the truth of *what is* in this moment.

Mature hope embraces the truth that no matter what we do or don't do, things will change. Change is constant and inevitable. Hope for an unchanging world quickly becomes discouragement. Instead, we need to trust in ourselves and each other, in right action and perseverance without despair.

I once met a man who planted ten thousand oak trees. He was at that time seventy years old. He didn't know how many had grown to be adult trees, and he certainly would never see any of them in their full maturity. He said hope was a shared promise between him, the trees, and the children who would one day climb the oaks' magnificent branches.

I never met Crystal. She just phoned one day out of the blue to ask if I would read *The Tibetan Book of the Dead* to her dying teacher, a world-renowned psychologist. I explained that it was a highly esoteric work and that some of its imagery could be quite frightening to the uninitiated. I wondered why Crystal thought her teacher might want me to read this book to her on her deathbed.

Crystal said, "She has been a remarkable teacher who has led a remarkable life, and we want her to have an equally remarkable death."

Sensing the pressure this expectation might exert on her teacher, I responded, "Perhaps she wants a perfectly ordinary death."

Crystal hung up on me, deciding, I supposed, to call someone else.

Later, she called back, explaining that after talking among themselves, she and the other students had realized that in their hearts, all they really wanted was to help their teacher die peacefully.

I agreed to help, provided we would make every attempt to learn what the teacher actually needed. I asked her to look and listen carefully to what the teacher was telling her.

"Oh, but I can't," Crystal replied. "She's in a partial coma. She can't talk."

"Look more closely. Is she perspiring?" I asked.

"Yes," Crystal said.

"Then go get a cool washcloth and place it gently on her head. She's telling you that she has a fever."

"Okay," she said.

I asked, "Is she grimacing with any obvious signs of pain?"

"No," Crystal replied.

"Wonderful. Then let's try the next step," I advised. "How is her breathing?"

"It's very fast, somewhat erratic," she said.

"Sit quietly beside her, following the rhythm of her breath. Breathe in as she breathes in; breathe out as she breathes out. There is no need to guide her. Just accompany her. In this way, you can provide a kind and loving presence, patiently attending to the moment-to-moment changes in her experience."

Crystal continued in this way for over twenty minutes. The change in atmosphere was evident even over the phone.

"What's happening now?" I asked.

"Well, her breathing is still quite fast, but I am much calmer now!" Crystal answered. Then she laughed. What a change from her tone when she'd first called.

So I said, "Just keep listening like this. Keep watching the tone of her skin. Listen to her breathing. See what happens when her eyes flutter. Watch her carefully. See everything as a communication with you. Let her show you the way. She'll guide you through. She knows how to do this. We've been dying for hundreds of thousands of years."

Then I expressed my admiration for Crystal's tender care, and we hung up. The next day, she phoned to say that her teacher had died quite peacefully during the night, when most of the students were out of the room.

In our culture, we like to nurture a story of what it means to have a "good death." We treasure the romantic hope that when people pass away, everything will be tied up neatly. All problems will have been resolved, and they will be utterly at peace.

But this fantasy is rarely the reality. The "good death" is a myth. Dying is messy. People who are dying often leave skid marks, dragging their heels as they go. Some people turn away from others and never look back. For many, the habits of a lifetime go unquestioned, and they fight fearfully to keep those habits in place. For others, their fight is like a badge of honor; they want to go down swinging. Very few people walk toward the immense challenge of dying and find peace and beauty there. But who are we to say how another should die?

In my experience, the romantic expectation of a good death places an immense and unnecessary burden on the dying. We may view it as a failure when people don't go calmly into the night. "Oh, my mother didn't see tunnels of light. She died terrified. It was an awful death," I once heard a man complain. Many people feel like failures simply for dying in the first place because our culture is so steeped in the language of "fighting until the end." Why should we further weigh the dying person down by judging how they go? As Crystal discovered, allowing our loved ones to have the experiences they need as they die is tremendously freeing for them and for us.

When I sit at the bedsides of people who are dying, my primary goal is to keep my heart open. I feel that I have a responsibility to support them wherever they are in their journey. I point to their internal resources. I try to illuminate capacities that they already have but may not recognize. Sometimes, people are able to see kindness in my eyes. This reflects back to them their own kindness, and suddenly, they are able to see themselves in a new way.

Emily was only thirty-four when she arrived at Zen Hospice dying of breast cancer. Before she fell into what a friend calls the "Twilight Sleep"—the sleep from which we rarely emerge—she shared with me the horrible torment she had suffered as a child at the hands of Ruth, her abusive mother.

When Emily's condition grew critical, Ruth came from across the country to be at her daughter's bedside. They hadn't spoken in years, and there was very bad blood between them. The mother sat there pouring out her apologies for her past behaviors and begging her only daughter for forgiveness. Emily remained silent and unresponsive, as she had been for days.

Suddenly, Emily sat upright in bed and looked her mother straight in the eye. Then, powerfully and with perfect clarity, she said to Ruth, "I hate you! I've always hated you." And then she died.

There was enormous suffering in that room. Ruth was in shock. She was living her worst nightmare. It was gut-wrenching that Emily's last words were so harsh.

It is difficult to keep our hearts open in that kind of hell. Yet when we do, we may see beyond the immediate anguish and become aware of another possibility. Emily was finally able to tell her mother what was true, what she had been afraid to say all her life. It was horrible, but it was real. Truth-telling seems necessary for a future based on healing and mature hope.

Was Emily's a "bad death"? Many people would say so. I've stopped judging. One person's "good death" is another's worst nightmare. Some want death to come suddenly, while others hope they will die slowly. Some people hope to be surrounded by loving family members, while some fear the interference of well-meaning others.

In the months after Emily's death, I worked with Ruth to support her through her grief. It was a tough road. Yet taking responsibility for her past actions and facing the seemingly impossible truth of Emily's hatred proved essential in her finding self-forgiveness. It was critical in healing the wounds and reconciling herself to her long-troubled relationship with her daughter that she not hope for a different past. Knowing that she could not alter conditions, that she could not change what had happened at Emily's deathbed or go back and be a different sort of mother, Ruth was able, eventually, to accept what was so and make peace with it.

In death and in life, should we "hope for the best" or "expect the worst"? What if instead, we cultivated a non-judgmental attention and commitment to being with the truth of whatever is present? Suppose rather than choosing sides, we developed the mental clarity, emotional stability, and embodied presence to not be swept away by the cycle of ups and downs, of hopes and fears? Balanced equanimity gives rise to a resilience that is fluid and not fixed, trusting, adaptable, and responsive. Perhaps we might accept our past, ourselves, others, and the continually changing conditions of our lives "as is"—neither good nor bad, but workable.

It's helpful here to take refuge in impermanence. Not in the expectation that things will turn out as we hope or fear, but in the fact that things will change whether we want them to or not.

We speak of living in the present moment. But where is *this moment* to be found? Is it a nanosecond that punctuates the space between past and future? To paraphrase St. Augustine, now is neither in time nor out of time. The elusive present moment is not measured by the tick-tock time of a clock, which we humans invented, nor is it separate from past or future. There is no time line, at least not as we conventionally think about it.

We all have experienced feelings of timelessness, when a moment expands a bit like a dream. When I remember my mother, who died more than forty-five years ago, isn't the past then happening in the now? The present moment includes the past and also the potency for the future. My granddaughter is still an infant, so at the moment she is not consciously shaping her future. Yet the potential for that future lives within her right now, as it lives within each of us.

This is where the energy of hope has a place—not as a wish to be fulfilled or a plan to be formulated and executed, but in how we meet the ever-changing moment. The present moment includes all time; it is the all-inclusive now. The present moment could best be described as *the flow of life.* We are continually being shaped by it, and we are shaping it through the way we meet and respond to it.

Don't wait is an encouragement to step fully into life. Don't miss this moment waiting for the next one to arrive. Don't wait to act on what is most important. Don't get stuck in the hope for a better past or future; be present.

David was living with serious Parkinson's disease. At first, his body's deterioration frustrated and frightened him. He noticed how often he would relate to his body from a wish for it to be another way.

If only I could slow the progress of this disease, he would think. *How and when will my illness get worse?* he would worry. Waiting for his circumstances to change, hoping for a different future, he would be mostly in his head and riddled with anxiety.

Fortunately, David is a dedicated meditator, and over time, he was able to shift his mind-set. His thoughts would quiet down. He would relax and become more peaceful, more reflective. He described such moments as "timeless" and told me, "I see now how the constant desire to

have things be other than what they were was blinding me to the positive aspects of my Parkinson's experience. Now I focus on my gratitude
for those who care for me. I trust in my capacity to meet whatever challenges come my way."

David said, "In my ordinary mind, I have a hope that I am going to
change my illness. It is the object of my fear, and I want to control that
fear. But I am only setting myself up for disappointment. I get lost. When
I emerge into a more peaceful state, the object comes to me, and I see it
for what it is: a 'scary thought.' Then I realize, if I am aware of the thought
and the accompanying fear, then the fear is not all that is present. Awareness is also present. And with that recognition, I can choose to function
from the fear or from the awareness."

He continued, "It's like how, when we saw the earth from the moon
for the first time, we could understand ourselves in ways that weren't
possible before. When I'm not so full of the hope of expectation, I can
see more of the picture. I see opportunities that I missed before. This is
not some passive, helpless state or a vacant lot in my mind. It is a pure
openness that has inherent dynamism. It is infused with curiosity and
discovery."

What David was describing so eloquently is a subtler dimension to
the idea of *don't wait*, which I call *non-waiting*. It is the antidote to the
trap of expectation—an open, receptive quality of mind. In non-waiting,
we allow objects, experiences, states of mind, and hearts to unfold, to
show themselves to us without our interference.

The difference between *don't wait* and *non-waiting* is like the difference between detachment and non-attachment. Detachment implies
distancing ourselves from a particular object or experience. It can feel
cool, like we are withdrawing or pulling away. Non-attachment simply
means not holding on to, not grasping, not getting entangled. There is
no need for distancing oneself.

Similarly, non-waiting is relaxed and spacious, a way of allowing
experience to come toward us without the need to reach out and grab
it. We come to know our experience by revelation, not by wrestling

meaning out of it or by manipulating it into being the way we want it to be, or by encumbering it with our previous knowing. Non-waiting is a quiet welcoming, more of an invitation than a demand. When we stop leaning into the next experience by hoping for a particular outcome, or leaning into the past by hoping we might somehow change it, only then are we free to know this moment completely.

Non-waiting offers us a new vantage point, a bit like Google Maps. In one moment, we may have a very narrow street view. We may be focusing on certain particulars, like the address of a house. Then we pull back to a more panoramic perspective, and we see how that one house is but a small dot in the city, the country, the hemisphere in which it resides. When we see the bigger picture, we can include more options.

Non-waiting is not patience. Patience implies expectation, waiting for the next moment, just doing it in a calmer way. The experience of non-waiting is more like *continuous contact* with reality. We are alert, awake, and fully alive. Whatever the experience—whether "good" or "bad," whether we like or dislike it—we give our full attention to it, to what is happening right now.

In living, as in dying, when we hold hope apart from expectation, independent of attachment to outcome, we develop a wise connection with reality. We show up and participate directly in life's unfolding. We engage in the journey instead of waiting to arrive at our destination.

Hope with an attitude of non-waiting gives rise to a timeless expansiveness, a joyful openness, a receptivity not contingent upon circumstances and conditions. It arises from an immediate connection with the benevolence of this human life. And, thanks to it, we are able to proceed with our lives without so much interference. Mature hope is a bit like Brahms's "Lullaby," a sweet reminder that helps us to relax and appreciate the potential for new life that always infuses the present moment.

4

THE HEART OF THE MATTER

Forgiveness is not an occasional act, it is a constant attitude.
—MARTIN LUTHER KING JR.

Forgiveness shakes loose the calcification that accumulates around our hearts. Then love can flow more freely. Blaze and Travis taught me that.

Blaze was the first person who lived and died with us at Zen Hospice Project. She was living alone in a dingy SRO hotel room when she was diagnosed with terminal cancer. A social worker introduced me to Blaze at San Francisco General Hospital. She couldn't go home, and she needed someone to love her, that much was obvious, so we invited her to stay with us at the San Francisco Zen Center. It wasn't a well-thought-through invitation. We didn't have a hospice yet. But Blaze needed a place to stay, and there were empty student rooms at our center. I figured it would all work out somehow. In those days, I was young, idealistic, a bit naïve, and not big on plans.

Blaze didn't have any friends, as far as we could tell. But shortly after she arrived, she asked us to track down her brother, Travis, saying that she hadn't seen him in more than twenty-five years. It wasn't easy. This was before the Internet, and Travis was a wrangler who rode the rodeo circuit. He never stayed in one place for too long. We contacted the

Professional Rodeo Cowboys Association, and eventually we found him.

"Your sister is dying, and she wants to see you," I told him over the phone. I really didn't expect anything to come of it.

Then late one night, Travis showed up at the Zen Center front door. He cut an imposing figure dressed in full cowboy regalia: a ten-gallon Stetson, a king-size silver belt buckle, and snakeskin boots.

"So what kinda place is this where you got my sis?" he demanded, looking around the modest interior.

"She's upstairs," I replied. "Would you like to go see her?"

He said, "Sure," so I took him to Blaze's room. But when we got there, it was clear that Travis was too scared to go inside. He just paced nervously in the hallway.

After a while, I suggested that he get some rest and try again tomorrow. When I offered him a room at the Zen Center, he agreed to stay the night.

The next morning, I found Travis in the dining hall in his cowboy getup, surrounded by Zen monks with shaved heads and black robes eating tofu. It was quite a sight.

After some time, he said that he was ready to head upstairs, and he found himself able to enter Blaze's room. I sat quietly in a corner, observing. I was surprised by how subdued this brother and sister were when they finally reunited. They didn't talk about Blaze's illness or anything serious. They just made small talk about the weather, rodeos, and listening to Hank Williams on the radio.

Travis visited daily. Gradually, their conversations deepened. Blaze talked about her experiences of hospitals, doctors, and what it was like to have cancer. There was some playful reminiscing and sharing of memories.

Ten days after Travis's arrival, Blaze's condition took a turn for the worse. While she rested, Travis and I went to the courtyard, where we would sometimes go to shoot the breeze. He would smoke a cigarette, and I would listen. Nothing important seemed to be happening, so I stood to go home to my family. Under his breath, Travis mumbled, "I want to tell 'er, but I can't tell 'er."

I sat back down. "You know, Travis, if there's anything you need to tell your sister, you should do it soon. Don't wait. Blaze hasn't got much more time."

"Not good with words," he replied.

I said, "If you can't tell her, why don't you tell me?"

A long story poured out of Travis. He told me about how he and Blaze were abandoned as kids. They had grown up in orphanages and foster homes all over the West, sometimes together and sometimes apart. It had been pretty miserable. Travis, who was a year older than Blaze, had hurt his sister badly a few times. He had done some really awful things to her, he said. He had been abusive to her in many ways. That was why they hadn't seen each other in so many years.

My initial reaction was, *Who am I to hear this confessional? I'm not a priest. I'm not a therapist. I don't have a psychology degree.*

But I remembered once meeting the great humanistic psychotherapist Carl Rogers, who was the grandfather of a good friend. Later, I studied films of him working with patients. I noticed that he rarely spoke, but that his listening was so devout it drew out the truth from his clients like a healing salve. Something he had written had always stayed with me:

Before every session, I take a moment to remember my humanity. There is no experience that this man has that I cannot share with him, no fear that I cannot understand, no suffering that I cannot care about, because I too am human. No matter how deep his wound, he does not need to be ashamed in front of me. I too am vulnerable. And because of this, I am enough. Whatever his story, he no longer needs to be alone with it. This is what will allow his healing to begin.

Sharing our stories helps us to heal. Intuitively, I sensed that the greatest gift I could offer Travis in that moment was my undivided attention. Listening without judgment is probably the simplest, most profound way to connect. It is an act of love.

When Travis finally finished his story, he was confused and apologetic. I think his outburst had surprised him as it much as it had me. "So that's what happened. Now what do I do?" he asked. It was clear that, as far as he was concerned, all he could do was suffer the consequences of his horrible behavior.

I suggested that we go talk to Blaze.

When we got to her room, Travis pulled up a chair next to Blaze's bed and said, "You know, Sis, there's something I've been meaning to tell you all these years, but, you know, I never could find the right words . . . I just wanted to say . . . about all those things I did . . ."

Blaze raised her hand like a traffic cop to stop him and said calmly, "In this place, Travis, I have somebody who feeds me. I have somebody who bathes me. I'm surrounded by love. There is no blame."

I was awestruck by what I had just witnessed. A whole lifetime of pain forgiven in a single moment. A powerful act of mercy, the slate wiped clean. We all cried together, then a liberating silence followed.

I remembered that one day not long before Travis had arrived at the Zen Center, I'd been sitting with the usually taciturn Blaze when she'd asked me a question. "There are these people who come in the room and tell me to love. Then there are these other people who come in the room and tell me to let go. Which should I do first?"

I hadn't answered her for a long while. Then I had said, "Blaze, you're going to know what to do, and you can trust that. But the thing is, they are almost simultaneous actions. Love is what allows us to let go."

Loving and letting go are inseparable. You can't love and cling at the same time. Too often we mistake attachment for love.

In Buddhism, loving kindness, or *metta*, is considered a sublime state of being. A heavenly realm. It's expansive, allowing, caring, and connective. Attachment masquerades as love. It looks and smells like love, but it's a cheap imitation. You can feel how attachment grasps and is driven by need and fear. Love is selfless; attachment is self-centered. Love is freeing; attachment is possessive. When we love, we relax, we don't hold on so tightly, and we naturally let go more easily.

Blaze understood something about letting go. In forgiving Travis, it wasn't that Blaze had forgotten what had happened to her. Nor was she condoning anything her brother had done. Basically, she was saying to him, "Look, if you want to carry this pain around for the rest of your life, be my guest. But I'm done." Approaching death, she had reached a point where she wanted to release herself from all the resentment and angst that had been her companions for decades. The past didn't define her anymore. She didn't want to die full of argument. She wanted to be free, full of love, and she understood that the only way she could do that was to forgive her brother completely. No questions asked.

Two days later, Blaze died.

Forgiveness is critical for two reasons. It heals us by allowing us to set down old pain, and it helps open us to love.

In order to be free, we have to forgive. When I speak of freedom in this context, I don't mean some sort of ultimate enlightenment, but something far more practical and immediate: freedom from the indictments, recriminations, and judgments that cause us so much suffering. Holding on to our pain is, quite simply, not in our best interests.

The refusal to forgive is a way we resist life. We can be very loyal to our suffering. Yet when we cling tightly to our past, we hold on to not just the memories, but also the tension and the emotional states that go along with them. Resisting forgiveness is like grasping a hot coal and saying, "I'm not going to let go until you apologize and pay for what you've done to me." In our effort to punish, we are the ones who get burned.

Forgiveness allows us to let go of pain not by sugarcoating it with positive thoughts, but by allowing our experience to come forward so that we can touch our pain with mercy. We don't have to let old hurts continue to define who we are in the here and now. We can let the past dissolve. We can leave it behind. We can say good-bye to old wounds. By forgiving, we can release ourselves from suffering that has been confining us ever since the event took place.

In forgiving, we get to know our pain more intimately. This is what

Travis did when he told me the story of his past. For the first time in his life, Travis took that old hurt out of his back pocket, dusted it off, and gave it a closer look. Only then was he able to receive Blaze's forgiveness.

Forgiveness has the power to overcome what divides us. It can melt the armor of fear and resentment around our hearts that keeps us separate from others, from ourselves, and from life itself. I once asked a young woman with cancer who had been abandoned by her family and had to live on the streets if she thought forgiveness took courage. "Yes," she said, "but for me it was a way to find out if I was capable of loving again." Forgiveness releases our hearts from the rubble of anger and other negative feelings, and clears the way to love.

Like the ama, Japanese women pearl divers of days gone by, when we dive deep in our wounds, we may emerge with treasure. Bare breasted, the ama wore nothing more than a short loincloth, a face mask, and a pair of fins. They filled their lungs with air and plunged courageously into the cold, dark waters of the sea, disappearing below the surface and emerging several minutes later with a pearl. Exploring our own hurt, in addition to contributing to our healing, helps us feel empathy for others who have suffered similar injuries.

Sometimes a vast accumulation of pain can be released all at once, as it was with Blaze and Travis, but forgiveness doesn't typically happen like that. I would say that 99 percent of the people I have worked with benefited from the practice of forgiveness, and they each came to it in their own way. Often, it is a long, difficult process. Usually, people are waylaid by the circumstances surrounding the wound, their relationship to the perpetrator, a lack of motivation, or simply the passage of time.

We all agree that forgiveness has many benefits. Why, then, do we resist it?

Forgiveness is a fierce practice. It takes real strength, a willingness to be with what is difficult. It asks us to face our demons. It requires absolute honesty. We must be willing to see things as they are, bearing witness to painful acts that happened to us or the harm we may have done to others. Sometimes we need to rage. Sometimes we need to grapple with our guilt. Sometimes we need to fall into a deep sorrow. Forgiveness isn't about squelching any of these emotions. It is about facing them with kindness, paying close attention to what is getting in the way of our letting go.

In my experience, people typically arrive at a place of forgiveness when they realize, "I don't want this to interfere with my capacity to love. I don't want this to be a legacy that I leave behind or with my children." We forgive because there is no point in waiting to unburden ourselves, no point in wasting time by holding ourselves back with old resentments. We forgive because we don't want to reach the end of our lives filled with sighs and regret. We forgive not because it is "bad" not to, but because holding on to our pain hurts too much and keeps us from loving fully.

A ninety-year-old woman named Magda attended one of my retreats. That week, she spent quite a bit of time complaining about her relationship with her ninety-one-year-old husband, Jerzy. They had weathered sixty years of marriage. But now that he was aging and increasingly frail, he began to create distance between them. He would tell her that he wanted to move out of their home and into a nursing home or go back to Poland, where he was from. She felt angered and hurt by his behavior.

"How could he do this to me after so many years?" she asked.

When we spoke about forgiveness, I could sense Magda's resistance. She was waiting for Jerzy to apologize. She wasn't ready to let go of her sense of being wronged. But even though the barriers to forgiveness may seem impenetrable, love can enter through the thinnest crack in someone's defenses.

Weeks later, I got a letter from Magda:

I learned from you on retreat that people are going to die. Jerzy is going to die. I don't want to spend the final days with him being mad at him. I saw that I had to shift my perspective toward him, overcoming my feelings of indignation and rage. I began to understand his constant threats of moving out as just his way of protecting himself. I realized that I love him, and I need to forgive him. I want to cherish every moment with him. I don't want to spend our remaining time squabbling.

It can be difficult to mercifully move toward our own or another's ugliness. The beauty of forgiveness is how the investigation of our feelings of disconnection, alienation, fear, and bitterness allow us to feel these painful emotions with kindness and to rediscover our common humanity.

We all have darkness within us, and we all also have the capacity to forgive.

I learned just how challenging forgiveness can be from my own experience. In the 1980s, I was traveling in the mountains of Guatemala, a country ravaged by a brutal civil war. I volunteered at a makeshift medical clinic staffed by a well-intentioned but young and inexperienced intern from Guatemala City.

Late one night, a Mayan couple rushed in carrying their five-year-old son. I didn't speak Mayan, and they spoke only a few words of Spanish and no English. After a medical exam, it became clear that the boy was suffering from a mysterious but severe abdominal pain and probably needed emergency surgery. The problem was, the nearest hospital was eight hours away by jeep. If the child didn't get help sooner than that, he surely wouldn't make it through the night.

Earlier in my trip, I had met the Guatemalan colonel in charge of the government troops in the area. He had bragged to me about all the wonderful things the army was doing for the indigenous people. So I ran to his house to ask him to use a nearby army helicopter to fly the boy to the hospital and save his life.

The colonel had an angry scowl on his face when he came to the door.

After I had described the situation in my broken Spanish, he made a dismissive gesture with his hand as if to say, "Why did you wake me up in the middle of the night to tell me about this irrelevant Indian boy?" Then he slammed the door in my face.

I was furious. I had to return to the clinic empty-handed.

When I arrived, the child was writhing in gut-wrenching pain, his mother crying out in Spanish, "Mercy, Madonna!" The parents thought I was a doctor. They didn't know there was nothing I could do. I just cradled the little boy's sweaty head in my two hands. His father and I took shifts holding him. Meanwhile, the mother fed her son a syrupy corn mush, a homemade medical remedy. Mayan prayers were whispered throughout the night.

I sat there helpless for hours as mother and father cuddled their five-year-old son and watched him die a horrible death, probably from a ruptured pancreas. Then they wrapped him up in a tattered, hand-woven blanket. The father rested the boy's body over his own shoulder and carried him away.

The experience filled me with a murderous rage. I was furious with that colonel. He could have prevented this horrendous, unnecessary death. I honestly believe that if I had had a gun, I might have shot the man. I don't think I have ever felt so much hatred before or since.

After I left Guatemala and returned to California, I continued my work on behalf of the refugees by lobbying Congress for policy changes and speaking publicly about the consequences of the ongoing civil war. But months later, the image of that little boy lying there in total agony, and my despair in being unable to help him, still haunted me.

One night, I was listening to a news program on the radio about the wars in Guatemala and the rest of Central America when my rage resurfaced. Without realizing it, I started screaming at the radio. I turned, and to my horror, I saw my two-year-old son, Gabe, cowering in the corner. He was crunched down, his hands over his face, terrified.

I imagine all of us parents have had moments like this, moments when we think to ourselves, *Oh my, I have done a horrible thing to my child*. It can be soul shattering. I realized then and there that I had to stop fighting the war—not the war in Guatemala, but the one in my own heart. I could never condone what that colonel had done; it was wrong and will always be wrong. There was evil in his actions that I will never forget. But my ongoing internal battle with him was tearing me apart and harming my relationship with my son.

Ultimately, my concern for my son's well-being served as the motivation to turn toward the thing I didn't want to look at—my extreme anger at the colonel—and eventually to let it go. I recognized that the next step would be the heavy lifting of practicing forgiveness. I had to stop the rage. It was hurting my heart too much. Love was driving me to forgive.

When my anger confused me, when obstacles came up, my intention served as a compass guiding me back home to forgiveness. Some days it was impossible. I would become overwhelmed by powerful resistance or seduced by doubt. "This isn't working. Forgiveness is just a story I'm telling myself." Returning again and again to my love for Gabe and my desire to let go of my own pain, I would touch my own confusion with mindfulness and mercy. I would say to myself, "I don't want to be chained to this resentment anymore."

To remind myself of this intention, I asked a master calligrapher to paint my favorite quote from the Buddha: "*Hatred can never cease by hatred in this world; by love alone does hatred cease. This is an ancient and eternal law.*" This work of art has rested at the center of my altar for more than thirty years and remains there to this day. It is the first thing I look at every day when I sit to meditate.

Next to the Buddha's quote on the altar, I placed a photo that I had found of the colonel. As I began my forgiveness meditation practice, I would gaze at both items and silently recite a phrase: "For whatever you may have done to harm me in your thoughts, words, and actions, I forgive you." Then I would allow all of the ugliness in my mind and heart to emerge.

To be honest, I often didn't feel very forgiving. I experienced more rage and anger than acceptance. Revenge strategies would fill my mind.

When this happened, I wouldn't try to force forgiveness to happen—that isn't possible, anyway. I knew that I had to experience it in an authentic way. So instead, I would move directly into sensing how much it hurt me to hold on to the pain. I would allow myself to feel my grief and suffering, my burning hatred and disgust. Trying to bury or ignore this unpleasantness was futile—it would only resurface of its own volition, like a zombie rising from the dead, as it did that day when I screamed at the radio. So I would allow those feelings to surface, and I would touch them with mercy.

At times, when it felt absolutely impossible to forgive, I gave myself permission to set the colonel aside. I remembered my teacher's kind counsel years before: "When you go into the gym, don't pick up the five-hundred-pound weight. Start with the twenty-pound weight." I practiced forgiving the smallest slights: A driver cutting me off on the freeway. A colleague who used sharp words to disagree with a point I made. I developed the muscle of forgiveness by working through everyday grievances.

I called forth allies to join me on my journey: compassion, kindness, and love. These served as the ground for my forgiveness practice, the resources I could draw upon. I would imagine the love I felt for my favorite friends and teachers, my family, and my son, consciously cultivating positive emotions while looking at the colonel's photo.

Sometimes, I would find myself clinging to my resentment and bitterness. The illusion would arise that the world someday would confirm my self-righteous point of view. But I also knew that that day would likely never come—the colonel would never pay a price for letting the Mayan boy die.

It is common for people to willingly carry around resentment. Some people would rather die than forgive. Every part of us might scream, "No! I don't want to forgive!" At the same time, many of us can't even remember what happened to cause us such fury in the first place. What we do remember, what we hold on to, it turns out, is not the story or even the hurt so much as the resentment we have built up as a result.

I found it liberating not to be driven by dreams of idealistic outcomes. At first, my entire practice was quite simply about this willingness to let myself feel my feelings fully. I had to grieve the loss of the little boy. I had to stew in my hatred toward the colonel for allowing it to happen. The key was investigating with an open heart the obstacles standing in my path at each step of the journey. When teaching a retreat, I often ask, "How does your resentment feel in your body, heart, and mind? Do your shoulders tighten? Does your jaw lock down? What happens in your mind? Do you run revenge scenarios through your imagination? Do you replay arguments with the accused, saying what you wish you had said at the time? Does it make you feel important? What are the honest feelings in your heart? Not just the anger, but what about the helplessness, hurt, or sadness that sits just under that rage? Get to know this resentment intimately."

We confuse forgiveness with forgetting. We are afraid that if we forgive, we will forget, and the harm may happen again. However, we don't need to cling to the mental tension and emotional anguish to benefit from the lessons learned. We don't need to punish ourselves—or anyone else—in order *not* to forget. We don't need our bitterness to prove that we have been wronged.

Similarly, we mistakenly imagine that forgiving means condoning another's bad behavior. As one middle-aged man I worked with put it, "You don't want to give up any weapons and let the other person off the hook." But forgiveness does not release others from responsibility for their actions, nor does it necessarily change their behavior. It is a tool for removing the roadblocks to our hearts and liberating us from the destructive hold on our past pain. Forgiveness is for the forgiver.

Many insist that there must be remorse, an apology by the perpetrator, justice, or even punishment before there can be forgiveness. This is a subject of much debate. The problem with this strategy is that in some cases, we may need to wait a long time for justice to arrive, if indeed it ever comes. In my mind, forgiveness isn't about justice—unless we speak of restorative justice, which aims at fairness and the healing of

relationships. Forgiveness is about the release of the contraction of bitterness in our hearts and a rediscovery of inner peace.

Outrage can indeed fuel change, but wanton anger is an act of ego, a
knee-jerk reaction and a cheap substitute for true strength. When we access the strength hidden in our anger, we have the capacity to take dynamic action and the resolve to stand powerfully against injustice when
needed.

When I spoke publicly and lobbied against the wars in Central America from a place of anger, people were less inclined to listen to me. Like
my son Gabe cowering in a corner, they shied away from my rage. As I
forgave the colonel, my activism became infused with love. I did what I
was doing—and more—because I loved the people of Guatemala, and
I didn't want to see them suffer.

Our identification with old pain can feed an absence of forgiveness.
After carrying pain for so long, we wonder, who would we be without
it? Our resentment, our self-righteousness, seeing ourselves only as
casualties—these feelings, in spite of being a burden, become familiar.
We know, *This is how it feels. This is who I am.* We would rather stay with
what is known than unburden ourselves of the negativity. This urge to
cling to our sense of having been wronged in the past can last a lifetime.

One woman I knew who was in her late seventies told me that she
had been haunted since childhood by her resentment. Her father had told
her, "You never seem to rise to your best." In an attempt to please him,
she had become an obsessive overachiever. But over time, she came to
resent how his lack of appreciation had colored her life. It wasn't until
late in life, when she allowed herself to get angry with her father, that
she finally forgave him.

Forgiveness does not imply or require reconciliation. Forgiveness may
lead to a meeting of the minds at some point—as when a child grows to
an adult and forgives his parents for not being perfect—but reconciliation isn't always the outcome. Reconciliation takes two people. It requires
the re-establishing of trust. When you reconcile, you make an agreement
for the future. Think of when you have a fight with your friend or part-

ner. Afterward, you both say, "I'm sorry. I see that I hurt you. I want to take responsibility for my actions. I love and respect you, so I'm going to try not to do that again—and this is how." That is reconciliation.

We can't depend on other people taking those courageous steps toward vulnerability and love. Sometimes they don't want to. Sometimes it is too late, and they already are gone from our lives for good. Fortunately, forgiveness only takes one person: you. It is a beneficial practice for letting go of your own pain. We can forgive someone without ever having a conversation with her. She can be dead, and still it isn't too late to forgive her.

Forgiveness does not ask us to welcome people back into our lives. We can still say to our abuser, "No, I don't ever want to see you again." But forgiveness empowers us to let ourselves off the hook: "I don't need to continue to carry all this tightness, rage, anger, and pain within me."

Forgiveness asks us to move closer to our suffering, and, in so doing, discover a larger, more compassionate part of ourselves that can touch our wounds with kindness and understanding. Gradually, we shift away from being someone who is only afraid of pain to becoming one who is capable of embracing it. As such, the practice of forgiveness opens the mind to the natural compassion of the heart.

In the process, we not only liberate ourselves from that particular moment in time when we suffered our wounds, but we also begin to recognize ourselves as something more than our pain. We free ourselves to be more of who we really are. Unconfined. Able to grow and re-imagine ourselves. Paradoxically, we become more of who we are, more than ever before.

The words of forgiveness I recited while gazing at the colonel's picture on my altar day in and day out didn't ring true for almost two years. But I continued repeating them, anyway . . . and one day they finally felt right. I was able to open my heart to the colonel. His actions were detestable, unforgivable, but over time, the man came into clearer view.

Eventually, I understood that the colonel's actions were the result of unknown causes and conditions in his life that had hardened into ignorance. That ignorance had caused the problem, and it wasn't going to help me to keep holding on to my hatred for him. I knew that intellectually all along, but I needed to experience my resistance in all its facets before I could let go.

Finally, I saw that my lack of forgiveness was acting as a defense against my feelings of failure. I was scared that if I forgave the colonel, I would be abandoning this boy again. But in reality, I had fought that battle—and I had lost. Buried far, far underneath the rage, like an ancient barnacle-crusted ship lost at sea, I found the hidden treasure, the crux of the issue: I had to forgive myself. I blamed the colonel for the boy's death, but I felt that I had failed the child, as well. This self-loathing was getting in the way of my letting go. I had to accept that I was human and had done all that I could. Circumstances were beyond my control.

It took another year for me to forgive myself for wanting to kill the colonel.

Perpetrator and victim live within each of us. If I could forgive the colonel for his ignorance, then surely I could forgive myself. Over time, this practice led me to the understanding that forgiveness is *always* for our own benefit. We might extend our forgiveness to others or ask for forgiveness from them, but primarily it is an act of self-interest, not about changing the other person. When we forgive, we give ourselves the medicine that is most helpful, touching ourselves with radical self-acceptance.

Forgiveness is not an intellectual exercise. We must fully engage the heart until it is felt in our bones. Working our way through hatred teaches us to love more deeply.

After Blaze died, we held a memorial service for her at Green Gulch Farm, a beautiful Buddhist retreat center along the California coast north of San Francisco. En route to the service, Travis asked me to pull over at a corner store. He bought a pint of gin and a couple of dozen roses. He polished off most of the gin by the time we arrived at his sister's memorial.

This was the first memorial we had ever done for one of our hospice patients, and we weren't really sure what to do. Most of the volunteers who had taken care of Blaze had come to pay their respects. To start things off, we asked everyone to share their memories of Blaze.

When it was Travis's turn to speak, he walked around the room and handed a rose to each volunteer. He didn't know most of their names, but he knew they had taken care of his sister, and for that he was grateful. As he offered the roses, he said, "Some of these roses are for gratitude; some of them are for love." Then he stopped in front of me and looked me straight in the eye. "And some of these roses, well, they're just roses."

I wondered if maybe we had had some kind of Zen influence on Travis. He was expressing the ordinariness of the experience, what in the Zen tradition we call "nothing special." It is an insight that emerges when we come to see and accept circumstances just as they are. Travis now saw himself in that way—as natural, imperfect, nothing special—just like those roses.

Who would have guessed that the rough-edged cowboy who had showed up at our door a few weeks earlier would have been capable of such wisdom and tenderness? Something had changed in Travis since Blaze had given him the gift of forgiveness. His heart had cracked wide open.

And that had happened in no small part because Travis had been ready to receive his sister's forgiveness. In telling his story in the courtyard of the Zen Center, in sharing every painful detail, he had finally found the courage to meet with mercy what he had been hiding from for most of his life. Without a doubt, Blaze's act of forgiveness had been very gener-ous, and it had set her free before her death. But Travis's true healing had come from his ability to forgive himself.

All forgiveness is self-forgiveness. It is a remarkable form of self-acceptance that allows us to release unbelievable pain. It's about realizing that as long as you hold on to the hot coal of your anger, resentment, and sense of having been wronged, you are only hurting yourself. Unless you release that burden, you will carry it with you for the rest of your life. You will never be free.

Don't wait. Don't wait until you find yourself on your deathbed to begin the process of forgiving those who have hurt you or those you have wronged. Allow the fragile nature of life to show you what's most important . . . then take action. It hurts too much to keep others or ourselves out of our hearts.

THE SECOND INVITATION

Welcome Everything, Push Away Nothing

Barn's burnt down—
Now
I can see the moon.

—MIZUTA MASAHIDE

My wife, Vanda, who is British, was initially confused by the way Americans use the term "You're welcome." It is more common in her home country to respond to "thank you" with something like, "Don't mention it." Similar, I suppose, to the informal French *de rien*, the Spanish *de nada*, or the *no problem* so common among millennials. The trouble with these other expressions is that they downplay an act of kindness, which "You're welcome" acknowledges. The word *welcome* connotes an invitation. When I first tried to translate what is meant by "You are welcome" to my wife, I opened my arms wide in a gesture that suggested my receptivity to every part of her.

In welcoming everything, we don't have to like what is arising. It's actually not our job to approve or disapprove. The word *welcome* confronts us; it asks us to temporarily suspend our usual rush to judgment and to simply be open to what is happening. Our task is to give our careful attention to what is showing up at our front door. To receive it in the spirit of hospitality.

A friend of mine was once invited for dinner at the home of a renowned psychiatrist named Sidney. Sidney was a man of unusual intelligence, insight, and grace. However, in the few years prior to this dinner,
his Alzheimer's disease had taken a toll on his short-term memory and
ability to recognize faces.

When my friend arrived, she rang the doorbell, and Sidney opened
the door. At first he had a look of confusion. He quickly recovered and
said, "I'm sorry. I have trouble remembering faces these days. But I do
know that our home always has been a place where guests are welcome.
If you are here on my doorstep, then it is my job to welcome you. Please
come in."

We like the familiar; we like certainty. We love to have our preferences met. In fact, most of us have been taught that getting what
we want and avoiding what we don't is the way to assure our happiness. Inevitably, though, there are unexpected experiences in our
lives—an unanticipated move, a job loss, a family member's illness,
the death of a beloved pet—that we want to push away with all our
might. When faced with the uncertain, our first reaction is often resistance. We attempt to evict these difficult parts of our lives as if
they were unwanted houseguests. In such moments, welcoming
seems impossible or even unwise. When I say that we should be receptive to whatever presents itself to us, do I mean that we should let
life walk all over us?

Not at all.

When we are open and receptive, we have options. We are free to
discover, to investigate, and to learn how to respond skillfully to anything we encounter. We can't be free if we are rejecting any part of our
lives. With welcoming comes an ability to meet and work with both
pleasant and unpleasant circumstances. Gradually, with practice, we discover that our well-being is not solely dependent on what's happening
in our external reality; it comes from within.

In order to experience true freedom, we need to be able to welcome

everything just as it is. At the deepest level, this invitation, like life itself, asks us to cultivate a kind of fearless receptivity. *Welcome everything,*
push away nothing cannot be done solely as an act of will. To welcome
everything is an act of love.

5

AS IS

The curious paradox is that when I accept myself
just as I am, then I can change.

—CARL ROGERS

I took a seat in the armless metal chair next to Lorenzo's bed. He was lying there, tangled up in a synthetic hospital blanket, turned toward the institutional green wall.

A recently homeless man in his sixties, Lorenzo had adopted a quality of resignation, having fallen into a deep depression after being diagnosed with terminal lung cancer. A few days earlier, he had tried to take his own life. Now he was a guest of the Psychiatric Emergency Services at San Francisco General Hospital. The staff told me that he had barely talked to anyone since being admitted.

I sat quietly. Time passed.

After twenty minutes, Lorenzo craned his neck over his shoulder and demanded, "Who are you?"

"I'm Frank. I'm with the Zen Hospice Project," I replied.

"Nobody has ever sat this long in silence with me before," he said.

"I get lots of practice sitting in silence."

Lorenzo was a thin, elegant-looking Italian-Argentinean man dressed in baggy sweatpants and a rumpled shirt. Beneath his despair and hostile attitude, I sensed a keen intelligence.

"What do you want?" I asked him matter-of-factly.

"Spaghetti," he answered without missing a beat.

"Spaghetti? Well, we make really good spaghetti at our place. Why don't you come live with us?"

"Okay, Frank." He nodded in approval.

That was the end of the admissions interview.

The next day when Lorenzo arrived at our hospice residence, we had a big bowl of spaghetti waiting for him. You see, to Lorenzo, spaghetti meant familiarity, nurturance, home, and a return to normalcy.

Lorenzo lived with us for almost three months. He didn't stop wanting to kill himself just because we gave him spaghetti. It was good spaghetti . . . but it wasn't that good.

However, Lorenzo and I did come to love and trust each other. Trust is built one day at a time, one interaction at a time. It begins with the practical. When you help move someone from the bed to the commode, the other person comes to trust that you won't let them fall. In time, they trust you with their secrets and fears.

Lorenzo was an educated man with an interest in art, literature, and philosophy. His life had spiraled downward after his marriage broke apart. He had lost his job and health insurance when he could no longer work due to his cancer. He was a self-determined man who never imagined himself as someone who would one day live on the streets. He needed to regain some semblance of control.

It is not uncommon for hospice patients to express a wish to die. Lorenzo wanted to read *Final Exit*, Derek Humphry's bestselling book about assisted suicide. This was many years before the current laws allowing physician-assisted death, so Lorenzo's request was considered radical. I bought him the book, anyway, and each night read him a chapter from it. Sometimes we have to go to the darkest places to find what heals.

In those late-night sessions, Lorenzo would talk and I would listen as he slowly began to reveal his deepest fears. Like many people, Lorenzo feared having to endure days of unbearable pain and distressing symptoms. I assured him that at our hospice, we had raised pain and symptom management to a high art form. He worried that he might be emotionally abandoned, that being sick meant giving up control or becoming dependent on others. I promised we wouldn't leave him alone and that he would get to choose how he wanted to be treated.

One day shortly before he died, Lorenzo called me into his room and said, "I want to thank you. I am happier now than I've ever been."

"Bullshit," I replied. "Not long ago you told me you didn't want to live if you couldn't walk in the park or write in your journal. What was that about?"

"Oh, *that*," he answered with a shrug. "That was just chasing desire."

"What do you mean? Those activities aren't important to you anymore?"

Lorenzo sighed. "No, it's not the activities that bring me joy. It's the *attention* to the activities. Now my pleasure comes from the coolness of the breeze and the softness of the sheets."

I smiled. What a remarkable transformation for a man I'd met in a psychiatric unit just a few months earlier.

In the non-judgmental atmosphere of acceptance and respect we had provided him, Lorenzo was able to discover a new way to be present for his experience. He developed a capacity to pay attention, to be open to what was happening. As a result, he found that all-important gap between stimulus and response. He saw through his mind's conditioning and freed himself from habitual thoughts and behaviors.

Now Lorenzo could relate more skillfully to his illness and imminent death. He could hold it and, in some sense, befriend it. No longer a victim of his condition, or shut down to it, he was free to experience and embrace his life directly, immediately, and fully.

Welcome everything, push away nothing is first and foremost an invitation to openness. In the Buddhist way of thinking, openness is one of the key characteristics of an awake and curious mind. It does not determine reality, it discovers it. Chögyam Trungpa Rinpoche, the charismatic

Tibetan Buddhist teacher, spoke of the heart of Buddhist practice as that of "complete openness." He described this openness as "a willingness to look into whatever arises, to work with it, and to relate to it as part of the overall process . . . It is a larger way of thinking, a greater way of viewing things, as opposed to being petty, finicky."

Openness doesn't reject or get attached to a particular experience or view. It is a spacious, undefended, non-biased allowing. A total acceptance. Openness is the nature of awareness itself, and that nature allows experience to unfold.

This openness welcomes paradox and contradiction. It permits whatever emerges to emerge. Openness means keeping our minds and hearts available to new information, experiences, and opportunities for growth. It means having tolerance for the unknown. It means welcoming the bad times and the good times as equally valid experiences.

Welcome everything, push away nothing is the opposite of rejecting. Denial breeds ignorance and fear. I cannot be free if I am rejecting any part of my experience. The rejected experience will keep showing up like a bad penny. It will come back again and again, finding new ways to express itself. Until I know it and see through it, it always will be the bane of my existence. It always will be a cause of my suffering. We must let go of our opposition to the experiences we are trying to avoid, whatever they may be—thoughts, feelings, and events included.

Like many of the people I have cared for, my younger brother, Alan, was a street alcoholic who had a very tough life. He went in and out of treatment programs over the years, but usually ended up losing the battle to drugs and alcohol. At one point in his life, he lived in the stalls of a racetrack. He also worked hard at recovery, graduated from college, and became a social worker supporting people living with HIV.

In time, however, Alan's demons would get the best of him. He would lose touch with his twelve-step fellowships, stop attending AA meetings, and fall back into old destructive patterns. He cycled through these ups and downs for years. Then he cleaned up long enough to get married and to have a daughter. But he relapsed, and a few years later, he had a heart attack and died.

My older brother Mark called to give me the news of Alan's death. We made plans to meet at a funeral home in Kentucky near where Alan had lived. I asked him to make an arrangement with the funeral director to allow me to sit with Alan's body. It is a common custom in certain Buddhist traditions to leave the body undisturbed for up to three days. During this period, people come to meditate with the body, perform prescribed ceremonies, and even help guide the departed through intermediate states referred to as *bardos* in the Tibetan system. Even if one doesn't subscribe to these beliefs and rituals, I have found that establishing an unhurried, respectful, and sacred space after death can aid family and friends in the grieving process.

"Why do you want to do that?" Mark asked me, not being familiar with or inclined toward Buddhist practices.

"It's just a California thing," I quipped.

"Well, we're not going to hold a service or anything. Alan didn't have a circle of friends," he said.

"That's okay. I'll just sit with him at the funeral home."

When I arrived at the mortuary, an attendant wheeled Alan's body out on a gurney. He hadn't been prettied up yet, he was not embalmed, but that didn't matter to me. I asked my brother to leave me alone for a while so that I could get a feeling for Alan. I wanted to reflect on his life and our relationship.

The moment I had settled into my breath, Alan's ex-wife, Lorraine, burst into the room. She was a drug addict, and she arrived in a highly agitated state. She rushed over to the gurney and started shaking the body, asking a flurry of questions. "Why is this tag on his toe? Where are his glasses? What's that scratch on his chin? Will he come back?"

At first I felt angry. I just wanted to sit quietly with my brother, and now there was all this chaos in the room. Lorraine kept going on and on, demanding answers, and I desperately wanted her to leave.

Then I stopped myself from attempting to force events to progress in the way I had imagined. I thought, *You wanted to be with your brother? This is what it is like to be with him. This is it.* I decided to welcome the anger rather than push it away so that I could see what was true in that moment. And as I did, I realized that there was strength in the anger, which I could harness to meet the situation in front of me.

I stood up, walked over to Alan's ex-wife, and laid my hand on her shoulder, hoping to provide some comfort. Occasionally, I answered one of her questions, but mostly I remained silent. After fifteen minutes, Lorraine quieted down. "I have to go," she said, and she left.

I felt a wave of relief and settled back into my chair. But only seconds later, the funeral director walked into the room. "Sorry. We're closing now," he said. "I'm going to have to ask you to leave."

And that was it. That was all the time I got with my brother.

Welcome everything, push away nothing, I thought to myself, my own teaching coming back to me. I could not change the situation. If I railed against it, I would only cause myself more suffering. So I let go of my expectations of what it would be like to sit with my deceased brother. In accepting what had happened, I found peace in the midst of the turmoil.

What are you pushing away at this moment in your life? What are you not allowing in? What nightmare are you trying to avoid?

Once I was advising a group of pediatric palliative care nurses. I asked them if it was okay with them if the children they were caring for died. Most said no. They thought it went against the natural order. Yet in America, almost sixty thousand young people under the age of nineteen, half of them infants, die each year. I brought that up with these caregivers, asking how they would help the children under their watch to relax and die in peace when they were pushing against the experience every time they walked into the room?

Welcoming what is, as it is, we move toward reality. We may not like or agree with all that we encounter. However, when we argue with reality, we lose every time. We waste our energy and exhaust ourselves with the insistence that life be otherwise.

In spite of what we have been led to believe, which is that destiny rests firmly in our own hands, we often have little control over the external circumstances of our lives. However, we have a great deal of choice about how we relate to and learn from the cards life deals us. We build resilience by allowing ourselves to experience what we are feeling in any given situation, whether it's good or bad. Until we come to accept life with all its madness and inspiration, we will feel cut off, separate, isolated. We will view the world around us as a dangerous and frightening place.

Acceptance is not resignation. It is an opening to possibility. And openness is the basis for a skillful response to life.

Of course, there are situations we cannot live with, such as when we are being physically or emotionally abused and we have no choice but to leave. But most of the external circumstances we encounter on a day-to-day basis are not a matter of life and death. We can practice meeting small, unpleasant conditions with grace, noticing our own relationship to what is occurring. How is our internal reaction and view shaping our response to the outer world?

When I think of welcoming, I have the image of an open doorway that allows for passage. Opening allows experiences to enter and allows for our responses to emerge and be expressed in the world. To be open is to allow things to be known, to be free of concealment, not to keep secrets from ourselves, to be all that we are and can become. Sometimes this requires necessary pain, like when we lance an abscess or open to a psychological wound. Openness is essential for true healing to be possible.

We tend to protect ourselves from the experiences and situations we don't like. But there is a sense of liberation and confidence that gets built up within us when we do the opposite, when we push away nothing.

Welcome everything, push away nothing is not just about learning to welcome changing conditions or moving beyond our preferences. It is about accepting life "as is."

My daughter, Gina, and I like to shop in consignment stores for vintage clothing. There are great finds in such shops—a silk paisley scarf, a retro leather jacket, sequined heels. While Gina tries on outfits, I peruse the racks for the next cool item. Many of the clothes have a small stain, a missing button, or a slight tear in the fabric. I noticed in one store, all of the clothes carried a cardboard tag with the price and the disclaimer *As Is.*

I like these tags. I think we should hang them on ourselves and each other like Christmas tree ornaments. What a beautiful gift to accept ourselves, others, and our circumstances *As Is,* with all the beauty, imperfections, and challenges that make up this very human life of ours.

To welcome everything and push away nothing is an invitation to discover a deeper dimension of our humanity, to tap into something beyond our habitual selves. We can gain access to some part of us that includes, but is not driven by, our reactivity.

My habitual everyday self is not going to be able to welcome challenging emotions and experiences easily. Little old me can make some decisions, like whether I want chocolate or vanilla ice cream, but it wants to push away pain, anger, death—the big-ticket items that require a more substantial investment from a larger part of myself. Why? My personality is always going to avoid the tough stuff. The personality is full of knowing and often has habitual interest in sustaining the familiar. We want what is happening to fit into our agenda.

The only thing our personalities have to work with is their own history. But if all we have to meet the current situation with is our habitual response, then we are bound to keep getting the same results.

We generally identify ourselves with the contents of our awareness—with our opinions, memories, desires, aversions, self-concepts, and other mental and emotional fixations. However, in welcoming everything, we allow our identities to rest in awareness itself.

Awareness offers a completely different vantage point that doesn't need to push anything away. It isn't separate from anything else. It is, by definition, open, receptive, and responsive. When we engage that aspect of our being, an open and unbiased awareness allows us to see through the obstacles that are clouding our view. Awareness gives us the possibility to know and understand, and this means we have the possibility to find happiness and freedom.

Welcome everything, push away nothing is neither a foolish nor an idealistic invitation. On the contrary, it is eminently practical. Accepting life *as is* means that we make peace with things as they are rather than trying to force them to be the way we want them to be (and getting frustrated that we can't). Instead of spinning a story that we then try to live into, we open to a way things are and accept that we are completely human.

To be human is much more than being born, getting an education, finding the right partner, and getting a pretty house on a nice street, just so that you can sleep, wake, work, go to bed, and do it all over again. It is an invitation to feel everything, to come into direct contact with the strange, beautiful, horrible, and often perfectly ordinary thing we call life. It is an opportunity to be conscious of the fact that some of us will make love while others make war. To recognize the truth that there are babies like my granddaughter born into loving arms and caressed by a mother who kisses her bright future into her child's cheeks, and there are babies like Carolyn, a woman I knew whose parents left her in a Dumpster. To embrace the night screams in refugee camps and the giggling of children in living rooms under tents made of couch pillows and bedsheets. There is devastation and hopelessness, and there is passion and holy commitment to creating a better future for everyone. There is me writing and you reading and the separation between us, and there is the unity we feel almost immediately when we are reminded that there is love.

6

TURN TOWARD YOUR SUFFERING

The journey from teaching about love to allowing myself to be loved proved much longer than I realized.

—HENRI NOUWEN

During a workshop in the rural Northwest, I was speaking on the possibilities that arise when we stop running away from what is difficult. One of the attendees, a burly middle-aged man with broad shoulders and an even wider smile, spoke up. "That reminds me of telephone poles."

I didn't have a clue what he was talking about. "Telephone poles? What do you mean?" I asked.

He explained that he once had a job installing telephone poles. "They're hard and heavy, standing up to forty feet high." There was a critical moment after you placed a pole in the ground, he said, when a pole was unstable and might topple over. "If it hit you, it could break your back."

His first day on the job, the man turned to his partner and said, "If this pole starts to fall, I'm running like hell."

But the old-timer replied, "Nope, you don't want to do that. If that pole starts to fall, you want to go right up to it. You want to get real close and put your hands on the pole. It's the only safe place to be."

When confronted by harsh realities in life, or even some small dis-comfort or inconvenience, our instinctive reaction is to run in the op-posite direction. But we can't escape suffering. It'll just take us by surprise and whack us in the back of the head. The wiser response is to move toward what hurts, to put our hands and attention gently and mercifully on what we might otherwise want to avoid.

Especially in Western culture, we are taught that if suffering exists, something is wrong. It is a mistake. I had a boss years ago who, when something didn't work out, demanded, "Whose fault is this? Who is to blame?" When I would explain that sometimes things just don't go ac-cording to plan, he would yell, "Don't be ridiculous! This is somebody's fault."

When we believe that suffering is a mistake, it's no wonder we do everything in our power to steer clear of it. Our avoidance instinct is also due to the fact that our culture has decided that suffering has no value. "Why suffer?" we have been trained to say to ourselves. "You're better off escaping this pain by any means possible!"

As a result, we have become masters of distraction. To a great extent, this is our primary human practice. A large portion of our day is consumed with activities that are attempts to protect ourselves from discomfort: surfing the Internet, watching TV, working long hours, drinking, eat-ing. Our approach naturally leads to epidemics of alcoholism and drug abuse; compulsive overeating, gambling, and shopping; and an insecure attachment to our technological devices. We have become a society riddled with unhealthy addictions.

Do any of these strategies really work? Sure, we get some temporary relief by ignoring problems or substituting a more pleasant experience for an unpleasant one. But when I look closely at my life, I see that such benefits are short-lived. What sticks around for the long run is the habit of self-deception and its negative consequences.

Suffering is exacerbated by avoidance. The body carries with it any undigested pain. Our attempts at self-protection cause us to live in a small, dark, cramped corner of our lives. We accept a limited perspective of the situation and a restricted view of ourselves. We cling to what is familiar simply in order to reassert control, thinking we can fend off what we fear will be intolerable. When we push back, hoping to get rid of a difficult experience, we are actually encapsulating it. In short, what we resist persists.

My mom wasn't the ideal mother. She could turn her love on and off in an instant. Yet one afternoon when I was about five years old, she taught me an invaluable lesson. I cut my hand while playing with a pocketknife. I was terrified because there was blood everywhere. My mother took one look at the wound and calmly said, "Oh, I think we need the magic towel for this one." Then she pulled me up onto her lap, wrapped my hand in a towel hanging from the stove, and held me until I began to calm down.

After a while, I caught my breath, and she said, "Let's take a look." I didn't want to; it was too frightening. But accompanied by her kindness and reassurance, I was willing to try. Slowly, she unwrapped the towel, and together we looked into the wound. I realized that I would be okay. In that moment, I saw that it is possible and even helpful to turn toward our pain and that there is always the possibility of healing.

That insight planted the seed for much of the work I have done in my adult life. The secret of healing lies in exploring our wounds in order to discover what is really there. When we allow the experience—creating space and acceptance for it—we find that our suffering is not a static, monolithic thing, but rather it is composed of many elements, including our attitudes toward it. Understanding this, we can work skillfully to alleviate the underlying reactions that exacerbate our problems so that we might ease our suffering.

Suffering will only be removed by wisdom, not by drenching it in sunshine or attempting to bury it in a dark basement.

Suffering is a pretty dramatic word. Most people don't think the term applies to them. "I'm not suffering," they say. They imagine children starving in a famine-struck African country or refugees fleeing war in the Middle East or people afflicted with devastating illnesses. We imagine that if we are good and careful, stay positive, play by the rules, and ignore what's on the news every night, then it won't happen to us. We think suffering is somewhere else.

But suffering is everywhere. This is one of the most difficult truths of existence.

Suffering is falling in love and then becoming complacent. Suffering is not being able to connect with our children. It's our anxiety about what will happen at work tomorrow. Suffering is knowing your roof will leak in the next rainstorm. It's finally buying that shiny new smartphone, then seeing an advertisement for an even newer device with incremental improvements. Hoping your company will get rid of your grumpy boss who still has a year to go before his retirement. Thinking that life is moving by too fast or too slow. Not getting what you want, getting what you don't want, or getting what you want but fearing you will lose it—all of this is suffering. Sickness is suffering, old age is suffering, and so is dying.

In Buddhism, the old Pali word for suffering is *dukkha*, which is sometimes translated as "anguish" or more simply as "unsatisfactoriness" or even "stress." *Dukkha* arises from ignorance, from not understanding that everything is impermanent, unreliable, and ungraspable—and wanting it to be otherwise. We wish to claim our possessions, our relationships, and even our identities as unchanging, but we can't. All are constantly transforming and slipping right through our fingers.

We think we need the conditions of our lives to reliably give us what we want. We want to construct an ideal future or nostalgically relive a perfect past. We mistakenly believe this will make us happy. But we all can see that even those people who realize extraordinary conditions in life still suffer. Even if we are rich, beautiful, smart, in perfect health, and blessed with wonderful families and friendships, in time these will break down, be destroyed, and change . . . or we will simply lose interest. On some level, we know this is the case, yet we can't seem to stop grasping for those "perfect" conditions.

Originally, the word *dukkha* referred to an axle that didn't fit quite right into the hub of a wheel on an oxcart. I've ridden in those wooden oxcarts in India. Bouncing up and down on dirt roads full of potholes made for a pretty rough journey. When the axle and hub weren't properly aligned, the ride was extra bumpy.

Let's say you get fired from your job. That is undoubtedly a stressful event. But the suffering is greatly exaggerated if you refuse to accept what has happened as the current reality. Under such difficult circumstances, we tend to say things to ourselves like, "This isn't fair. This can't be true. This isn't the way it should be," which only causes us to suffer more. A critical point here is that *acceptance* doesn't require *agreement*. We may still want to work to change our life circumstances. But you can't make a change until you first accept the truth of what is right in front of you, eyes wide open.

Dukkha comes from the mental and emotional confusion of not seeing and accepting the conditions of life as they actually exist. We always want something. What we have never seems to be enough. We want to ignore the temporality of permanence. And that creates an unsatisfactoriness, a dread, that rumbles beneath our awareness and drives us to behave in ways that exacerbate rather than ease our pain.

What is an alternative way to handle life's inevitable *dukkha*?

The first step is to realize that pain and suffering actually are two intimately related yet different experiences. The familiar adage says, "Pain is inevitable; suffering is optional." That about sums it up.

If you are alive, you *will* experience pain. Everyone has a different pain threshold, and yet we all experience it throughout our lives. Physical pain is the nervous system's internal alarm, your body reacting to a potentially damaging stimulus. It creates an unpleasant sensory experience, such as hunger, exhaustion, an upset tummy, a pounding headache, or the aches of arthritis. Pain also can take emotional form, such as the crush of heartbreak or the sadness of loss.

So there is pain, from which there is no escaping. And then there is suffering, which we can do something about. Suffering generally occurs as a chain reaction: *stimulus-thought-reaction*. Many times, we have no control over the stimulus that causes us pain. But we can shift our relationship to the thoughts about and emotional reactions to the pain, which frequently intensify our suffering.

Suffering is about perception and interpretation. It is our mental and emotional relationship to what is first perceived as an unpleasant or undesirable experience. Our stories and beliefs about what is happening or did happen shape our interpretation of it. When things don't go according to plan, some people believe that they are helpless victims or that they "got what they deserved." This leads to resignation and apathy. When we get caught in anxiety and worry about what might happen in the future, it can quickly proliferate into a web of fear that is not easily corralled.

Opening to pain in the present moment, we may be able to do something to improve the situation, maybe not, but we can certainly notice how our attitudes toward the experience are impacting what is happening. My reaction to pain, even to the thought of pain, changes everything. It can increase or decrease my suffering. I have always liked the formula:

$$Pain + Resistance = Suffering$$

If we attempt to push away our pain, whether it is physical or emotional, we almost always find ourselves suffering even more. When we open to suffering, inquiring into it instead of trying to deny it, we see how we might make use of it in our lives.

After my heart attack and a triple bypass surgery a few years ago, a famous Tibetan Buddhist teacher kindly called to wish me well. I knew he had heart problems himself, so I asked him how he dealt with it all— the drama, the confusion, the precariousness, and the beauty. I half expected him to offer me some esoteric meditation practice.

Instead there was a pause, after which he said, "Well, I thought to myself, it's good to have a heart. And if we have one, then we should ex-pect it will have problems!" The teacher giggled in his very Tibetan way, reminded me to get plenty of rest, and hung up the phone.

I realized he was right. It was true. All humans have problems. All be-ings feel pain. Once I was able to accept that I had a fragile human heart and that it would take some time to heal, I could relax into acceptance of this temporarily painful situation. In so doing, my suffering also relaxed.

After some time, I came to the conclusion that I wouldn't trade in my heart or its suffering even if I had the option to do so. Without my heart, how would I know all the love that was surrounding me during my illness? Without suffering, how would I feel empathy for others or meet their suffering with a compassionate response?

We can shift our relationship to pain by the way we give our atten-tion to it—by turning toward it rather than trying to bury it or run in the opposite direction. One teacher of mine suggested that we begin by "putting out the welcome mat." We invite in what hurts; we sit down with it and get to know it really well. In this way, we come to under-stand the nature of the experience and the deeper causes not always evi-dent at first glance. In the end, the only way through suffering is for us to allow what is happening, welcoming the experience and introducing awareness and compassion where denial was predominant.

We sometimes fail to remember that pain has an essential role in our lives. If we didn't feel the discomfort from the heat of a fire, we would burn our fingers. The painful emotions of shame, loneliness, and guilt highlight deeper troubles in our relationships. Pain can motivate us to take action, to identify and address its causes, and even to seek happiness.

The journey through life is already pretty difficult. There's plenty of unavoidable pain. But when we are not aligned with the way life actually works, we add a great deal of unnecessary suffering to the mix. In such moments, it seems useful to stop fighting circumstances, come back to reality, and get ourselves centered again. There can be no suffering with-out suffering. Suffering can open us to freedom, to compassion, to love.

This concept is so important. It is the medicine many of us crave when we realize that suffering is an attitude of mind. We have a choice to break the momentum of habit. We can release old attitudes and turn toward the difficulty to see what it has to teach us. Instead of trying to avoid it, deny it, endure it, or become resentful of it, we can discover another way.

One day, in the middle of writing a foundation grant report, I got a call from a man I didn't know. He explained that he was the father of a seven-year-old boy who had been very ill with cancer. Some people had told him that I might be able to help him out.

I said certainly, I would be willing to help the family through their grieving process. I made some suggestions about how I might be able to support when the time was right.

The man paused. It was clear that I didn't understand yet what was happening. He practically whispered, "No, Jamie died a half hour ago. We'd like to keep our boy at home in his bed for a little while. Can you come over now?"

Suddenly, the situation wasn't hypothetical; it was real and staring me in the face. I had never done anything like this before. Sure, I had sat at the bedsides of people who were dying, but I had not attended the death of a young child with two grieving parents in unimaginable pain. I honestly had no idea what to do, so I let my fear and confusion arise. How could I possibly know in advance what was needed?

I arrived at the house a short while later, where the dispirited parents greeted me. They showed me to the boy's room. Walking in, I followed my natural inclination: I went over to Jamie's bed, leaned down, and kissed him on the forehead to say hello. The parents broke into tears because, while they had cared for him with great love and attention, nobody had touched the boy since he had died. It wasn't their fear of his corpse that kept them away; it was their fear of the grief that touching him might unleash.

I suggested that the parents begin washing the boy's body—something we often did at Zen Hospice Project. Bathing the dead is an ancient ritual that crosses cultures and religions. Humans have been doing it for millennia. It demonstrates our respect for those who have passed, and it is an act that helps loved ones come to terms with the reality of their loss. I felt my role in this ritual was simple: to act with minimal interference and to bear witness.

The parents gathered sage, rosemary, lavender, and sweet rose petals from their garden. They moved very slowly as they put the herbs in warm water, then collected towels and washcloths. After a few moments of silence, the mother and father began to wash their little boy. They started at the back of Jamie's head and then moved down his back. Sometimes they would stop and tell one another a story about their son. At other times, it all became too much for the father. He would go stare out the window to gather himself. The grief filling the room felt enormous, like an entire ocean crashing upon a single shore.

The mother examined and lovingly cared for each little scratch or bruise on her son's body. When she got to Jamie's toes, she counted them, as she had done on the day he was born. It was both gut-wrenching and extraordinarily beautiful to watch.

From time to time, she would look over at me as I sat quietly in the corner of the room, a beseeching question filling her eyes: "Will I be able to survive? Can I do this? Can any mother live through such loss?" I would nod in encouragement for her to continue at her own pace and hand her another washcloth, trusting the process. I felt confident that she would find healing by allowing herself to be in the midst of her suffering.

It took hours for the parents to wash their son. When the mother finally got to the face of her child, which she had saved for last, she embraced him with incredible tenderness, her eyes pure reflections of her love and sorrow. She had not only turned toward her suffering; she had entered into it completely. As she did, the fierce fire of her love began to melt the contraction of fear around her heart. It was such an intimate moment. There was no separation between mother and child. Perhaps it was like his birth, when they had the experience of being psychologically one.

After the bathing ritual was complete, the parents dressed Jamie in his favorite Mickey Mouse pajamas. His brothers and sister came into the room, making a mobile out of the model planes and other flying objects he had collected, and they hung it over his bed.

Each one of them had faced unbelievable pain. There was no more pretense or denial. They had been able to find some healing in each other's care and perhaps in opening to the essential truth that death is an integral, natural part of life.

Can you imagine yourself living through what these parents did? "No," many of you will say, "I cannot." Losing a child is most people's worst nightmare. *I couldn't endure it. I couldn't bear it*, you may think. But the hard truth is, terrible things happen in life that we can't control, and somehow we do bear them. We bear witness to them. When we do so with the fullness of our bodies, minds, and hearts, often a loving action emerges.

Humans are amazing. I find our courage astounding. People everywhere experience unbelievable hardships—wars, unanticipated catastrophes, financial upheaval, the loss of their homelands, the deaths of their children—and yet they go on, they turn toward, they recover, they live. And sometimes they act with enormous compassion toward others who have suffered similarly or who may yet in times to come.

One of the most stunning images of this that I can recall came after the major earthquake and tsunami disabled the Fukushima nuclear power plant in Japan. A photo in the newspaper revealed a dozen elderly Japanese men gathered humbly, lunch baskets in hand, standing in a line outside the plant's gates. The reporter explained that they were offering to take the place of younger workers inside who were attempting to contain the radiation-contaminated plant. In total, more than five hundred seniors volunteered.

One of the group's organizers said, "My generation, the old generation, promoted the nuclear plants. If we don't take responsibility, who will? When we were younger, we never thought of death. But death becomes familiar as we get older. We have a feeling that death is waiting for us. This doesn't mean I want to die. But we become less afraid of death as we get older."

Suffering is our common ground. Trying to evade suffering by pretending that things are solid and permanent may give us a temporary sense of control. But this is a painful illusion because life's conditions are fleeting and impermanent.

We can make a different choice. We can interrupt our habits of resistance that harden us and leave us resentful and afraid. We can soften around our aversion.

We can see the way things actually are and act accordingly, with wise discernment and love.

The Thai meditation master Ajahn Chah once motioned to a glass at his side. "Do you see this glass?" he asked. "I love this glass. It holds the water admirably. When the sun shines on it, it reflects the light beautifully. When I tap it, it has a lovely ring. Yet for me, this glass is already broken. When the wind knocks it over or my elbow knocks it off the shelf and it falls to the ground and shatters, I say, 'Of course.' But when I understand that this glass is already broken, every minute with it is precious."

After being with Jamie's parents as they bathed their son, I returned home, and I held my own child very close. Gabe was also seven years old at the time. I saw clearly how precious he is to me, what a joy he is to have in my life. While I felt devastated by what I had witnessed, I also was able to appreciate the beauty in it.

The experience clarified for me the value of suffering. Facing suffering head-on helps me to see the true nature of life, which is that it is unpossessable. Furthermore, it deepens the empathy I feel for others, making me more aware of our common humanity. When I reflect on suffering, I can see where I'm getting caught up in my own pain, and that keeps me from generating unnecessary suffering for myself. Finally, it shows me the possibility of taking a more balanced view of life, how it is possible to live in a world of constant change with more ease.

When we welcome our suffering, it shakes us out of our complacency. It can bring clarity and help us find meaning, without which the pain might be too much to bear. It tenderizes and opens us to vulnerability that gives us the capacity to sense, make contact with, and experience more of life. We access our courage to be with what otherwise would be intolerable.

Furthermore, when we bear witness to our own suffering, we stop separating ourselves from it. We realize that it is an integral part of the human condition; it's not personal to us. Then we can say to ourselves, "Hey, this suffering may be moving through me in a unique way, but it is not just mine. It has been going on since the dawn of time."

That perspective, in turn, gives rise to compassion and action. When we take off our armor, our hearts are more available to love, and the mind is free to see the fundamental causes of suffering. We not only come to terms with our deepest fears, but also connect with others who have similar wounds. We are motivated to find ways to reduce suffering—our own and other people's. "A good half of every treatment that probes at all deeply consists in the doctor's examining himself," wrote Carl Jung. "It is his own hurt that gives a measure of his power to heal."

Turning toward our suffering may plunge us into the very sadness, fear, and pain that we usually try so hard to avoid. But if we are willing to brave the darkness by welcoming everything and pushing away nothing, the energy that had been consumed by our resistance to life's unwelcome events will now be available to contribute to healing, building resilience, and acting with love.

An integral part of healing is letting go. But there is no letting go until there is letting in. I learned this the hard way.

When I was thirteen, an experience shattered my innocence. My family lived in a house on land given to my grandfather by the Catholic Church. It was across the street from the parochial grade school that my brothers and I attended and that my grandfather, a bricklayer, had helped to build. A block away was our parish church, where my grandfather had served as sexton, my father attended early Sunday Mass, and my mother prayed devoutly.

Like all my family members, I was a practicing Catholic. I loved being an altar boy, taking part in the rituals, and being that close to God. I was happy when I got a job in the rectory where the priest lived, answering phones and doing odd jobs on Sunday nights.

My dream job became a nightmare when one of the priests, a portly man in his fifties who had clearly had too much to drink, called me up to his room one night and started asking me questions about school. He seemed friendly enough at first, but when I told him what my grades were, he pulled out a paddle and said that I needed to be punished. He demanded that I pull down my pants and lie half-naked across his knees. I felt frightened, vulnerable, and weak. He was the one with all the power, and he used it to molest me.

Tragically, this became a regular event. Over time, the abuse became more twisted and violent, the betrayal more devious, and the confusion over my own sexuality more unmistakable.

I felt trapped. I tried to quit my job at the rectory, but my parents wouldn't allow it. I was too ashamed to tell them the real story. In fact, I couldn't tell anyone about what was happening because the priest was "a man of God," a protected authority, revered in the community. I was just a kid. Why would anyone believe me? There was no one I could turn to. I couldn't even go to confession.

One Christmas Eve when I was fifteen, my mother and I celebrated by attending midnight Mass together. My oldest brother was in Vietnam at the time. After the service, my mother brought me into the chapel with this priest who was abusing me and sobbed to him about the danger her older son was facing. She asked the priest to pray for him.

I wanted to scream, "Are you kidding me? This man is a fraud! A monster! He can't help your son survive; he is practically killing me!" But I could only stand there, frozen, as my abuser consoled my mother in his priestly role. I was overwhelmed by the duplicity of it all, but unable at that young age to take any action on my behalf.

We altar boys alluded to what was happening, but none of us spoke honestly about it. I later learned that the priest had regularly molested other boys who trusted him, as well. All of us were afraid of his power and had troubles elsewhere in our lives that left us feeling weak and isolated. He was trolling for innocents.

The sexual abuse continued for the next few years. I dreaded Sundays. Like other victims of abuse, I learned how to live a lie. I buried the secret deep inside and pretended it didn't exist. I carried the shame. I became adept at keeping the shadowy parts of myself pushed far below consciousness. Increasingly, I felt disassociated from my body, in an almost constant state of disorientation. I walked through life numb, emotionless. At other times, I wanted to kill him. I hated him, and sometimes I projected that hatred onto everyone and everything that crossed my path. I felt dirty, like there was something wrong with me. I was broken, unrepairable. I tried to suppress my memories, to deny what had happened. I didn't want it to define me.

For years, I had horrible nightmares and flashbacks, which I never spoke about out loud. This habit of not facing my wounds may have made me susceptible to still more sexual abuse by others as I became a teenager. This led to further distortions in my own mind. Unconsciously and ignorantly, I began to conflate pedophilia, homosexuality, and child molestation. Of course, we now know that child molestation and child sexual abuse don't imply a particular psychological makeup or motive on the part of the perpetrator. Not all incidents of child sexual abuse are committed by pedophiles. And people who sexually abuse boys are not necessarily homosexuals. There is, in fact, no reputable data showing a linkage between homosexuality and child molestation.

Yet none of this made sense to my hurt adolescent mind. I was scared, confused, and just wanted to be loved. I became estranged from formal religion. I saw all religious clergy as hypocrites and didn't trust any spiritual teachers, regardless of tradition.

When I was in my late twenties, after having been exposed to Buddhism and meditation while traveling in Asia, I returned to Northern California and started studying with Stephen Levine, a pioneer in the field of conscious dying. Stephen was the first spiritual teacher I ever confided in. It was my trust in him that allowed me to share my history of abuse. Stephen listened intently without judgment or comment. It took time for the full story to unfold. When there is shame, our telling the details of the story makes it more real. This starts to heal the sense of disconnection with our experience and supports integration of the wounds.

Stephen, who was very intuitive, knew my deep commitment to seeing the truth and my heart's wish to heal no matter what was required. He said, "I think you should start working with people with AIDS." The illness had just appeared on the scene and at that time was primarily infecting gay men. Stephen said, "You should serve this population. I'll help you."

I grabbed him by his shirt, threw him up against the wall, and yelled, "Are you crazy?" My inner hurt adolescent was exploding. In that moment, all I could experience were prohibitions against this idea and a great deal of pent-up anger. What a ridiculous notion, how absurd, I thought, that I should serve the very type of person who, in my confused mind, had caused me so much harm.

But even as the word *No!* left my mouth, I knew that Stephen was right. It was a moment of sudden awareness, a recognition of the meaning that was to be found in my suffering. I had to do it. Stephen was sending me straight into hell to face my demons. In a flash, it became clear that the victim, rescuer, and perpetrator all lived within me. I certainly knew the experience of being identified as a victim. And I had developed a distorted sense of the wholesome rescuer. But in that moment, the perpetrator was also present. I was now the one allowing my views to cut me off from others who had nothing to do with my wounds. It was evident to me that all three needed to be welcomed, known, and held in love. I had avoided this hurt for a dozen years, turning away from my past experiences, righteous in my aversion. Clean, transparent, compassionate service was the necessary antidote.

Not long after that, I signed on to be a home health aide serving gay men with AIDS. I worked the graveyard shift, caring for men during the lonely hours between midnight and dawn, when my deep, dark, shameful experiences often surfaced. Caring for others became a way of nurturing myself. It wasn't a sudden fix. It was what Stephen would call a "gradual awakening." It was a path of healing that I would walk for another twenty years.

Along the way, I found that, as with the cut on my hand as a child, I could summon the courage to look right at the damage, horrifying as it was. Becoming mindful of our wounds and the associated beliefs we have about them is not a passive process. This turning toward, with full acceptance, allows us to take action. We gain insight, and then we can do something about it. In time, once the hidden pain and shame had seen the light of day, the broken child was mended and the wounded healer began to emerge.

I know what it is like to have pain. To run away from it, to hide. And I know what it is like to have wounds that we feel can never be healed. While those painful experiences left scars, challenged my faith in God and my trust in fellow humans, something basic in me didn't get destroyed. I was fortunate. Not everyone has the support of wise friends who can help remind us that we are more than our suffering.

The childlike belief in a personalized God and a church that would protect me no longer served me. I found a deeper faith in an essential love that manifests through our fellow human beings, through our own bodies, hearts, and minds—in our human ability to embrace what seems impossible to embrace.

The willingness to be with our suffering gives rise to an internal resourcefulness that we can carry forward into all areas of our lives. We learn that whatever we give space to can move. Our feelings of discomfort or anxiety, frustration or anger are free to open, unfold, and reveal their true causes. Often in allowing our pain to arise, we discover a point of stillness, even peacefulness—right in the middle of the suffering.

Turning toward our suffering is a critical part of welcoming everything and pushing away nothing. This invitation means that no part of ourselves or our experience can be left out: not the joy and wonder, nor the pain and anguish. All are woven throughout the very fabric of our lives. When we embrace that truth, we step more fully into life.

7

LOVE HEALS

Life begins with love, is maintained with love,
and ends with love.

—TSOKNYI RINPOCHE

When I was in my late teens, I put my Red Cross lifesaving certificate to work teaching swimming to children with severe disabilities. Jasmine was a beautiful sixteen-year-old who would have been the high school homecoming queen if she hadn't had spina bifida. The way the disease contorted her body made her too self-conscious to put on a bathing suit and join us in the pool. But she loved to watch, make wisecracks, and flirt.

I spent months patiently encouraging her to give swimming a try. Each day, I tried to playfully reflect back to her the strength, courage, sense of adventure, and beauty I saw radiating from within her. When someone believes they are beyond love, you cannot convince them to love themselves. But you can show them that they are loved. As the poet Galway Kinnell wrote, "Sometimes it is necessary to reteach a thing its loveliness."

One day, Jasmine slipped out of her wheelchair and onto the raised marble ledge of the pool. Weeks later, she took off her braces and heavy orthopedic shoes to dip her toes in the water. And after six months, she showed up in her turquoise bathing suit. Without prompting, she maneuvered her twisted, skinny legs onto the pool's edge, called me closer, and with a huge smile leaped into my arms like a seven-year-old child.

In the horror of my own suffering, I always had held out the hope that one day someone would rescue me. I had imagined that I would be saved by love coming toward me. Just the opposite. I was rescued when love came *through* me. I discovered love through acts of kindness . . . not offered *to* me, but coming *from* me. I think of the words of the late John O'Donohue, who wrote, "We do not need to go out and find love; rather, we need to be still and let love discover us."

The experience with Jasmine and the other disabled kids unlocked a compassion hidden deep in the heart of my suffering. I discovered an essential love that was reliable, vast, and undamaged. This became a source of true support, my steadfast guide throughout many years of sometimes amazing, sometimes trying experiences in hospice care.

Love has been my mentor. Love itself has taught me to love.

The boundlessness of love is made evident when the veils between this world and the invisible world are thinnest. At birth and death, love melts any division. It often allows us to move beyond what we thought possible. We do things we couldn't have imagined. I have known women who labored through the powerful, strong contractions of childbirth, moving through exhaustion, pain, and sometimes fear only to discover a deep upwelling of love. A love that is unlike any they have known before. There are countless stories of similar discoveries near the time of death, like the daughter who thought she could not live without her father, yet out of love she released him, saying, "It's okay, Daddy. I love you . . . You can go."

In such moments, we glimpse a love without limitation, a love unlike the commerce-like reciprocal exchange that characterizes many romantic relationships (as when someone else expresses love for us and we feel obliged to react in turn). This is an entirely different order of love, one that springs from the very source of our being. It recognizes and responds to the intrinsic goodness of the human heart. It is both profoundly receptive and dynamically expressive.

This facet of love represents a more universal aspiration that all beings, including ourselves, will find happiness and the causes of happiness. It exists both before and beyond conditions. It is not something to be achieved by our personalities. It is not an idealistic love to be attained by following a certain path, nor is it the result of reaching a special spiritual state. It is always present. In a way, it is the background for all experience, the very essence of our being.

Because this love lives within us, it is always available. It is available to help us face the stuck, wounded, rejected aspects of ourselves and to meet the challenges that are yet to come. Dissolving our defenses, it enables us to grapple with the demons of negative self-image, shame, confusion, and unresolved loss, rather than continuing to avoid them. Then we can heal.

We may imagine that the tension and holding we have used to forge the armor around our hearts will keep out the pain, making us invulnerable. Instead, our armor cuts us off from love, dulling our sensitivity, steeling us to our experience, and locking out the tenderness, comfort, mercy, and joy that we need. Often, we remain frightened behind this shield and grow increasingly isolated from other people and ourselves.

Gradually, as we explore and relax the habitual strategies that once enclosed us, giving ourselves more space, we see that even our armor was never separate from love. Just as when the sun comes out it melts the ice, turns it to water and then into gas, and then absorbs it back into the atmosphere, so, too, there is nothing separate from this unlimited love of our being—not even the ugliest and most unloved parts of ourselves.

This love is the source that allows us to welcome everything and push away nothing. The sort of fearless openness required to turn toward our suffering is only possible within the spacious receptivity of love.

Carl was a homegrown philosopher. A conversation with him could easily become a never-ending stream of questions and more questions. I appreciated his keen intellect and logical mind, but I loved Carl's heart. I noticed how graciously he welcomed people into his room. He had a grandfatherly way of making space for them. Once, when two teenage volunteers visited him at hospice, he listened for almost an hour to their scene-by-scene replay of their favorite movie. He listened generously, not so much out of interest, but out of care for them as human beings.

With so many Buddhist volunteers around, it was inevitable that Carl's curiosity would lead him to ask about meditation. He was using a self-administered morphine pump that released prescribed amounts of pain medication to help with his stomach cancer, but it left him foggy at times. He thought he could use mindfulness to manage his abdominal pain instead of morphine. So he asked me to teach him how to meditate. I agreed to try.

In meditation, pain is considered a great teacher. There are many different techniques for working with the experience. I began with the most common, encouraging Carl first to notice the pain by directing his attention to the general area of his body, then to precisely sense the tension, the sharpness, the sometimes searing, ever-changing sensations. We would alternate between this pinpointed, concentrated attention and coming back to the breath in order to stabilize and refresh so that his mind wouldn't become too exhausted.

Carl was very determined. I noticed his furrowed brow and the tightness around his eyes. He was at war with his pain, enduring it rather than allowing, opening, or softening to the experience. He was trying to use mindfulness to conquer his pain, and he grew frustrated with the lack of immediate results. The pain was too much for him. He started screaming.

We needed to find another way.

Gently, I laid my hands on Carl's belly. This time I encouraged him to feel into the space between the center of the pain and the warmth of my hands.

"It still hurts too much," he groaned.

I pulled my hands farther away from his belly. "How's that?" I asked.

"That's a bit better."

I pulled my hands out still more, encouraging him to soften the muscles around his stomach, relax his forehead, and let the pain float in the space he was discovering.

"Oh, that's better," he said.

"Now a little more," I suggested. My hands were two feet away from his body.

"Oh, that's lovely," he whispered.

I wasn't doing energy-healing work. There was no magic being performed. All that was happening was that Carl was making space for his pain. He was breathing easier now. The muscles around his jaw had relaxed. He lay back against the pillow, eyes closed.

"Can you just rest there?" I wondered aloud.

"Rest in love," he murmured.

The words didn't come from me, but from some deep, innate place within Carl. His awareness was now infused with love. He had found the reliable resource in love that he could draw from when he needed to. He didn't have to generate the love or do something special to make himself worthy of it. Love was already present and in ample supply within him.

From then on, whenever Carl felt overwhelmed by his pain, he would push his morphine pump and say to himself, "Rest in love, rest in love."

His wife came to visit a few days later. She was a nervous woman, more anxious about Carl's condition than he was. She sat by his bed, her legs bouncing and fingers twitching. Carl reached his hand through the bed rails, touched her lightly, and said, "Rest in love, my dear. Rest in love."

I later shared this story with my old friend Ram Dass one morning over breakfast. Ram Dass is the beloved spiritual teacher best known for his book *Be Here Now*, which first brought awareness of Eastern philosophy to the West in 1971. He has been a guiding light for three generations. In late 1997, he suffered a near-fatal stroke, which left him paralyzed on the right side of his body, along with other challenging ailments like expressive aphasia, which limits his ability to speak. His teachings stem in part from his personal experience facing pain.

Ram Dass suggested that Carl had tasted the fruits of "loving awareness." He explained that to understand loving awareness requires only a short journey "from ego to the spiritual heart." Ram Dass illustrated this with a simple gesture, moving his left hand from his head to his chest while repeating gently, "I am loving awareness."

He went on to say, "When I am loving awareness, I am aware of everything outside and inside. I'm aware of the waves on the ocean, the hibiscus flowers in the garden, my scary thoughts and dark feelings. Loving awareness witnesses it all without getting identified with any of it. When I merge with love, there's nothing to be afraid of. Love neutralizes fear."

Ram Dass was speaking about an open, all-embracing love. Of course, we all get caught up in our likes and dislikes. Love doesn't mean we should tolerate bad behavior or say yes when we need to say no. We will fall prey to doubt, unworthiness, boredom, desires, and resentments. At times, we will be driven by our temperaments, beliefs, and lifestyles. Love doesn't eliminate any of these. Rather, it provides us with a way of approaching life that softens the identification that keeps unskillful habits from hardening into character.

Love is what helps us to accept ourselves, our lives, and other people *as is*. When something unwanted—such as death, illness, loss of a job or relationship—approaches, it is natural for fear to arise. In such moments, we need to find some part of us that is not afraid.

When you are afraid, don't you know that you are afraid? Then that means some part of you, the part that is witnessing your fear, is *not* afraid. It is not caught by the fear. We can learn to relate to difficult thoughts, strong emotions, or challenging circumstances from the vantage point of the witness, of loving awareness. When we do, it all becomes a lot more workable.

We love the positive experiences of our lives. It's relatively easy to accept them without questioning their origins. But one of love's most exquisite capacities is its ability to embrace whatever it comes into contact with—even if, at first glance, the situation, experience, or person seems unlovable. Love has its own freedom. When we feel love, it doesn't seem to concern itself with who or what we should love. Loving awareness helps us to embrace our sadness, loneliness, fear, depression, and physical pain. It shines a light in the darkness and reveals the actual sources of our suffering.

Love is not a gated community. Everyone and every part of ourselves is welcome. "No part left out," they say in Zen. This is the receptive function of love.

Once we have found this treasure, there is no point in keeping it to ourselves. The ground of love is limitless. We don't have to be stingy about it. We get caught up in scarcity about it, but it's not a commodity to be traded. There is an endless supply of love, and so we can endlessly give it away. One way to tap into this bountiful harvest of expressive love is through the Buddhist practice of *metta*.

Metta is a practice in which we consciously evoke a boundless warm-hearted feeling. Through the recitation of phrases such as "May all beings everywhere be happy and free," we gradually establish benevolence, friendliness, and love in our own hearts, and then we extend the wish for well-being and happiness to all beings in every direction. *Metta* expresses the strong desire for peacefulness and the welfare of others. It recognizes that love cannot be owned, but that our contact with it can be cultivated with practice. It is my belief that loving kindness is the essential human quality most beneficial in the lives of those who are dying and their caregivers.

I had the joy of working with a man named Michael who was an artist and longtime Buddhist practitioner. Michael had been ordained a

Zen priest and had been living with Parkinson's disease for twenty-five years. It was now in its final stages.

His wife invited me to come to talk to Michael about dying, but he wasn't so interested in the subject. Instead, we discussed his paintings, how his love for detail had to be surrendered now that his hands shook uncontrollably, how something new was emerging in the process. We spoke of the beauty of the plum tree that stood outside his window.

We had several visits, each with a different focus of his choosing. One conversation was about tools, especially pruning tools and paintbrushes, and the necessity of carefully caring for and choosing the right tool for the job. Other times, he would reminisce about his early years, or we would sit quietly in the backyard listening to the birdsong.

Sometimes we would talk about our wives, as men do more than women might imagine. Michael had an unusual marriage in which there was a great deal of love but also strain and separateness. He spoke of his stubbornness and habits of control that had taken their toll. He and his wife lived in the same house, but they also lived apart. Within their commitment and marriage, they were often at odds.

Of course, we also spoke of Zen, the power of silence, and the paradoxical teachings that made our minds spin. Ultimately, we touched on the simplicity of relinquishment, the total dropping off of body and mind.

I asked Michael what he thought of *metta*, or loving kindness practice.

"Crap," he said. In Michael's mind, *metta* lacked the clarity and sparseness that he found so satisfying in his own Zen practice. Then he added, "But I could do with a little love right now."

Metta practice generally proceeds in a very structured and specific way. Traditionally in Asia, you start this practice by first calling to mind yourself or your mother or sometimes your most beloved teacher. But Westerners often have the most complex relationships with those people, and many of us stumble when we try to begin our loving kindness practice in that way. So I asked Michael to name the one person it was easiest for him to love, or the person who had loved him without hesitation.

He took his time.

Then he said, "My dog Jonesy." His childhood companion, he explained.

"Your dog, huh . . . Why?" I asked.

Michael replied, "Well, no matter what I did, my dog loved me. If I went away for the day or even longer, he was at the door to welcome me when I got home, tail wagging, a big doggy smile. He was full of love for me." Michael went on to say, "It didn't matter whether I was grumpy or happy-go-lucky. He never judged me. He just loved me."

So we began with Jonesy. Michael lay in his bed, repeating traditional and creative phrases of his own making about loving his dog. "May you be happy." "May you be free." "May you have all the dog bones you want." "May you know you are loved."

As Michael repeated these phrases, his face broke into a joyous grin. Later, there were tears of gratitude. He kept up the practice over the next month. He would always start with Jonesy. Gradually, his love was like a cup spilling over. He now had so much love when he practiced *metta* that he naturally came to include his teachers, his mother, and, in time, his wife—demonstrating the expressive, contact-oriented function of love.

When Michael died, his wife was lying in the bed next to him, holding him. They had made their own form of reconciliation. It wasn't so much about words. It was about re-discovering love. The love that always had been there, hidden behind habit.

If love is bountiful and endless, why then do we get caught up in scarcity, feeling that we must hold on to our beloveds so tightly? In part, it is because we confuse love and attachment.

Attachment likes to impersonate love. It says, "I will love you if you give me what I need." Love is focused on generosity; attachment is obsessed with getting needs met. Love is an expression of our most essential nature; attachment is an expression of the personality. Love engenders faithfulness, aligning with our values, moving with purpose; attachment clings in fear and grasps tightly to a particular end result. Love is selfless and encourages freedom; attachment is self-centered and engenders possessiveness. Attachment leaves scars. Love inclines us to gratefulness.

Consider the experience of unhealthy attachment: It is tight, irritated, closed, fixed, and often compulsive. It creates an unwholesome dependency. We come to believe that our ability to feel pleasure and happiness, to have our needs met, is dependent on the words and actions of something or someone outside of ourselves. But love encompasses everything. We can love someone even if we don't agree with them and even if we don't like all their habits. My wife loves me, but she still gets annoyed with me when I forget to close the kitchen cabinets. Love is not blind to our day-to-day human challenges, yet it is not limited by them.

Healthy attachment is essential in forming and sustaining human relationships, as in the attachment between mother and child. However, love is possible without forming an unhealthy attachment, in which we cling to the point of not recognizing or allowing for the inevitable truth of impermanence.

There is an old Buddhist story of a family whose love was a model for the whole village. They lived in harmony and cherished each other. One day, the oldest son died. The villagers went to the home to console the family in their bereavement. When they arrived, they found the family was happy. They explained to the villagers that the secret of their love and harmony was that they understood how one day they would part. When and how this would happen was uncertain, so they lived as if it could happen at any time. Now, when the time had finally arrived, they were prepared.

A teaching story like this isn't a demand for an idealized response to death. All of us grieve. Even the most awakened people I know mourn. Rather, stories such as these challenge us to rethink our current actions, to consider what might contribute to a beneficial outcome. They help us consciously consider how we love the people in our lives.

As people come closer to death, I have found that only two questions really matter to them: "Am I loved?" and "Did I love well?"

When my heart attack and emergency open-heart surgery brought me close to my own death, I truly began to understand the depth of these questions. I now allow them to guide me in living well.

Recovery from heart surgery was daunting. I was fundamentally shaken up. I was caught up in the pain, identified with my deficiency, and experiencing a great deal of fear. I questioned my self-worth and value. I felt an objective helplessness that was without reason. I worried that I would be forgotten. I felt lost.

Initially, I couldn't get to the toilet by myself or shower without assistance. I was fragile, weak, inadequate, dependent, and my body was covered with ugly scars. At times, my mind wandered aimlessly; at other times, it was like a barking junkyard dog. I felt unacceptable, unattractive, and unlovable. I was a mess.

Fortunately, I had people around me who loved me in spite of myself. My name was placed on altars in Buddhist centers everywhere, and friends and students chanted my name during their prayers and practices.

I hadn't known I was so loved. The love of others opened me to personal self-love and more profoundly to the recognition of the very boundless love that we have been exploring. It was not simply an emotional response. It was palpable, warm, pleasurable, and included a sense of deep contentment. I felt nourished, reminded of some basic goodness within me. There was a melting, an intimate appreciation that the essence of my being was indeed love.

For months I just cried, as I recognized again and again what a blessing it was to know such love in my lifetime. I said to friends, "The doctors told me I couldn't get my incisions wet, but I have been bathing in love every day."

This experience of love opened me to trust not in the actions of others or even my past experiences, but in an intelligence within me that was a wise, loving guide in unknown territory. It was a trust in the process, that what was happening was optimal and that whatever happened to me, I would ultimately be fine. A natural buoyancy filled me. It wasn't a belief; it was a non-conceptual, implicit trust that I could lean back into, as if it were supporting me. I had witnessed this many times in other people as they came close to death.

This love and trust gave rise to a profound rest. I felt a deep sense of ease, like warm, golden honey running through my veins, soothing, comforting. It freed me from my obsession with trying to make things other than what they were. There was no need to resist, to grasp. I simply rested with things as they appeared, changed, or disappeared. Body at rest. Heart at rest. Mind at rest.

Rest in love, I thought to myself. *Rest in love.*

When people are sick or wounded, just love them. Love them until they can love themselves again. This has worked for me. It makes me wonder if maybe love really is the best medicine.

Love is the very human quality that allows us to welcome everything, not just what we prefer most. Love is the motivation that enables us to move toward fear—not in order to conquer it, but in order to include it so that we might learn from it. In love, there is no separation. Caring for all things is therefore a natural action of love. Nothing remains isolated from its care.

Why is love the quality that allows us to welcome everything? When we view reality from the vantage point of our personalities—from a small, separate self—we are constantly looking for what distinguishes us from one another. But when we live from the vantage point of boundless love, we begin to see all the points of connection that join us together.

Love breeds love.

THE THIRD INVITATION

Bring Your Whole Self to the Experience

Watching the moon
at dawn,
solitary, mid-sky,
I knew myself completely:
no part left out.

—IZUMI SHIKIBU

Imagine you had a photo of yourself printed on thick, stiff cardboard. Now imagine that the photo was not just of your face or even the length of your body, but somehow represented a multi-dimensional image of your whole being, including all the parts of your personality. Suppose you fed that board through a laser-cutting die to make it into a jigsaw puzzle. Visualize spreading all one thousand interlocking pieces out on a table and starting to assemble the puzzle.

You might begin with the corners, or an easily recognizable part like your hand or ear, or perhaps your eyes since they are said to be the windows to the soul. But as you progressed, you might come upon a puzzle piece you didn't like—for example, your fear. You might muse, "I think I will leave this piece out." Or you might come upon your lust and say,

"No, my spiritual teacher told me that lust is no good. I can't include this piece."

And so it would continue, with you deeming certain aspects of yourself acceptable and other parts totally unacceptable. After a while, you wouldn't be able to recognize yourself in the puzzle because you would be looking at such a fragmented image. You wouldn't be able to see the full picture.

We all like to look good. We long to be seen as capable, strong, intelligent, sensitive, spiritual, or at least well adjusted. We project a positive self-image. Few of us want to be known for our helplessness, fear, anger, or ignorance, or want others to know that sometimes we are more of a mess than we'd like to admit.

Yet more than once I have found an "undesirable" aspect of myself, one about which I previously had felt ashamed and kept tucked away, to be the very quality that allowed me to meet another person's suffering with compassion instead of fear or pity. My own experience of abuse allowed me to empathize with both the abused and the abuser, to help each find forgiveness for their anger and open toward their fear. It is not our expertise, but rather the wisdom gained from our own suffering, vulnerability, and healing that enables us to be of real assistance to others. It is the exploration of our inner lives that facilitates us in forming an empathetic bridge from our experience to theirs.

To be whole, we need to include, accept, and connect all parts of ourselves. We need acceptance of our conflicting qualities and the seeming incongruity of our inner and outer worlds.

Wholeness does not mean perfection. It means no part left out.

8

DON'T BE A ROLE, BE A SOUL

Don't sell your soul to buy peanuts for the monkeys.
—DOROTHY SALISBURY DAVIS

When I am sitting at a person's deathbed, I feel my own fear. I'm in touch with my grief. In the service of healing, I draw on my helplessness as well as my strength, my wounds as well as my passion. This is how we discover an authentic meeting place with other people: through the vulnerable and courageous exploration of our own experience.

Years ago, back in 1989, I was caring for my dear friend John, who was dying of AIDS. I loved him very much and always wanted to offer him the best care possible. There were several of us in his support group. We took turns accompanying him for twenty-four-hour shifts.

Monday was my day. This one unforgettable Monday, a strange neurological complication swept through John, causing him utter confusion and forgetfulness, a sudden change in his thinking and speaking skills, and a loss of sensation in his hands and legs. In one fell swoop, John lost his ability to hold a spoon, stand, or communicate in any sort of intelligent way. When I entered his apartment, there he was, sitting in a plaid robe at his painted kitchen table, hunched over a bowl of Kellogg's Cocoa Krispies, his hair a mess and his face absolutely blank.

I couldn't find my friend. Where had he gone? A few nights before, we had been laughing as we watched Johnny Carson together. Now I couldn't recognize him. Honestly, I was terrified.

As the day wore on and morning rolled into afternoon and then evening, a palpable darkness settled around us. I'm embarrassed to say that at times, in an attempt to manage John's unfamiliar behavior, I was manipulative and cajoling. At other times, I treated him like a child. I didn't know what to do. I was lost and confused.

Taking care of John in this condition was hard work. He had anal tumors and constant diarrhea. I had to move him from the toilet to the bath and lift him back to the toilet again dozens of times in the middle of the night.

When the dawn light finally began to cast shadows across the bathroom tiles, I was exhausted. I just wanted to go to bed. I longed for John to sleep and wake up as the man he used to be. I wanted this nightmare to be over.

Then, between one of those moves from the bath to the toilet, I was washing my hands in the sink. Looking in the vanity mirror, I could see John sitting behind me, his pajamas down around his ankles. He was mouthing words.

I turned.

Out of his garbled mind came a whisper. "You're trying too hard."

I stopped, sat down beside the toilet, and began to cry.

That moment turned out to be the most intimate of our whole friendship. There, next to the toilet, shit everywhere. You see, in that moment, there was no separation between us. We were both helpless together. We cried and after a while laughed at the complete absurdity of the circumstances.

Up until that point, I had been afraid to enter that territory of helplessness where John was living, fearing I would get lost there. Instead, I stayed busy trying to be helpful, to assert control and hide out behind my well-defined role: Mr. Hospice.

It's common and perfectly natural when caught in the grips of fear to become defensive, controlling, emotionally unavailable and irritable, and to lose patience with ourselves and others. We want to feel safe, so we cling to roles with their established rules and prescriptive behaviors.

But in order to connect with and truly serve John, I had to see how my fear was triggering a sense of powerlessness. I needed to slow it all down, to soften and open to what was present, instead of continuing to insist that the situation conform to my preferences.

After all, we wouldn't be helpless forever. The situation would show us what to do next. But we couldn't see the road through until I relaxed my identification with the caretaking role and allowed my helplessness to enter the room.

We are social animals, and as such, each of us has multiple roles that we perform in society. I am a husband, father, and grandfather at home; a neighbor when I walk down my block; a customer when I step into a café; a teacher in my spiritual community; and a patient in the hands of my heart surgeon.

Roles are neither good nor bad. They are primarily functional and provide for some needed predictability in our lives, especially when it comes to interpersonal relationships.

Developmentally our roles change as we move through life. Until mid-life, we generally focus on accomplishment, creating our identities, rebelling, developing a career, building a family, and forging the structures we need to thrive in the world. When we find the courage to change in the second half of life, we often turn inward. The skills we developed to address first-half-of-life tasks are not sufficient or appropriate to support us on this next stage of our journey. In this period, we usually orient toward exploring the meaning of life, embracing mystery, cultivating wisdom, and relaxing a certain striving. It's age-appropriate behavior.

Each role comes complete with its own expected set of behaviors, functions, and responsibilities (batteries not included). It gets complicated when one role conflicts with another. Single mothers who struggle to balance full-time work and parenting regularly report the emotional and physical exhaustion that accompanies role conflict. The night the massive San Francisco earthquake struck back in 1989, I was torn between my role as a father, caring for my family's needs, and my role as a hospice director, needing to assure the safety of the patients and staff. It is harder still when personal beliefs conflict with our professional roles. Sometimes we know what is right, but feel powerless to act on our good judgment.

Roles are a choice. When we choose to be in one role, we also choose not to be in another. If, as a young girl, I commit to the one-pointed, rigorous life of becoming a professional ballet dancer, I may choose to give up a traditional education or certain aspects of my social life. If in my role as a lawyer, I think it's important to project the image of a strong, knowledgeable male, that I am cool in a crisis, I may find it difficult to disclose my weaknesses or embrace my more nurturing qualities.

When we disown parts of ourselves, we tend to judge others who display those same qualities. We lay claim to moral superiority. Thus holding too tightly to a role can create a chasm between people that is difficult to cross.

Life asks us to continually adapt. Roles, like most things, are fluid. When parents get older, roles reverse and children frequently step into being caregivers. If I am the nurturer in my family and I get sick, someone has to agree to take care of me. If I am the decision-maker and now I have Alzheimer's, someone else must take charge of certain decisions. Or let's say I'm an alcoholic and I get treatment. Suddenly, I am no longer the black sheep of the family, and I have to be let back in to participate in decision-making.

When we over-identify with a role, it defines us, confines us, and reduces our capacity for conscious choice. It sets up an expectation about how life is supposed to proceed. That means more fragmentation, more fixed positions and entrenched beliefs, and less access to our innate wisdom. Often—especially in our public, professional roles—we don't allow our whole self to show up.

When I go to a party, inevitably someone will ask, "What do you do?" But of course, if I only define myself by what I do, who am I when I am not doing? The truth is we are not what we do, what we think, what we feel, what we say, or what we have. We are more than all that.

Ram Dass says, "Don't be a role; be a soul."

We are not our roles, and we are not our conditions. You may have cancer or bi-polar disorder, but you are not your disease. You may be born into wealth or poverty, but you are not rich or poor. You may find yourself happy or sad, old or young, in supportive conditions or in conditions of despair, but you are not these things.

We are first and foremost human beings, with all of the complexity, fragility, and wonder that life encompasses. When we only look through the lens of a role, it narrows our vision of the world. We don't see things and people as they actually are, but rather project our story onto them. This frequently causes us to attribute a particular significance to an experience and miss the true meaning that is trying to emerge.

Too often in caregiving and other helping careers, we find ourselves not so much looking to see what serves others, but to confirm our socially approved identity. We want to be somebody who helps. We say, for example, "I work with the dying," with the emphasis on I. And so we invest in the role instead of the function. I call this "helper's disease," and in my view, it is a more rampant epidemic than cancer and Alzheimer's put together.

I am speaking about the way that we try to set ourselves apart from other people's suffering. We do this with our pity, our fear, our professional warmth, and even our charitable acts. It alters the way we make decisions.

Once there was a woman in our hospice who was just a few days from death. As she looked back on her life, she felt regret about many of her choices. As a result, she was quite sad—a little depressed, but not clinically. This seemed natural to me.

A visiting nurse pulled me aside after meeting with the patient and suggested that we start her on an antidepressant medication. This particular medication takes four to six weeks before its mood-altering benefits take effect.

"Why do you want to prescribe this medication?" I asked.

The nurse responded, "Well, she's so uncomfortable, and it's hard to see her this uncomfortable."

I said, tongue in cheek, "Maybe you should take the medication."

Helping can be egotistically or altruistically motivated. The social psychologist Dr. Daniel Batson identified two distinct emotions that motivate people to help others. The first is what he called "empathetic concern," which he proposed could be considered altruistic in that it focuses on the other person. It is the tenderness and care that are evoked in us when we see another person suffering.

He called the second motivation "personal distress" and posited that this could be considered egoistic in that it is self-focused. Here, the motivation to help comes from the desire for personal gain, like improved self-esteem, or because we are trying to avoid the pain of guilt, self-criticism, or other unpleasant feelings. It is the opposite of empathy in that instead of fostering connection, it can lead to self-protection, withdrawal, or doing more, whether or not the extra interventions are wanted or have any real value.

It's not uncommon in health care for physicians to fend off their own feelings of fear, futility, or helplessness by prescribing a treatment program, drug, or procedure that is unnecessary, ineffective, or unwanted.

Jackson worked in a wire-hanger factory. He had three TVs in his room, which he liked to watch all at once. Each had its own handmade rabbit ear antenna because of course Jackson had an unlimited supply of wire hangers. He preferred watching horror movies and thrillers at night. Often three at the same time. In the morning, he would wake groggy and complain of terrible nightmares. I suggested that maybe he could turn off the TVs before sleeping.

He looked at me like I was crazy and said, "No, man. The TV helps me go to sleep." I realized that for Jackson, TV was company, perhaps his longest relationship, and that being left alone terrified him. His terminal cancer scared him for similar reasons. He was afraid that his disease would cause others to abandon him because there was no future in a friendship with him.

Jackson never wanted to disappoint others, especially his doctor, whom he believed held his future in her hands. He was adamant about keeping his commitments to her, even when it wasn't in his own best interests. "You can't expect people to help you if you don't show up to be helped," he said, insisting on making it to his oncologist's office for a checkup that had been scheduled a month earlier. It was an ordeal for Jackson to make that trip to the hospital. He had stopped eating a week before, he felt nauseous much of the time, and he was very weak and unable to walk.

The physician clearly was upset when she saw the dramatic change in Jackson's condition—his gaunt body, protruding eyes, and the changes in mood caused by his glioblastoma. Yet she barely made eye contact with him during the entire fifteen-minute visit. She kept her fear well concealed behind her white coat. Speaking abruptly, she suggested a new course of intensive radiation to shrink the brain tumor.

Jackson responded by saying that he was nauseous and tired and wanted to rest. The oncologist scribbled a prescription for an anti-nausea medication and scheduled the radiation treatment for the following day.

I took Jackson back to the hospice, where he died later that night.

It was difficult to watch the doctor's cool, indifferent, almost robotic interaction with Jackson. She might have paused, taken a beat, listened when he said, "I'm tired. I need to rest." But she railroaded right over him. She couldn't let the pain in. And in so doing, she missed a healing opportunity—not only for Jackson, but also for herself. Glued to the safety and privilege of her medical role, she sacrificed a bit of her humanity that day.

In the increasingly technological environments of medical centers, where treatment protocols change rapidly, clinicians frequently are pressured to accomplish more with fewer resources. As a result, it's easy for them to become exclusively task-focused. But human beings are not task delivery systems. In caring for each other, we must attend to both task and relationship. Without a relationship to each other and the realization of the intrinsic values of purpose, meaning, and spiritual growth, there is a loss of soul. We split off the secular from the sacred. We've all encountered a doctor or other clinician who is fulfilling the role, performing the job, but is not present with us. Soul is about presence. When we get stuck in our roles, we stop caring. Patients feel ignored and objectified, and their autonomy is lessened. Often, they actually end up suffering more from the treatment they receive, enduring their suffering without complaint while tolerating all sorts of unpleasant side effects.

Nurses and doctors, people with good hearts, also frequently become closed to their own pain. Driven ruthlessly by the unrealistic expectations of the systems in which they work, trained to use coping strategies that have them ignoring what hurts most, they lose touch with their compassionate hearts. Often, they meet their own discomfort and alienation with rejection instead of love. Like the oncologist treating Jackson, when they are overworked, they become shut down; molded by their training, they see only symptoms and not the person in front of them. All they have left to offer is their expertise.

Most of us are naturally inclined to help people; we want to try to reduce others' suffering. Yet some of us reach too quickly for our version of a prescription pad, doling out unsolicited advice. Usually, our first instinct upon hearing of someone's difficulties is to try to fix them. While our intentions may be genuine, we can be blissfully insensitive to the way we impact others. We've all been there. You meet a friend at Starbucks and mention in passing that you didn't sleep well the night before. Your helpful, well-meaning friend launches into a discourse on the health risks of drinking coffee, maybe some diet tips, and the importance of an exercise regime.

We like our opinions. There is nothing wrong with having a point of view. What's problematic is imposing it on others. Giving people advice that they can't use and don't want won't make you feel less helpless. If you feel helpless, you might try acknowledging your helplessness first, at least to yourself, before you speak out or take any action. If you haven't been specifically asked for suggestions, chances are they're neither wanted nor appreciated. I always find it best to inquire before offering guidance. Respect a "No, thanks," and move on.

The attachment to the role of helper goes deep for most of us. If we're not careful, if we become wedded to this role, it will imprison us and those we serve. Because let's face it: if I am going to be a helper, then somebody has to be helpless.

This was so clear to me when I was in the hospital recovering from my heart attack and surgery. People would come in to be with me—doctors, nurses, aides—and oftentimes, they were so busy doing whatever task they had to accomplish that they wouldn't see me. I was touched all the time, but rarely did that touch feel healing. Mostly I was "monitored." I'm sad to say that my health care providers often had more of a relationship with the devices and machines they were using than they did with me. The staff tried to manage their anxiety through well-constructed professional scripts and coping strategies that were meant to create a buffer, keeping my suffering at arm's length. It rarely worked. Their anxiety simply got passed on to me.

No one really asked me how I felt, only, where was my pain on a scale of one to ten? Did I have a bowel movement yet? Was I doing my breathing exercises? I was information to be charted.

At one point in the hospital, I lost my stability. I couldn't concentrate. I got swept up in the fear, the pain and dependency. I started identifying with the anxiety, with my shrinking world. I felt myself getting smaller and smaller.

Hospitals have a "fix it" mentality. They are environments of expectation. There is a protocol for everything and a plan to move you through the anticipated process. Some of this is necessary and helpful to recovery. I would not be alive today if it were not for the brilliance of medical procedures. However, the emphasis is completely future-oriented.

Immersed in such conditions, I found it difficult to stay present. The health care professionals who came into my room would ask, "How are you today?" But inevitably, when I said, "Not so good," they would reply with the refrain, "You're going to feel much better tomorrow." Even when friends came to see me—including some lovely Buddhists who have beautiful souls and have steeped themselves for years in meditation and mindfulness—I found they mostly pointed my attention toward the future. "Tomorrow will be a better day," they would say, intending to reassure me.

Gradually, I lost contact with myself. I got swept up in solution consciousness and joined with the predominant mind-set of using only external measures to evaluate my state of being. Stuck in my role as a patient, I was nothing more than a problem to be solved. It was hell.

After a few days, I finally got fed up. I said, "I don't want to talk to anybody. I don't want any visitors. I just want to go for a walk and listen to the Blind Boys of Alabama." I pulled a set of headphones over my ears like a teenager slumped and sulking in the back of his parents' car, and I shut them all out. My friends, the health care workers, everybody.

I love the Blind Boys of Alabama because of their contagious spirit and faith. They are a gospel group who first sang together in 1939. They have such confidence in the benevolence of God. I walked the hallway, listening to their music until their faith infused me. It's not that I had to believe exactly what they believe, but I needed to be with somebody who had trust in the basic goodness of life. In that moment, for me, it was the Blind Boys. I borrowed their confidence until my own could rise up again.

Slowly, I started to feel the return of my capacity to be with my experience. I came back to my hospital room, went straight into the bathroom, closed the door, and cried. It was the first time since the operation that I'd had the ability to cry, and I just let the tears flow. I let my body shake and heave. At last, I could be with what was uncomfortable, miserable even. I felt so relieved because I—and everyone around me—had been deflecting the difficult stuff. But now I could access it. I could feel the helplessness and the fear and the pain and the "What is this going to mean about the rest of my life?" and the "Do I have any value anymore?"

and "What will I be able to *do* after this?"—all those big questions that had arisen from the physical and emotional trauma of the heart attack.

A nurse came into the room. "Are you okay?" she asked, rapping loudly on the bathroom door. "You're crying in there. Are you okay? You know it's okay. We're all out here. We're here to support you."

I said, "Please, just leave me alone."

But she didn't want to. Stuck in her helper role, she kept pushing her agenda. "You know it's okay. Everything is going to be okay. You're going to be fine tomorrow. Come back out here with us, and I'll call a social worker."

"No," I said, more firmly this time. "Leave me alone. Let me be with this. I've been trying to get access to my feelings for days, and I'm finally here. Let me be with myself."

And she left. She let me be.

I trusted that if I could touch my suffering, my own innate compassion would emerge as a loving response. It did.

Too often, caregivers tend to amplify the patient's fear or exacerbate the condition of confusion by focusing exclusively on *problem solving*. In so doing, they may intensify the contraction. Soon, just as I had, the patient loses contact with their innate resourcefulness.

In the chaos of illness, one calm person in the room can make all the difference. In caring for someone who is sick, we use the strength of our arms and backs to move a patient from the bed to the commode. We lend the patient our bodies. We can also lend people the concentration of our minds and the fearlessness of our hearts. We can be a reminder of stability and confidence. We can expand our hearts in such a way that it can inspire the individual who is struggling to do likewise. Then we become a compassionate refuge. Our presence restores trust in the patient's capacity to heal.

I don't heal because my problems are being solved. I heal by reconnecting with what I feel I lost in the fear and contraction. I heal by connecting to my innate capacity to heal. This is felt as loving self-acceptance, a quality of openness to my condition that is expanded and strengthened through the dynamic companionship of compassion. It breeds courage and allows us to go toward and learn from the suffering. When we reflect this intrinsic wholeness in others, we can be a portal to a larger possibility. As caregivers, as friends, our work is to be portals, not just problem solvers.

I like the old word *service* better than *caregiving*. Service speaks to the depth of the heart's intention, an embodiment of unselfish values, and the action that springs from wisdom. Service is always mutually beneficial. Caregiving too often turns into helping and fixing.

My friend Rachel Naomi Remen, M.D., says this better than anyone I know when she writes, "Helping, fixing, and serving represent three different ways of seeing life. When you help, you see life as weak. When you fix, you see life as broken. When you serve, you see life as whole. Fixing and helping may be the work of the ego, and service the work of the soul."

Fixing and helping are draining. Over time, we may burn out. But service is renewing. When we serve, our work itself will renew us. In helping, we may find a sense of satisfaction, but in serving we find a sense of gratitude.

Try it sometime. Sit with another person without a solution to their problem, without playing a role. No analyzing, no fixing, no meddling, no mending. Listen generously, as if the other person has all of the resources that they need inside of them. Just respect and receive what is being offered. It's not even important that you understand. Imagine your listening presence is enough, exactly what is needed. Often a receptive silence heals more than all the well-meaning words.

It's not that roles have no value; it's that they are not sufficient for our well-being. For that, we need the courage to be authentically whole.

What is authenticity? It is saying what is so when it is so. Showing up, doing what we say we will do, remembering our commitments, and honoring our agreements. Authenticity engages the will and points to what has heart and meaning, while simultaneously diminishing reactivity. It means taking personal responsibility for both the tasks at hand and the relationships we build as we perform those tasks. Acting authentically builds trust.

Sarah was a student at one of our trainings on compassionate caregiving. A skinny, shy white woman in her mid-twenties, she worked as an attendant in an inner-city hospice, Joseph's House in Washington, DC, where she cared mostly for African-Americans on the verge of death. We had a wonderful talk about "helper's disease" and showing up authentically as ourselves rather than hiding behind our roles. A few weeks later, she wrote me the following letter.

There is an excerpt I love from John O'Donohue. He asks, "What have you done with your wildness?" This experience has been wild for me. Radical. Learning to embrace the reality of what's arising within me has required courage from my heart. I've witnessed myself going into scary, dark, overgrown, overwhelming places. I can't believe it, but I've had moments of thrusting my head into Mara's* mouth, rather than running away from her. Of course, it's hard, and I don't do it all the time. But in my body a seed has been planted. I'm continuing to nourish that seed of understanding: the understanding that going into, not away from, those scary places is the very courageous act that enables my humanity, my sensitivity, my power, my authenticity, my own exciting and unpredictable wildness to be.

At work, I've noticed that the lovely residents intuit when I'm in that wild space. It's at those times that they trust me most. I will take risks to be there for them. I will think outside the box. I will refuse to abide by limited conceptions of roles and regulations. I will be unapologetically myself. I will trust my intuition in giving care. Not only do I provide the care that's actually needed by others, but I create healing—not draining—spaces for myself, too.

*Mara is the Buddhist figure of temptation.

It's that trusting intuition that guided me to jump into Ms. Helen's bed with her and sit there for an hour with my hand on her leg, not asking her again if she'd please take her meds. It's why I told everyone else that I was busy and I couldn't come; even though it may have looked like I was just sitting doing nothing. It guided me to talk back to Helen when she swore at me, to shake my ass and say, "Oh, you know it's hot, Helen," when she told me how fat my ass is (she tried not to smile). The wild intuition enabled me, when she called me a "stupid white bitch," to stand tall on my own two stupid white legs, and to do so while stretching my heart open and taking her in and taking in my own insecurity and self-loathing about my racial identity and racial privilege and managing to love us both through the whole inner drama.

Now Ms. Helen happens to be one of my favorite people I've ever met in my life. Without your training, I wouldn't have had the courage to receive the gift of that relationship. I wouldn't have had the courage to see, with as much clarity as I can muster, that it's not personal, that love is there, and that the way to it is by really, truly showing up and being there with her, grounded in my own body and my whole self.

Authenticity requires trust in a deep inner wisdom and the willingness to bring that wisdom into conscious action. Wisdom is not about age or expertise, tools or roles. I have a lot of tools that I have collected over the years, but in serving, I don't lead with my tools. I find that if I start pulling those tools out and setting them down between myself and my client, then one of us is sure to trip over them. So instead I lead with my humanity.

We tried to keep it simple at Zen Hospice. When someone new arrived, I would meet them at the front door and escort them to their room. I rarely told them my title, preferring to introduce myself by my first name. Roles might come later. What mattered more in the beginning was finding our common ground with one another.

Before we would bring in the nurse or start any medical evaluations or procedures, I would tell new people about the neighborhood. I'd explain about Mrs. Mahilia Kennedy, who lived two doors down with her granddaughter, or Jeffery and Francis, who lived just to the left. I'd mention the preschool down the street and how they might hear the children laughing as they passed by on their way to the park next door. Finding one's place is important. In some cultures, it's the way you introduce yourself to others. On our first meeting, one patient said, "I am the daughter of Hannah, and our people come from Tensas Parish in northeastern Louisiana. I've got seven brothers and sisters. They call me Jerline. Pleased to meet you."

Before we talked about illnesses, we would talk about food. When you natter on about food together, you are equals. When a person speaks of what they most like to eat, you learn a lot from their face, the way their eyes open wide or they lick their lips or how their voice trails off. When we share about food, we share details about our families, the way we grew up, and how we were loved or not. What people used to love to eat but can't anymore says a lot about their relationship to their health conditions.

I learned to see myself in each person that I serve, and I would try to see them in me. This was both a beautiful and challenging practice, especially when working in San Francisco's multicultural communities. On the surface, it was easy to focus on our differences: they were black or Latina or Vietnamese, I am white; they shot heroin and had AIDS, I didn't; they were homeless and alone, I paid a ridiculous amount of money for rent and was raising four teenagers. At one time, we might have walked past each other on the streets, unseen. But now in hospice, we were thrown together in the most intimate way.

And in the midst of the service activities—changing residents' diapers or calling their long-estranged family members or advocating for services they needed—we found a meeting place. It wasn't sameness; we didn't need that to connect. It was a belonging that came about because all parts were honored. Honestly, we often failed miserably in connecting, blinded as we were by our privileged view. But we kept at it, and the people we worked with kindly taught us a bit more every day about respecting difference while aiming at inclusivity.

I was often guided by the good counsel of George Washington Carver, the African-American author who was born into slavery and later became a leading scientist, botanist, and educator. He said, "Anything will give up its secrets if you love it enough. Not only have I found that when I talk to the little flower or to the little peanut they will give up their secrets, but I have found that when I silently commune with people they give up their secrets also—if you love them enough."

While service is natural, even instinctual, it isn't always easy. Sometimes we wander away from what we love when we get caught in a role. We become drained. To find our way home, we have to remember what called our souls to serve in the first place. We have to discover how to love what we do, even if we don't always do what we love.

A young woman came to one of my workshops. Athena worked as a physician in a large medical center on the night shift. Part of her job as an intern was to pronounce the deaths of patients she did not know. It was not a technically difficult task, but a sad one, especially in the wee hours of the night. Athena complained that she had grown indifferent to the task. She was exhausted, disheartened, and felt desperate because the practice of medicine had lost all meaning for her. She asked me to introduce her to a Buddhist ritual or practice that might help restore her sense of purpose, the love that had once inspired her to be a doctor.

I also told Athena that a Buddhist practice was unlikely to help. She needed to find the healing she longed for in her own lineage. I suggested that the practice of medicine could be seen as a spiritual path. I reminded her that she was a lineage holder, that the foundation of her practice went back to the Greeks and beyond. She had, after all, upon the completion of her medical school training, taken the Oath of Hippocrates. I offered the possibility that when she put on her white coat, she could imagine it to be a ceremonial robe of Asclepius, imbued with his wisdom and healing powers. She seemed content with these suggestions.

I did not see Athena again after that workshop. But almost a year later, I was teaching a workshop with Dr. Rachel Naomi Remen. She mentioned Athena by name, reporting that Athena had participated in a physician support group that Rachel facilitated. Rachel had been struck by Athena's story. Rachel told me that Athena had become revitalized in her medical practice after she and I spoke. Apparently, when I told Athena to turn toward her own lineage to find the healing she sought, the direction had resonated with her. Athena came from a family of physicians. Her father and grandfather were both doctors, and both had recently died. But with their help, Athena had found her own healing ritual. Her grandfather had been a country doctor, and she had inherited his shabby old black doctor's bag. In it, she placed her father's stethoscope, a small candle, and some essential rose oil favored by her grandmother. She kept this kit in her locker at work.

Now when she was called upon to declare a death, Athena fetched her bag and carried it to the patient's room. Often, she would pause quietly at the threshold to gather her breath and call on her ancestors for support. Sometimes there was a nurse present who pulled out the intravenous lines and removed the stickers that were used to track heart rhythms. Athena placed the small votive candle on the bedside table, lit it, and removed her father's stethoscope from her grandfather's bag. In silence, she examined the patient, listened for the sound of a heartbeat, and mindfully watched to see if the breath had stopped. She felt intimacy in these simple actions. Then she removed the small vial of rose oil and, taking a bit on her fingers, placed a few drops on the forehead of the person who had died, adding a short intuitive prayer: "May you be at peace, may you find rest, may all your suffering come to an end."

Athena felt that she could no longer play the role of a doctor in the way she had been trained: to be self-denying; to trade her humanity in for expertise. However, finding this personal ritual had restored her love of medicine and inspired her to continue to be the healer she had always hoped she would become.

In listening to the call of her soul, Athena had found the courage to step out beyond her role and into her authentic self. There, as she cared for others, she found peace, contentment, renewed inspiration, and access to her innate kindheartedness.

9

TAMING THE INNER CRITIC

The way we talk to our children becomes their inner voice.
—PEGGY O'MARA

No matter how you try, you can't please your inner critic.

There is no fooling it. The critic knows your every move, every trick up your sleeve, every bit of your past. It has been right there with you throughout your life. You shower with it. Take it to work. It sits next to you at every meal and even sticks around for dessert. It's there during and after sex. And yes, it's definitely there when you are dying.

It compares, praises, devalues, diminishes, invalidates, blames, approves, condemns, and attacks your appearance, job performance, the way you conduct relationships, your friends, your health, your diet, your hopes and dreams, your thoughts, and your spiritual development. Pick something, anything, as it is all interchangeable. Let's face it: in the critic's eyes, nothing you do is good enough.

The critic is the enforcer, demanding compliance to an acquired set of standards and moral codes. It's the voice that says, "My way or the highway." And it wields brutally its chosen weapons of fear, shame, and guilt in order to get you to do what it wants.

Often in our most vulnerable moments, when we would benefit from tenderness, we club ourselves with self-judgment. Even near the end of life, it is common for people to look back with regret, to become obsessed with "if only" conversations, or to tell themselves that they aren't doing a good job of dying. Friends and relatives add to the pile of guilt by projecting their own inner critic's voice onto the person who is dying, suggesting that he *should* fight harder or she *should* let go more gracefully.

The inner critic is ambivalent about change, shifts in identity, creativity, and inner work, and it is downright terrified of anything bubbling up from the unconscious. The judge prefers status quo, the familiar, the predictable. It insists on homeostasis. "Don't rock the boat," it advises. "It's not safe."

That's why focusing on self-improvement or making any attempt to fix what the critic views as "the problem" never works. In seeking the approval of others, conforming to an external standard, and trying to please, we are looking for love in all the wrong places. Praise and blame are symptoms of an infectious disease. And as with any illness, we need to do more than treat the symptoms; we have to address the underlying causes. We need to go to the heart of the matter. We need to see how the habit of constant self-judgment diminishes our life force, steals our inner peace, and crushes our souls.

The pursuit of perfection is learned early on and, for most of us, becomes a lifelong addiction. It is an ego-based quest that easily can eclipse the soul's journey to wholeness. This is why, in order to *bring our whole self to the experience*, we must address the often unconscious, corrosive voice of the inner critic. It is the primary obstacle to self-acceptance, trust, and the expansion of our dynamic potential. It stops all growth, arrests inner development, steals our power, and makes negative self-talk the norm. Furthermore, the judge impedes our ability to connect and empathize with other people. Chances are if you're extremely critical of yourself, you'll be a harsh critic of others. You may think it even if you don't say it.

When we bring our whole self forward, we include our brokenness. We make room for blemishes as well as purity, strength as well as vulnerability, success as well as screwups. Judgment focuses on what's wrong;

it feeds an "either/or" mentality. Embracing wholeness is a loving act of reclamation, a "both/and" way of meeting life.

To free ourselves from the inner critic, we have to understand something of its origins, how we are impacted by it, and how we can successfully disengage from its negative influence. In short, our treatment plan includes the application of wisdom, strength, and love.

When my son was seven, he built a fort behind a small desk in his bedroom. He often would crawl into this private place when he was upset, disappearing for an hour or more after one of our disagreements or when I was nagging him.

A few years later, we moved. When I pulled the desk away from the wall to dismantle his fort, I got quite a surprise. The back panel of wood was completely covered in swear words, profanity, angry rants, and cusses at his sweet old dad.

It's natural for a child to experience aggressive energy like this toward a parent. But usually, it feels too dangerous to express, and so we repress it. Once I had recovered from my initial shock and bruised ego, I laughed. I felt relieved that Gabe had found a way to vent his anger with me.

When all of us were children, our parents and grandparents, older siblings, teachers, spiritual advisors, and other responsible adults in our lives did their best to show us right from wrong. By and large, they were well intentioned. Their goal was to foster our development and protect us from harm. Without a doubt, we needed some guidance or we wouldn't have made it to adulthood alive and healthy, nor would we have been able to successfully enter into a society that relies on certain codes of conduct.

And so these grown-ups imbued us with their values and standards. They taught us the basic rules they believed we would need in order to cope in the world. This natural socialization process only becomes problematic when it spills over into a forced attempt to align a child's behavior with the adult's view of life. Most grown-ups are not ogres, yet inevitably they pass along their unconscious assumptions, unskillful strategies, prejudices, and biases from their own unexamined lives. Maybe your parents were embarrassed by your fascination with your sexual impulses, or exhausted by your unstoppable energy. Perhaps your teachers and spiritual leaders used warnings and reprimands to control your behavior, manage your emotions, and keep you from doing things that made them uncomfortable. Or maybe your mother or father wanted to get you to do things you didn't really want to do, like go to sleep when you weren't tired, dress a certain way, have different friends, or eat what was offered, whether or not it looked and tasted good to you.

When we were small, the adults had all the power. We were completely dependent upon them for our budding self-perception and, more importantly, for our survival. To a young child, such approval or disapproval often feels like a matter of life and death.

Out of self-preservation, we learned to get and maintain approval and avoid shame and punishment by bending to adults' wishes. Along the way, we internalized their voices of authority, adapted to their values, or rebelled against them. This conditioning—the "should" and "should nots," the message that something was "wrong" with us—formed the basis of our inner critics.

As we come into adulthood, the harsh, coercive voice of the judge outgrows its usefulness. But it continues to live on in us as a powerful psychological structure that wants to protect us by managing our lives. It's a bit like our wisdom teeth: once, when we existed on a diet of raw meat, nuts, and roots, these teeth were necessary for our survival. Yet as we evolved, we learned how to use tools, cutting and cooking the food we eat, and as a result, we no longer needed our wisdom teeth. Similarly, as we mature, we have access to a less reactive and more discerning wisdom that is objective, positive, and can function as a reliable and creative guide in our lives. We don't need the critic's constant appraisal and attacks, its humiliation, repression, and rejection, or the suffering it generates.

But mostly we still think we do.

Recently, the topic of the inner critic came up in conversation with a friend and neighbor. Beth is about the same age as I am, healthy and fit, and most would view her as highly successful, living a well-balanced life in which she is happily married, close with her children, and enjoying retirement.

When I mentioned how important I feel it is for us to tame the critic as we journey through life, Beth argued, "But what would I have left without the voice of my inner critic? Who would I be? A lazy, miserable person who had never gone after her dreams? Without it, I wouldn't get anything done. The critic tells me the truth about what I'm getting right and wrong. It is the reason why I want to be my best self. It motivates me toward productive change."

"Does it?" I asked her. "I find the inner critic berates me more than it motivates me. It is neither a conscience nor a reliable moral guide, and it isn't the voice of wisdom. Yes, there may be some kernel of truth wrapped up in the critic's commentary. It may have a useful tidbit of information to offer. But I certainly don't need its delivery system. It has a particular tone of voice that is often mean, dismissive, and manipulative. I've been with many wise spiritual teachers over the years, and none of them has ever transmitted their wisdom to me in such a nasty tone."

"But sometimes my inner critic praises me," Beth replied. "It congratulates me for working hard to get the job done."

I nodded. "It's true, the critic can offer praise. And that tone is far stickier because we like it; we crave approval. However, not all praise is equal. We should question the critic's motives. Upon closer examination, we find that we only receive praise for gaining a narrow set of outcomes or displaying the few qualities approved of by the critic."

"It's true," Beth said. "I realize I've been getting pushed around by my critic for fifty years. I've been so busy trying to earn its praise and prove my worth by trying to be smarter, younger, stronger, and more successful. I've started three profitable companies, and I still feel like an imposter."

Some of us, like Beth, have a mistaken loyalty to our critic. We think it keeps us sharp and leads to more critical thinking we need in our jobs or to understand the world. Looking closer we see that the mechanism of the critic is pretty simple and unsophisticated; after all, it was formed when we were children.

People often imagine that the negative, grating voice in their heads is helping them. But it's not. The critic doesn't believe in our basic human goodness. It only believes in rules and moral codes. Psychologically, the critic is the protector of ego. It denies everything else. It doesn't know your soul. It doesn't trust your heart to know how you feel, to be empathic and compassionate in relationships. It doesn't have faith that your intuitive *gut sense* can guide you in situations you're encountering for the first time. The inner critic only wants you to heed its advice. It doesn't trust in your ability to reason and evaluate as a way to navigate through life's dilemmas.

There is an alternative to the critic. It's found in the movement from judgment to discernment. Judgment is the harsh, aggressive habit that shuts down the conversation, binds us to the past and old behaviors, and closes off our access to other capacities. Discernment makes space, helps us to have perspective, and allows more of our humanity to show up. Discernment helps wisdom to emerge and enables us to choose a more beneficial future. Our innate discriminating wisdom is a kind, more objective voice that is available to all of us. It can differentiate, discern, and intelligently guide us forward.

The critic may have served a purpose back in kindergarten, but it's time to trade in our old model.

I was teaching a workshop in central Italy and had an insightful exchange with a student named Stella. She was a doctor, a warmhearted and attractive woman in her late thirties. After my talk about the inner critic, she approached me and said quite seriously, "I don't have a critic."

"Are you sure?" I asked.

"Yeah, I can't find one," Stella said. She told me how successful she was at work, how she had achieved her goal of becoming a doctor at a young age, how proud her parents were of her.

Now, in Italy there remains a strong cultural bias, or we might say a cultural critic, that places significant pressure on women of childbearing years to have babies. Italian women often find it daunting to balance work with the traditionally demanding expectations for mothers. Increasingly, many are opting not to have children at all. Yet the conditioning and beliefs run deep and are often the cause of considerable internal conflict.

I said, "Do you really want me to try to help you identify the voice of your critic? It could be quite painful."

Stella was insistent. "Yes, yes, please. I want to understand."

So I took a guess. In a very calm tone of voice, I asked, "How come you haven't had any babies yet?"

Immediately, Stella burst into tears. I didn't have to add anything to that one line, nor did I need to speak it harshly. I knew my words would pass through her inner critic and the judge would make my question sound like an accusation. "You're right!" she cried. "I hear that voice all the time . . . not just in my head. From my parents, my neighbors, my co-workers, even taxi drivers—and it always upsets me."

Identifying her critic shook Stella to the core. She cried as I held her, yet she wanted to keep inquiring into her experience to help surface more of the story. I suggested to Stella that she might want to explore this issue with the support of a good therapist.

In fact, the incident did inspire Stella to go into psychotherapy to work on this issue. She came back to the workshop a year later and announced that she was very happily pregnant. She'd told herself that she had written off children because she had been so wrapped up in her career, but in truth, her critic was telling her that she wouldn't be a good mother and would never find a partner to have children with her.

Thanks to therapy, Stella confronted her judge. She acknowledged a deep part of herself that wanted badly to be a mother—and always had. If the nasty, demeaning voice that called her a "loser" for being single at thirty-seven and "incapable" of raising kids had gotten its way, Stella never would have discerned the best path forward. She had to tune in to the far quieter voice of her soul. Then and only then was she able to figure out a plan for how to have a successful career as a physician and be a mother.

Our essential nature has certain attributes that are innate, meaning they already exist within each of us, and we all have access to them. One of these innate qualities is wisdom. People don't usually think of wisdom as innate. They believe it is something you must acquire over the course of a lifetime through experience. It's true, there is an analytical wisdom that needs to be trained and developed over time. But we also have an innate wisdom. Buddhism refers to a self-revealing *wisdom-nature* that we can attune to through meditation. As with Stella, we all have access to this inner wisdom, if only we listen carefully to what it has to offer.

As we move through the vicissitudes of daily life, our essential nature passes through cultural, familial, and societal conditioning. These innate qualities bump up against our personalities, our belief systems, and the hindrances of our very human minds. As that contact occurs, the qualities of our essential nature go through a process of constriction. They become twisted. Then, instead of being expressed in a free, open, and natural way, the various qualities appear distorted. Strength gets tangled up in desires or expectations and gets expressed as frustration, anger, and destructiveness. Compassion passes through fear and shows up as pity or an obsessive need to fix others and protect ourselves from pain.

The critic is particularly fond of distorting wisdom. In fact, the critic likes to substitute its own voice for the softer, gentler guide of our inner wise person. The critic says, "Trust me. I know you so well. I've been through this before." Wisdom says, "Relax into your experience. You can trust yourself to know what to do." Instead of telling you what might *appear* to be true, as the critic does, wisdom teaches us how to discover what is really true.

It's important to realize that even in its twisted expressions, the fragrance of our essential nature remains. We tend to view distortions as obstacles blocking our way home. We feel defeated and give up, or we wage war against our anger, our fear, and our inner critics by trying to overcome or get rid of them. Instead, we might see the obstacles as door-ways. We could move toward them, gently and persistently, in order to understand what they are all about.

Once, a leader of a spiritual organization used me as a scapegoat to push forward a plan without considering the community's readiness. As a result, I was forced to leave the community and part with the people who were most central in my life at the time.

Some years later, I was reflecting on the incident and became over-come with hatred toward my accuser. In my mind, I kept replaying my version of the story of how I was wronged, imagining it to be completely true. As I did, I noticed that my right hand was making a chopping mo-tion into my left hand. The hatred grew in intensity. Wanting to under-stand this obstacle, I allowed myself to imagine my darkest and most bitter thoughts. I let the hatred rip, feeling the full range of emotions as I fantasized about how I might cut this man out of my life. My hatred felt cold, calculating, indifferent, and temporarily powerful. My right hand was like a knife, slicing and destructive.

Just then, I recalled the statue of Manjushri, an iconic, archetypical form of Buddha that is often found in Zen meditation halls. He wields a sword in his right hand. It is known as the sword of discriminating wis-dom. The sword is said to be able to cut through ignorance and the entanglements of deluded views.

In that moment, I realized that wisdom was true power. Within the hatred I was experiencing, there was a flavor, a fragrance of that wisdom, but it had been distorted. When I could see more clearly, I understood that my hatred was only impersonating power; it was a counterfeit ver-sion of power.

With the emerging wisdom, I saw that while my anger at the rejec-tion had seemed to be only outwardly focused, it had been eating at me inwardly for years in the form of obsessive self-hatred. I had this inner narrative going about what I should have done years ago. My critic had been on my back for over two decades, wanting me to change what had happened or to get over it, to stop being such a baby. It became clear how my drive toward self-improvement, as with so many other people on the spiritual path, had a religious zeal to it. I never left myself alone. I was constantly comparing myself to others. I was never good enough.

I thought of the American Buddhist nun and bestselling author Pema Chödrön, who wrote, "The problem is that the desire to change yourself is fundamentally a form of aggression toward yourself." That doesn't mean that we ought to condone wrongdoing, abandon plans and goals, or resign ourselves to being stuck in our old stories. It means that we should do our best to hold our imperfections with kindness. We can bring self-acceptance forward, befriend ourselves, and get curious about the twists in our innate qualities rather than trying to beat them into submission.

In order to stop the pattern of self-betrayal that occurs when we are at the mercy of an unchecked inner critic, we have to stand up for ourselves. We have to act on our own behalf. I find it helpful to remember how you reacted as a child when your parents didn't approve, or when an authority figure imposed rules on you that you didn't think were fair. What was your automatic response?

Karen Horney, the German psychoanalyst credited with founding feminist psychology, wrote about three human coping strategies for dealing with basic anxiety. They are applicable both to how we reacted to criticism as children and to how we continue to respond to the inner critic today:

- Some of us *move away* by withdrawing, hiding, collapsing, keeping secrets, and silencing ourselves. We avoid conflict. Maybe you went to your room, perhaps you quietly watched TV as you tried to absorb the judgment or simply endure it.
- Some of us *move toward* by seeking to please and accommodate, negotiate, persuade, and explain. Maybe you did extra

schoolwork, tried to be helpful around the house, or always were well behaved in order to earn approval.

- Some us *move against* by trying to gain power over others. We rebel or fight back. Maybe you talked back, yelled, acted with hostility, slammed doors, or snuck out the window and did what you wanted.

Here is the problem with all of these strategies: they still give the inner critic all the power. We remain caught up in reacting to authority instead of creatively choosing our own path. To undo this old habit, we need strength.

Essential strength comes from repeated encounters with our basic nature, through which we develop confidence in its presence and wise guidance. That becomes the foundation on which we stand, the essential strength that we carry into action. When our strength gets distorted, for example, by righteousness or resentment, it takes shape as anger. But we can harness the energy of strength that lives in our anger. We can tap into its vitality, intensity, and aliveness.

Suppose you brought awareness to a negative reaction as it was first arising within you. As I did when I examined my hatred toward the spiritual leader whom I felt had wronged me, you might contain the hurtful expression of your anger before acting out, focusing instead on the visceral physical experience within your body. Perhaps then you could channel that energy honestly into protecting yourself from the attack.

There are a dozen books out there offering myriad strategies for defending against the critic. For me, it boils down to this: summoning the courage to face a powerful and coercive force head-on. I side with the poet e. e. cummings, who wrote, "It takes courage to grow up and become who you really are."

Once when I was teaching about the inner critic, a woman raised her hand and asked to speak. Her frustration was palpable, her face turning red and her whole body trembling. "I can never defeat the inner critic!" she said. "It always gets the best of me. Why am I so weak?"

I pulled a chair right up next to her and stood on top of it so that I was a good four feet taller than she was. Then I pointed my finger down at her and said in a firm, loud tone, "You are bad!"

She burst into laughter. "Oh yeah, look at that!" she said. "That is what the critic is like when it has the best of me. No wonder I feel weak. I couldn't fight back against that adult voice when I was a small child. It was too big, too powerful."

Then I asked the woman to stand up on the chair so that she was a head taller than I was. I guided her to breathe deeply, feel her way into her body, center herself in awareness, and think about her innate goodness. "Now how would you respond to the inner critic when it tells you that you're bad, you're weak?" I asked.

"Don't speak to me that way," she said, her voice strong and confident. "It hurts me when you talk to me like that. And it doesn't help me do any better."

Telling the emotional truth, expressing disinterest in the critic's advice, using humor, staying connected to your physical center, harnessing your strength—all these strategies are meant to restore our contact with the dynamic expansiveness that is our essential nature. When we have successfully defended against an attack and disengaged from the critic, we may feel a shift in physical energy, perhaps a release of tension, a free flow of breath. Emotionally, we may feel increased confidence and compassion for what hurts. Mentally, we may have more clarity and less confusion. However, be prepared for residual feelings and sensations, questions and doubts to linger for a period of time. In other words, don't expect to feel warm and fuzzy right away.

Defending ourselves against the inner critic is tough work. It takes practice.

Matthew was a gay man and a longtime Buddhist practitioner. Hospitalized with pneumonia related to his HIV diagnosis, he was running a high fever, occasionally crying out, and constantly writhing and wriggling in his bed as if he wanted to crawl out of his own skin. Matthew was also battling the inner critic, who, in his case, was dressed in the robes of a spiritual authority. He had been overtaken by anxiety, fearing eternal damnation, as well as shame at how he had lived his life.

Matthew had been raised in a fundamentalist Christian family. The commandments of a punishing god had literally been beaten into him by his fire-and-brimstone preacher man of a father. Now, believing he was close to death, he felt certain that God would condemn him for eternity to hell due to his sexual orientation.

It is not uncommon for long-buried cultural mores and early religious training to suddenly resurface at the time of death, even if the person has deliberately left those beliefs far behind. I tried to support Matthew by orienting him to the mindfulness and compassion practices that he had studied and loved for many years. We created an altar at his bedside with his beloved Buddha statue and a healing *thangka*, a traditional Tibetan painting. When that failed to calm him, I held his hand, massaged his feet, and played him his favorite chanting music. Still no change. Finally, the doctor ordered a sedative. Even that didn't work. Matthew was spinning in a world of confusion, shame, and dread.

By two in the morning, I was exhausted and, feeling ineffective and powerless, chose to go home and get some sleep. On the drive there, for some unknown reason, I thought of my first Holy Communion, the Catholic ritual that ushers young innocents into the loving lap of God. When I got home, I searched through my storage closet to find my memory box, a small collection of mementos I hold dear. Here, I located a five-inch plastic figurine of Jesus surrounded by lambs and little children.

Instead of going to bed, I drove straight back to the hospital. As Matthew continued to moan, shout, toss, and turn in agony, I took down the *thangka* and replaced the Buddha statue with this small plastic Jesus.

Just as I was smoothing the altar cloth, a cleaning woman named Deana came into the room and spotted the figurine. Setting her mop to one side, she said with great enthusiasm, "Merciful Jesus! When his kindness is with us, everything is all right."

At once, Matthew's eyes locked onto Deana. An angelic smile spread across his face as he pivoted toward the altar to gaze at the plastic Jesus statue and then back in Deana's direction. His entire body relaxed. In that moment, the punishing God of Matthew's childhood, the one whose wrath he had been taught to fear and whose judgment had made him feel like a terrible person, was transformed into the merciful God he also knew and loved. The one who adored all his children, no matter their so-called faults and flaws. A kind, forgiving, all-accepting, and benevolent God.

Deana's faith in God's love was so secure that it lent Matthew exactly the strength he needed to defeat his inner critic. I left them together there. They didn't need me.

When I eventually returned to the hospital later that afternoon, Matthew was sitting up in bed, smiling and eating a bowl of Jell-O.

Most of us have notions from our childhood religious experiences about how a "good spiritual person" ought to function in the world. I'm a Buddhist, so I'm not supposed to get angry. Matthew had been raised an evangelical Christian, so he wasn't supposed to be gay. But really, these ideas are just our inner critics projecting themselves onto every dimension of our lives. The voice of the authority figure who lives in our heads can just as easily come from cultural conventions or religious canons as from parents or teachers.

Matthew was able to release his spiritual superego. In the final days of his life, he was able to truly accept himself as the kind, giving, beautiful man he had become. He could see clearly that the delivery system of his youth, the hellfire and brimstone and judgments, was the cause of his self-rejection. He had always felt, on some level, that he was "wrong" for being gay. But finally, letting go of his inner critic, he realized that he was all right.

How did this happen?

With love. Love is what helps set us free. Love is the ally that makes acceptance possible.

However, we often confuse acceptance with approval. Acceptance is a loving act of an open heart. Approval is generally tied up with judgment. Our hunger for approval is partly why we are so easily hooked by the critic. We try to fend off unworthiness by seeking our value from external authorities whose voices we long ago internalized. We try to satisfy the enormity of our wanting through accumulation. We hope that if we get enough, do enough, change enough, one day we will finally be enough.

We worry that acceptance means conformity and mediocrity. We wonder if it puts us in danger of becoming a doormat for others. But here's the truth: We can't change something that we haven't accepted. So first we need to accept. That doesn't mean we won't shift behaviors or skillfully intervene when necessary. Acceptance gives us the opportunity to know ourselves and our inner voices, to examine our relationships with them. Then we can use our discerning wisdom to determine what is useful and what isn't. And then we can decide our course of action.

With acceptance, what emerges is a deep trust in what is. We release ourselves completely from the comparison, assessment, and rejection of the inner critic. We stop blaming ourselves for having desires and wants, and instead accept these desires as a flavor of love, one that expresses our hearts' deepest longing for what is true and real.

True acceptance begins an alchemical process. The undesirable can be changed into the desirable by mindfully embracing our flaws, shortcomings, warts, and all those rejected, painful, and scary aspects of ourselves. Even the seemingly unlovable pieces are loved because they are seen as part of the whole. We expose our imagined imperfections to the fierce fires of wisdom, strength, and love, and in so doing, we learn to turn lead into gold. Confusion dissolves into clarity. We discover courage in our vulnerability. We melt internal enemies and transform them into friends. This process reveals the real treasure, which is the pure potential that exists in everything, the glimmering properties of our essential nature.

10

THE RAGING RIVER

*What is to give light
must endure burning.*
—VIKTOR FRANKL

How do we cultivate our essential nature without sidestepping our human nature? This is at the heart of *Bring Your Whole Self to the Experience.*

It is a most beautiful and difficult thing to be human.

Waking up in this human experience is not easy. Authentic spiritual practice is not about maintaining high altered states, transcending the body, bypassing difficult emotions, or healing all that remains unresolved within us. It is more grounded, real, and alive than that. Spiritual practice helps us settle into the utter simplicity of being ourselves. The healing that it engenders happens when we bring awareness to the places that have hardened in us through the conditioned habits of grasping, resistance, and avoidance.

Mindfulness is a de-conditioning. It cultivates a merciful, awake presence of mind that no longer blocks the heart. Then things are free to be as they are. We allow the difficult, dark, and dense. We become more intimate with our pain and difficulties, our joy and beauty, embodying our full humanity and discovering an ever-deeper, vast sense of wholeness.

Sometimes what is *over there* seems more valuable than what is *right here*. But being who you are can only arise from accepting where you are.

My daughter, Gina, and I were walking on a stunning thin strip of beach on an island in northern Thailand. As a young person, she was prone to emotional upheaval. This day was being swept away by her unrequited attraction to a boy back home. As we walked, she talked, explaining how she had to get to a phone to call him. I asked her if she was sure she wanted to spend her time in paradise strategizing about how to reach this guy.

Wisely realizing that she wasn't even seeing the turquoise water surrounding us, she replied, "No, but what am I supposed to do about this? How do I get rid of this feeling?"

I might have dismissed this as a teenage drama, but I saw a small opening. I asked Gina to sense her body, particularly in the area of her chest. She reported the tension and heat she found there. She took a few breaths. I asked if she could name the feeling she was experiencing.

"Sadness and the fear that I will be rejected," she replied immediately. As she spoke, she realized how this feeling was opening up a deeper pool of unacknowledged grief that she had been carrying around.

With all the love in my heart, I said, "Sweetie, don't sell yourself short. Your thoughts and emotions are not who you are. They pass through you, but they are not you."

She stood still. It was like Moses seeing the burning bush. Her mind momentarily stopped. That simple truth had the power of a holy revelation for her.

We lay down in the sand and looked up. I said, "You are as amazing as the blue sky above us. Your emotions are like the clouds passing through the sky. This story of unrequited love is just another passing show. Like clouds, emotions can be powerful and painful. Sometimes they appear big enough to block out the sun. But it's only temporary. Don't be fooled."

I asked if there was any part of her that could be with her sadness. I could see her searching, eventually finding a more spacious part of herself. I asked her to place attention on the relationship between the sadness and the newfound openness.

Gina said, "Wow, the relationship between the two is like a third thing."

"Great," I said. "Let them mingle with one another and get to know each other really well."

Gradually, her crush on the boy faded, and her relationship with herself became far more interesting.

The ability to watch our inner dramas without getting lost in judgment or reactivity is essential to spiritual growth. When we try to push away difficult emotions or the bodily sensations and states of mind that accompany them, we actually keep them in place. When we lock them in, we don't give them the space they need to unfold and reveal themselves, to show us what they have to teach.

Resistance does not assist our inner work. In *Unfolding Now*, A. H. Almaas sums it up beautifully:

When you are resisting, you are basically resisting yourself. It is a kind of self-resistance. Instead of being with yourself, you are resisting being with yourself. Instead of being yourself, you are resisting being yourself . . . Resistance implies some kind of division. It signals that we are not recognizing that what is arising is a manifestation of our own consciousness, of our awareness. When hatred arises in us, for example, or fear, it is our souls, our consciousness, taking that form at that time for a reason we perhaps don't understand yet. If we are able to allow the fear or hate, embrace it, hold it, feel it fully in its totality—in all its texture, color and vividness—we give it the space to be itself.

We generally feel we have two options with difficult emotions: *repress* or *express*.

We repress because an experience seems threatening, upsetting, or somehow inappropriate. Repression can be a choice to defend against, as when we become conscious of a feeling or an experience and then push it below the surface of our awareness. Or the repression may be so power-ful that it completely prohibits an experience, and we block it from ever coming to the light of day.

When we repress an experience, it does not go away. It still lurks below the surface, encapsulated in its original form with all its associated energy. When we bury feelings or bypass them, the material is not available to us. We can't understand it. We can't use it in a constructive way. Repressed anger easily turns to depression, resentment, or fear. Repression gener-ates mental reactivity and skews our perceptions. It leads to what in Bud-dhism we call *papanca mind,* which refers to a proliferation of thoughts and reactions. We re-enact the play as we have scripted it, plot our re-sponse, and act out compulsive, mechanical behaviors. Physically, re-pression can manifest in symptoms like tension, dullness, and a lack of aliveness, and can even become a contributing factor to serious illness.

Emotional expression can be positive and healthy. Sharing our stories is often how we discover the meaning and value of a particular experi-ence. Expressing grief over our mothers' deaths and letting the tears flow can help us metabolize the loss. On the other hand, emotional reactivity usually means that our response is out of proportion to a given stimulus. Unconscious or unresolved feelings get triggered and erupt with an in-tensity that overwhelms us. Frequently, we act out on others. We kick the cat, rage at being stuck in traffic, or otherwise try to displace these uncom-fortable feelings because we are caught by the desire to discharge them.

There is a third option: *contain* the emotion. This is a more balanced and creative response. We hold the emotions and the related material in a caring way. We accept the reality of their presence, regardless of whether we like them or not. We bring them forward with respectful interest. We get curious about our experience. Maybe we explore the tightness in our chest, or sense the heavy weight of our arms or the feeling of longing without attaching any of it to a story. Reminding ourselves to instead gen-tly hold in steadiness apparently differing experiences and perspectives.

With equanimity, we can regulate, reflect, and reappraise. Breathing, sensing, and bringing mindfulness to the physical experience stabilizes our attention and allows the body to become a safe container in which emotions can be embodied and regulated. Then we can reflect on the possible consequences of acting out the emotion or unnecessarily dwelling on it, the potential impact of hurting ourselves or others. We can re-evaluate the automatic negative response and possibly even reinterpret our perceptions of events to discover a new meaning that helps us relate to our emotions in a constructive way. We realize that we have a choice to turn in a healthy direction, or at least to bring patience and kindness to our reactivity.

Grief is a normal, natural response to loss. It is also natural to want to avoid it completely.

There is a well-known Buddhist teaching that is often referred to as the parable of the mustard seed. It tells the story of a woman named Kisa Gotami, whose eight-year-old son suddenly died one day. She was out of her mind with grief. She picked up her son's dead body and walked through the village pleading with people to help her, to give her some medication that might help her son.

Someone sent her to the place where the Buddha was teaching. She approached him for help. "Please, save my son," she begged.

The Buddha responded, "I can, indeed, help you, but first you must complete a task." (There is always a task in these mythical stories.) "You must bring me a single mustard seed. This mustard seed must come from a home, from a family, that has not been touched by death."

Now, mustard seed was a common household spice at this time. What the Buddha understood was that Kisa Gotami needed to believe, for the time being, that her child would live again—she couldn't accept his death yet. The Buddha had no agenda to take away her denial or refuse any part of her experience. Instead, he skillfully guided her toward the discovery of a powerful truth.

Kisa Gotami set out to the village in the hopes of finding the seed. And as the story goes, she moved from house to house, but couldn't find a single home that had not been touched by death. No one could give her a mustard seed. Recognizing that death comes to us all, she was freed from her isolation. This enabled her to rest and bury her child. Rather than being defeated by the truth, she was consoled by it.

The difficulty with such stories is that we sometimes struggle to collect the wisdom from them, keeping them at a safe distance. "Oh yes, but these events happened twenty-five hundred years ago," we tell ourselves. Or "Oh yes, but this is just a story." That is why I like to imagine what it might be like if these events actually took place in the here and now.

Suppose this grieving woman walked through your neighborhood, to your street, and knocked on your door, holding a dead child in her arms. Can you imagine what it would be like to find her there? What would you do when you opened the door? Take a moment to reflect. What would you do, really? Imagine your response.

Some of us would invite her in, hug her, possibly even take the child into our own arms. We might make food, offer a cup of tea, or otherwise try to comfort this grieving mother. Others of us might sit with her on the couch, listen, cry with her, and, if it seemed appropriate, share stories of our own losses. Unsurprisingly, most of us would not know what to say or do. In our confusion, we might rely on hollow clichés like, "He is in a better place. He is with God now," or "There is a reason for everything." If we are honest with ourselves, we may admit that we would be too frightened to even open the door. Instead we would call the professionals, dial 911.

Probably those things happened even back in the day in Kisa Gotami's village. I suspect that her story wasn't as tidy as it is usually told. Death is messy. Grief is even messier. I imagine that Kisa Gotami, in walking from house to house, encountered the sadness, rejection, loneliness, and compassion of others. As she did, she began to realize not only that death comes to us all, but also that grief is our common ground. It is a connective tissue that joins us together.

Most of us wouldn't be able to contribute a mustard seed. Certainly none of us is exempt from loss. Each of us has our grief. Our tendency for self-protection leads us to store these difficult, sometimes shameful, experiences in a dark, cramped corner of our minds. But every new loss triggers the memory of another. In the intense grief arising from the loss of someone we love, we rediscover the pool of grief that we have always carried, the ordinary, everyday grief that inhabits our lives.

A while back at Zen Hospice, we cared for a young woman named Cindy, who had breast cancer. Her parents lived in Iowa, where her father, Clyde, had worked for the past forty years in a meatpacking plant on the night shift.

Knowing that Cindy's death was coming soon, I called to tell Clyde that if he wanted to be with his daughter before she passed away, he needed to come to San Francisco right away.

"All right," he said. "I'll take the train. I'll be there in a couple of days."

When I inquired as to why he didn't just fly, Clyde revealed that he had never been in an airplane before. I said, "You know, Clyde, I think you've gotta come quicker than that."

So he told me that he would come by plane and that he would arrive at ten o'clock that night. I went to Cindy's bedside and whispered in her ear, "Your dad's coming. He'll be here at ten."

She started mumbling over and over again, "Ten o'clock, ten o'clock, ten o'clock."

As her father's plane touched down at the San Francisco airport at ten in the evening, Cindy died. Honoring her indigenous roots, we bathed her body in a brew of herbasanté and covered her in a bed of herbs and flowers from our gardens: sage, lavender, lemon balm, bay laurel, scented geraniums, and rose petals.

It was my job to meet Cindy's father at the door an hour later and tell him that his thirty-year-old daughter had already died. Shocked, at first Clyde just paced the hallways. One of the volunteers stayed with him, and one of us stayed with Cindy. One person to accompany a man in his grief, the other to bear witness to death.

Eventually, Clyde was able to enter Cindy's room. Hours passed, some in silence, some filled with him telling stories about Cindy as volunteers generously listened. We mostly stayed close without interference, modeling that it was possible to be with grief.

Around three in the morning, I said, "Clyde, I'm tired. I've got to go to bed now and be home to get my children off to school in the morning."

He said, "It's all right. I'm going to stay up with Cindy."

At eight, I returned to see Clyde sitting on the edge of the bed with his daughter. His right hand had slipped under the bed of flowers, resting on Cindy's foot. He was holding a bagel in his left. He had the phone tucked into his shoulder, and he was making the funeral arrangements for his daughter.

Clearly, there had been a major shift in Clyde. Now he was willing to be with his grief. I asked him what had changed, adding, "As a father, I can't even imagine what you must be experiencing. It must be so strange to have your daughter die before you do."

Clyde was a plainspoken man. He said, "You know, I realized something. It's kinda familiar."

Most often, we think of grief as an overwhelming response to a singular event, usually the death of someone we love. Yet when we look more closely, we see that grief has been our companion for a good part of our lives. Clyde was talking about everyday grief, the response to the multiple losses and little deaths that occur almost daily. The loss of a treasured piece of jewelry, being let go from a job, the abrupt breakup of a relationship, infertility, financial crises, kids going off to school, the loss of our vitality or a physical or mental capacity, the loss of control, the loss of our dreams. Everyday grief arises when we remember how the carelessness of our actions has caused harm to others. It comes in moments of not being recognized, at times when our expectations aren't met. Sometimes our grief is about what we've had and lost, and sometimes it is about what we never got to have in the first place.

Sadness is just one of the many faces of grief. I find it useful to think of grief as a constellation of responses, an ever-changing process. The author C. S. Lewis, after the death of his wife, wrote, "No one told me grief felt so much like fear." Our grief manifests as anger, self-judgment, regret, and guilt. We experience loneliness and relief, blame and shame, and periods of numbness when we feel like we are walking through molasses. Rarely are we prepared for the intense feelings that engulf us when someone we love dies.

Karen, a longtime Buddhist meditator, master gardener, and lover of nature, experienced the death of both of her parents in about a year's time. Her father's suicide was unexpected and particularly painful for her. She described her grief as an all-consuming rage. Not long after these events, an environmental group invited her to speak at a rally to save the old-growth redwoods. In response, Karen shouted into the phone, "My father has died! There are no trees!"

In managing the grief of others and ourselves, we are generally afraid and impatient. Our own unexplored fear of grief can lead us to hurry others along the path of healing. But grief has a unique rhythm and texture for each of us. It is a deep, slow process of the soul. It cannot be rushed.

Dotty's son died of AIDS. Years later, she told me how an overzealous bereavement volunteer from a large hospice agency had continually asked her, "How do you feel about your son's death?" Dotty, a rather private person, said simply, "I hurt. How else could a mother feel when she has lost her son?"

Over the course of several months, the bereavement volunteer, with the encouragement of her support group, persisted in trying to help Dotty "get in touch with her feelings." In telling the story, Dotty said, "I felt so much guilt and confusion in those days, not about the death of my son, but over my inability to give that volunteer what she was looking for and obviously needed."

We need to allow for the full spectrum of expressions of grief, from the numbness and absence of expression to wild, out-of-control displays of emotion. The sometimes almost deranged explosions of grief are rarely allowed in conventional bereavement support groups. Yet grief is unpredictable, uncontrollable. You can be going along having a great day, and then suddenly, a memory is triggered and you find yourself overwhelmed by sadness. Intense emotions hit you when you least expect them. One friend whose mother had died said that it happened to her in the cereal aisle of a local supermarket. "I just lost it, right there between the Cheerios and the Raisin Bran."

Our fear of this lack of control leads us to ideas about managing our grief or getting over our grief. It is curious to me that we never speak about "managing" our joy or "getting over" our happiness. Grief is like a stream running through our lives, and it is important to understand that loss doesn't go away. It lasts a lifetime. It is our relationship to a particular loss that changes. It won't always hold the same intensity for us, or take the same expression. But the grief as a natural human response to loss will remain, and our resistance to it will only intensify the pain.

In challenging our notions of control, grief cracks our defensive shell of invulnerability. It exposes the ways we hide from the truth and asks us to acknowledge what has always been here but was previously unrecognized: our human frailty.

Grief can be so powerful that instead of surrendering to its force, we reach for information and models that outline predictable stages of grief in the hopes that they will take us through our grief more easily. In so doing, we run the risk of confusing the map with the territory. Journeying through grief, it can indeed help to get familiar with the terrain, to know something of its patterns. But there is no "right" way to grieve, no timetable, no one path. And there certainly are no shortcuts through grief. The only way is straight through the middle.

We don't get past our pain. We go through it and are transformed by it.

At Zen Hospice Project, our volunteer coordinator Eric Poché came up with a simple formulation that we often used to describe grieving. We speak of *loss, losing, and loosening*. These are not stages, nor are they meant to be a map. There is no linear progression through grief. Loss, losing, and loosening are simply common experiences that we might cycle through as we grieve, or that might suddenly explode to the surface of our awareness.

The initial experience of *loss* is often visceral. Even when death is expected, our bodies and minds can't seem to take it in right away. We don't want to believe that the person we loved has died. Just as when you've been punched in the belly, grief can take your breath away. A common reaction is shock and uncertainty. You might feel disconnected from other feelings or people. It can seem like you are sleepwalking or living in a dream. It can be difficult to find your balance.

When her sister, Piper, breathed her final breath after a long bout with cancer, Linda was down the hall. When Linda returned to the room, she let out a gasp, and then her body doubled over in pain. She wrapped her arms around herself, and although she was crying, no sound came out. She sat in a chair next to the bed, holding Piper's hand and staring off into space, shaking her head from side to side, repeating over and over again, "She was so young. This isn't possible. This can't have happened. This can't have happened."

There is no explaining to be done at a moment like this, just accompanying. After an hour or so, following our custom, I invited Linda to join us in a ritual bathing of her sister's body. Linda sternly shouted back, "She's not dead yet!"

Clearly Piper was dead. There was no breath, no pulse, and already her eyes had begun to milk over. Rationally, it's hard to imagine how Linda could deny these truths. Yet in the moment, her mind couldn't allow the reality to sink in. Intuitively, I asked Linda, "When was your sister most alive?"

She replied, "Oh, Piper was a rascal when she was a little girl. Always getting in trouble with our parents. As a teenager, she was even more mischievous. After high school, she became this adventurer, spelunking, climbing mountains. Later, she was the editor of a left-wing political magazine. She was hell on wheels, incredibly alive."

Gradually, more of the story emerged. Linda said, "Piper got sick a few years back. We didn't know what it was at first. Then she started the chemo, and after that she had trouble walking. Remember, Frank, just after she came to the hospice, Piper took that fall and broke her arm and you brought her to the ER? So stubborn! She wouldn't accept any help getting around.

"Everything happened so quickly. In the past few days, she stopped eating, then she stopped talking and even drinking. Her breathing really changed today, didn't it? It got slower and slower, and then there were those long gaps. I only went down the hall for a few minutes to use the bathroom. When I returned, she'd slipped away."

After a pause, Linda said, "Now we can bathe her."

We did so, then we dressed Piper in a beautiful white kimono and surrounded her with flowers. Telling the story of her sister's life helped Linda to accept the reality of Piper's death. It helped Linda become current. She told me later that bathing her sister's body with the utmost care, touching death directly like that, became a refuge for her. She would return to those moments when confusion or denial surfaced again to block the truth.

Shock and disbelief usually give way to guilt and regret. We judge ourselves mercilessly. I commonly hear statements such as "I should have taken her to the hospital sooner," "We could have tried other treatments," "I wish I'd spent more time with her," and "I wanted to be there at the moment she died." Our capacity to be cruel to ourselves never ceases to amaze me. If only we could stop for a moment and listen to the sounds of our voices, surely our hearts would open to embrace our pain.

Without acknowledging it, it's easy to be swept away by the powerful and uncontrollable emotions that rise up with grief, often unexpectedly. After months of exhausting caregiving, continuously witnessing the suffering of someone we love, we may be ashamed that we feel relief when they die. At other times, we get angry, incredibly angry. We want to blame somebody, anybody. "The damned doctors, they said she had six more months," or "What kind of God takes someone in the prime of life?" It is especially confusing when our anger turns toward the person who died. But the truth is we might be angry at that person for leaving us behind with all this pain and loneliness and confusion.

There is no avoiding these painful states of mind. If you're supporting a survivor or you are yourself the survivor, it is important to acknowledge the feelings and understand that they are perfectly normal. Some people cry oceans of tears, others feel numb. Men grieve differently from women. There is no right way, only your way.

Grief is disorienting. We forget our keys, arrive at places and can't remember why we went there. This is the state of grief that at Zen Hospice Project we called *losing*. We can't concentrate. We live in a confused reality. And this goes on for a while after the death of someone you love.

A few months after her mother's death, a woman described walking down the street and stopping at a store window. Inside, she saw a lamp that her mother would have really loved. When she got home, she picked up the phone to call her mother and tell her about it. Then she thought to herself, *Oh my goodness, I've gone crazy*. But this sort of experience is a normal reaction during the grieving period.

In the old days, people used to wear black armbands to let each other know that they were mourning because grief is like being in an altered state. And people treated mourners differently. They took care of them. In the first days and weeks after someone you love dies, don't expect yourself to be able to function fully. Ask for help. Let somebody else make the meals and do the laundry. Cancel your appointments. Take time. Walk if you can. Your body will be rebelling in all sorts of odd ways. Incredible fatigue. Your legs will feel like lead. Restlessness will rule. You may not want to sleep or eat. Or you might need to sleep all day. Find someone to hold you, or find a shirt with your loved one's scent on it and hold it close. Distracting yourself only postpones the experience. It doesn't make it go away.

Losing can go on for weeks, months, even years. When someone we love dies, we keep on losing that person over and over again, especially at holidays, in times of difficult decisions, and in those little personal moments we long to share.

During this period, we realize most clearly the roles that the other person has played in our lives, and we grieve the loss of those also. We don't just lose a wife when she dies. If she was the person who worked out all the battles with our kids, or earned the money, or touched our bodies with love and tenderness, we lose all those things, as well. One man told me that his wife did the banking and that every time he went to make a deposit he would cry. "Whenever I go there I feel like I lose her again," he said. If our parents die, we may find ourselves feeling really fragile. They were the buffer standing between us and death, and suddenly, we become much more aware of our own mortality.

This is the phase of grief when we feel most alone. Friends drop away, others give us unwanted advice. After the death of her husband, one woman told me that her friends suggested that she should get a dog for companionship. Others tell us to keep busy or to get on with our lives. It is their fear of pain and our cultural predisposition toward avoiding anything unpleasant that is driving them. Unfortunately, their advice doesn't help.

My friend Caroline told me that the one thing that did help after her husband's death was a friend who called her every week to invite her out to dinner. The friend said, "I know you may not want to go, and it's okay to say no. But I want you to know that I'm here when you need me. I will call again next Monday."

Losing is the time to be around the people whom you trust the most, those who have earned the right to listen. It helps alleviate the feeling of being disconnected from life. Those who have consciously lived through a loss of their own also know the importance of listening without judgment or agenda.

In this period of *losing*, it is critical that we allow ourselves to feel the pain. Some say time heals. That is a dangerous half-truth. Time alone doesn't heal. Time and loving attention heal.

Some begin this process by writing letters to the person who has died, speaking what was left unsaid, or repeating whatever they feel needs to be said again. Others make scrapbooks or photo albums. Rituals can help. I usually recommend that people find some place in their house to create an altar. Place on that altar a photo and some special objects of the person who has died. Spend some time there each day. Talk to the

person, tell them how you're feeling, maybe spend some time in meditation or in prayer. Use this moment to extend your wish to the person
who has passed that they may be free of suffering, that they may be
touched by compassion.

One Zen teacher brings together women whose babies have died.
They gather for a weekend and sew a *rakusu*, a miniature version of the
standard Buddhist monastic robes. It looks like a bib and is made of sixteen or more strips of cloth sewn together into a brick-like pattern. As
the women sew, they speak of their babies. They share how their bodies
and hearts ache.

The weekend concludes with a ritual that involves placing the *rakusu*
on a statue of Jizo, who is said to be an embodiment of the Bodhisattva
Vow, the aspiration to save all beings from suffering. In Japan, Jizo is
the protector of travelers and children, especially *mizuko*, which literally translates as "water child" but refers to the souls of aborted, still-
born, or miscarried babies. Some of the unborn babies who were unnamed
are given names. Often this is the first and only time these women's
losses have been acknowledged and ritually honored. They find it deeply
healing.

For many years, I led an annual retreat for people living with HIV. On
a certain night, we would gather round the campfire and introduce ourselves to each other by relating the losses of our lives. For some, this was
the loss of hope or the loss of faith. For others, it was the loss of identities.
For many, it was the numbing, multiple deaths that they had experienced
when their ten or twenty or thirty close friends had died of AIDS.

As we listened, we would bear witness to one another. And we would
discover that it is possible to open to and even heal such devastating grief.
We would find that our grief was workable.

It is not the pain that awakens us; it is our attention to the pain. Our
willingness to experience and investigate our suffering gives rise to compassion and kindness. Consistent, loving attention melts our well-
constructed defenses and unleashes old holdings. We begin to invite the
pain into our hearts. The thoughts, the physical sensations, the emotional

turmoil that we have so long rejected and had so little room for . . . they begin to be held in the comfort of our awareness.

Loosening is the period in which the knot of our grief is untied. It is a time of renewal. You can't go back to life as it was before because you are a different person now, changed by your journey through grief. But you can begin to embrace life again, to feel alive again. The intensity of emotions has subsided somewhat. You can remember the loss without being caught up in a stranglehold of grief. You can move forward without abandoning the one you love.

One elderly woman explained it this way. She said that she and her husband had made all of their important decisions together. For several months after her husband's death, she continued to set a place for him at the dinner table. She would sit down, talk to him, and ask his advice, as if he were still sitting there across the table from her.

Gradually, she said, that habit stopped, but she would still hear his voice inside her head. And when it came time to make decisions, she still would base her plans on what he would have said or done. After about a year of loving attention to him and her grief, she began to notice that the responses to her questions were coming in her own voice, not his.

"I lead my own life now," she said. "He travels with me everywhere, but I decide where we'll go on vacation!"

When someone close to us dies, we experience a tremendous sense of loss. At first, it's like reaching for a hand that has always been there, only to discover that it is no longer available. Gradually we see that the relationship continues. The person is in some way internalized, and you can carry them with you wherever you go. They might surprise you when a memory of them shows up when you least expect it. You can talk to them, they can talk to you, they can be with you, and you can be with them. You are not crazy because you feel the presence of your loved one in your heart.

The grieving process is like a transitional space in your relationship. The physical presence of the other person used to be at the center of the relationship, but now that there is no physical presence, the center of the relationship is the sensitivity and love that lives within you.

Grieving the death of someone we love is like being thrown into a raging river of powerful and conflicting emotions. It pulls us down, down beneath the surface of our lives and into dark waters where we cannot breathe. Frantically, we try to escape the whirlpool of this inner journey. Surrendering, we feel ourselves carried forward by gentle currents to a new destination. Emerging from the water, we step ashore with refreshed eyes, and we enter the world in a new way.

To accompany a dying person, to make the journey through grief ourselves—these may be the greatest challenges we will ever face in our lives. But don't turn away. Bring your whole self to the experience. When we take care of someone we love and do it with great integrity and impeccability, when we feel that we have given ourselves fully and completely to our grief and didn't hold anything back, then we will surely feel great sorrow. But also we will feel gratitude and the possibility of opening to a reservoir of joy and love that we may have never known before. I call this undying love.

In grief, we access parts of ourselves that were somehow unavailable to us in the past. With awareness, the journey through grief becomes a path to wholeness. Grief can lead us to a profound understanding that reaches beyond our individual losses. Every time we experience a loss, we have another chance to experience life at a greater depth. It opens us to the most essential truths of our lives: the inevitability of impermanence, the causes of suffering, and the illusion of separateness. We begin to appreciate that we are more than the grief. We are what the grief is moving through.

In the end, we may still fear death, but we don't fear living nearly as much. In surrendering to our grief, we have learned to give ourselves to life.

11

HEARING THE CRIES OF THE WORLD

If you want others to be happy, practice compassion.
If you want to be happy, practice compassion.

—HIS HOLINESS THE DALAI LAMA

California condors are magnificent creatures. The largest birds in North America, these spectacular, almost mythological beings can have wingspans of close to ten feet and soar like gods above the Big Sur coast. At one time, hundreds of condors roosted in the tall redwoods of the coastal mountains along the Pacific Ocean. But the last of the free-flying condors were taken into captivity in 1987 in order to save the species from extinction.

In the late '90s, California condors raised in captivity were reintroduced to the wild to restore the endangered breed. Unfortunately, these birds didn't adapt well to their release. They were ill prepared to live in the wilderness and were often found in places they didn't belong, flying in confused circles around buildings and near people, too afraid to venture into the woods.

Wildlife experts quickly learned from the error of their ways. For subsequent releases, they made sure the birds were reared by adult condors from early in life and were therefore less imprinted on people. This new generation of young captives, upon introduction to the wild, adjusted well. The California condor population is now thriving.

In Buddhism, wisdom and compassion are spoken of metaphorically as the two great wings of our practice. If the balance between the two is underdeveloped or immature, we cannot take flight and find freedom. Like those early young captive condors, we don't make smart choices and can end up flying in circles. Attempts at compassion without wisdom easily become sentimental and mushy. Attempts at wisdom without compassion can seem cold, indifferent, and cerebral.

The wisdom that gives rise to compassion is the clear understanding of our interdependence, an appreciation that we are not separate. We may appear so, but this is misperception, a conditioned view that shapes how we see ourselves and how we engage with each other.

I have several surfer friends who are always trying to teach me about waves. They talk to me about the elemental forces that create ocean waves thousands of miles offshore, how wind generates moving energy in the ocean, the way swells become surf. They point to the effects of tides and currents, the shape of the ocean floor, the length of a reef, wave height, the fetch and face of waves, and how they get arranged into sets. They spend endless hours studying waves. Honestly, I don't always see what they see.

I do see that each wave is completely unique. No two waves are the same. They come into form dependent on many differing conditions, live for a while, and express a distinctive beauty before they disappear, thrown up on the beach before flowing back out to sea. Each wave is distinct, yet not separate. All are part of the same ocean. The ocean is one big body, and the waves are its individual expression.

We human beings are like that: exquisitely unique and differentiated, but not separate. With all our extraordinary differences, we share the same basic nature. We are part of the same vast ocean.

When we release ourselves from a narrow sense of separateness, we open to a wider worldview. One that wisely appreciates that we are not alone, nor can we manage this life alone. We recognize that we are tangled up with each other and completely interdependent with everything else, including the earth, sky, and sea, the creatures that dwell in those places, and the seen and unseen forces that impact our lives.

This realization doesn't require religion or any esoteric spiritual beliefs. It is grounded in everyday observation. We share similar needs for water, food, a home, and love. We also have similar desires for attention, affection, to be seen, and to be happy. No matter how vast our differences, we human beings are really the same in fairly normal and essential ways.

A simple but effective meditation practice emphasizes this truth and serves as a way of evoking the compassion that is hardwired into our nervous systems. Choose that elderly person riding the bus with you, or call to mind the individual featured in the heartbreaking news story you just read, or bring it still closer to home to break the cycle of attack and withdrawal when you argue with your partner. Try it when you meet someone new. Silently repeat a few phrases to emphasize your common ground with the other person and feel the connection of simple human kindness:

This person has a body, heart, and mind, just like me.
This person worries and gets frightened, just like me.
This person is trying their best to navigate life, just like me.
This person is a fellow human being, just like me.

Now, allow some benevolent wishes for well-being to arise:

May this person have the strength and support to face the difficulties
    in life.
May this person be free from suffering and its causes.
May this person be peaceful and happy.
May this person be loved.

Once we have seen ourselves in others and seen others in us, it fundamentally transforms the way we live in the world. The shift in perception brings about a change of heart. We can no longer fool ourselves into believing that the intentional disrespect of others, placing ourselves above or below others, or acting only in selfish ways will ever bring us real happiness. As the poet says, "Only kindness makes sense anymore."

I love how His Holiness the Dalai Lama explains complex concepts in plain language:

There is no denying that our happiness is inextricably bound up with the happiness of others. There is no denying that if society suffers, we ourselves suffer. Nor is there any denying that the more our hearts and minds are afflicted with ill-will, the more miserable we become. Thus we can reject everything else: religion, ideology, all received wisdom. But we cannot escape the necessity of love and compassion.

We see that caring for another person is, at the heart of it, no different from caring for ourselves. Altruism is a natural expression of that wise understanding—action that arises from the recognition of our common humanity.

If I cut my left hand, my right one reaches out spontaneously to care for it. It doesn't ask if it is deserving of my attention, or a member of my same church, or if it shares my political views. Nor does it worry about becoming overly involved and getting swept up in suffering. One hand just embraces the other with love and compassion. Acting altruistically on behalf of another person is just like this.

Children possess a natural sense of altruism and compassion, perhaps because they do not experience such rigid boundaries between themselves and others.

When my son Gabe was young, we would walk around San Francisco together. His heart would always break when he saw homeless people living on the street. So we used to carry around a bag of change, and he would give the money out to people we passed by.

One day when he was about four years old, we walked past this rag-gedly dressed old man with a shaggy white beard. Honestly, he looked a bit scary to me. But Gabe's immediate response was, "Dad, can we take him home?"

"No," I said. "We can't." And we walked on.

After a block, Gabe stopped walking and frowned. "Somebody should be nice to him."

"How about if we treat him to dinner?" I suggested. So we did. We went back and invited the man to a diner right across the street and asked him questions about his life. As so often happens when you take the time to hear someone's story, it turned out that this man, Joseph, was just a regular guy. He used to be a construction worker but had fallen on hard times due to the housing slump. He had lost his job, gone through his meager savings, and the next thing you know, he was out on the street.

Our capacity to share feelings with others can be both gratifying and problematic. We may experience vicarious delight when a friend announces they are newly in love, excitement when listening to travel stories, or a sigh of relief when a family member reports positive results of a recent health exam. The experience can be multiplied through the sharing.

In the same way, when we see someone we love suffer, it can trigger shared emotions. When another person cries in grief, we, too, may share that sadness and begin to cry. Seeing an image of a helpless refugee child washed up on a foreign beach may give rise to a sense of powerlessness within us.

It's useful to draw a distinction between empathy and compassion. Empathy is this capacity to feel *as* the other person. And as such, it is a necessary and essential glue in forming relationships and social net-works.

Yet we need to balance and regulate the initial empathetic response in order not to confuse ourselves with the other person. This is particu-larly important for those who face continued exposure to suffering, such as nurses, teachers, counselors, therapists, and first responders. Otherwise, empathetic concern can easily slip into empathetic overload, which can have a negative impact on our health and well-being, leading to exhaustion, isolation, burnout, and even selfish behaviors such as acting out on others to relieve our personal empathetic distress.

Carl Rogers best described a grounded, healthy empathy when he wrote:

> It means entering the private perceptual world of the other and becoming thoroughly at home in it. It involves being sensitive, moment to moment, to the changing felt meanings which flow in this other person, to the fear or rage or tenderness or confusion or whatever he or she is experiencing. It means temporarily living in the other's life, moving about in it delicately without making judgments; it means sensing meanings of which he or she is scarcely aware, but not trying to uncover totally unconscious feelings, since this would be too threatening. It includes communicating your sensings of the person's world as you look with fresh and unfrightened eyes at elements of which he or she is fearful.
>
> To be with another in this way means that for the time being, you lay aside your own views and values in order to enter another's world without prejudice. In some sense it means that you lay aside your self; this can only be done by persons who are secure enough in themselves that they know they will not get lost in what may turn out to be the strange or bizarre world of the other, and that they can comfortably return to their own world when they wish.

While empathy can be a primer for compassion, we can also feel concern for another's suffering and be motivated to help even when we don't necessarily share their feelings. A useful distinction, then, is that with empathy, we *feel with* the other person, and in compassion, we *feel for the other*.

Furthermore, compassion is differentiated from empathy by a strong motivation to reduce suffering and advance the other's well-being. Without the presence of compassion, we cannot be open to suffering. Compassion serves as a kind of inner guide, which helps us respond to the exact face of that suffering.

I love romance, and so did Catherine. One night when we were watching *Pretty Woman* on TV at the hospice, she made an announcement. She probably had only six weeks to live, but she wanted to get married to her sweetheart. She asked me if I would perform the ceremony.

"Sure, I would be honored," I said. "But what you really need is a wedding coordinator, and lucky for you, I'm really good at that. You know, there are a lot of details to plan for a wedding."

So every day, I would come into her room, and we would talk about the wedding. I would ask her questions about every aspect of getting married: The guy she was marrying, why did she love him? Did she have any concerns about their compatibility? Were they going to write their own vows or not? What kind of cake did she want? Did she want to be in a wheelchair or in bed for the service? What dress would she wear? All the while, I was aware that there was more happening in these conversations than bridal details.

One day, in the middle of deciding what to do about the cake, Catherine broke into tears and blurted out, "I just want my mother to be here."

Catherine's mother had been dead for six years, but that was what mattered most to Catherine in the moment. Not her cancer or even the fact that she was dying. It was that her mother wouldn't be there to witness her wedding. That was the face of her suffering. I might have missed it or offered a cliché "Oh yeah, wouldn't that have been nice." Instead, we went right to the heart of the issue, exploring how we might bring her mother's presence into the wedding.

"We could have pictures of her there," Catherine offered.

"Great idea," I replied. "And, if she were there, what would you have wanted her to say on your wedding day?"

Catherine thought about it, then asked shyly, "I would have loved for her to read aloud the poem she wrote me before she died. Would you read it?"

"With all my heart," I replied.

When our nonjudgmental attention responds to exactly what hurts in another, the heart opens. It feels cared for and seen. Compassion is cognizant of the spectrum of considerations, but attuned to what matters most in this moment. Sometimes that attunement is so intimate that we may feel ourselves engaged in a "soul-to-soul" meeting with the other.

Both Steven and Rick were living with AIDS a few rooms apart from each other at the Zen Hospice Project. Rick, in addition to his HIV diagnosis, had suffered a stroke that had paralyzed his right side, leaving him with aphasia that made his speech garbled and unclear. He was quite angry with his condition, prickly with most people. This, combined with his inability to communicate, caused him to become isolated.

Steven, on the other hand, was open and radiant in his demeanor. When you entered his room, you felt like you were walking into a sanctuary. Steven had done his homework, the inner journey of facing his demons. Now there was a great sense of peacefulness and gratitude present in him.

One day, I explained to Rick that Steven was coming close to the end of his life. Rick decided to say good-bye. I helped him limp down the hallway to Steven's room, where Rick sat on the edge of the bed. I sat in the corner, not wanting to interfere.

For the next twenty minutes, I watched the most incredible unfolding: the two men entered into a profound silent exchange. No words were spoken, but their eyes never left one another's faces. At the end, Rick nodded, and Steven said, "Yes, thanks, that was wonderful." They hugged, and then Rick returned to his room. Steven died later that night.

Rick had shown up with his fear and darkness. He knew he was staring at his own destiny. He, too, would die within a matter of weeks, and that scared him. But because Steven had opened to his own suffering, he could be with Rick's fear without adding more fear. Steven looked at Rick with such unbelievable love and compassion. It was a soul connection that, at least in that moment, provided Rick with a healing salve.

. . .

A misconception many people hold about compassion is that we should help the other person to feel safe, that there is no danger. This is fine, of course, if you can do it. But I work with people who are dying, and for many, dying does not feel safe.

I have found that when I am really present, sitting in my own seat, so to speak, and grounded in compassion, the other person can sense that and begins to trust and open up—not because there is no danger, but because they feel that they are not alone. Genuine understanding and compassionate companionship offer them the support and encouragement they need in order to go toward what feels dangerous.

Even when we've devoted our life to compassionate action, we will at times become overwhelmed by suffering. In such moments we need to temporarily pull back and engage the resources that are needed to meet the situation in front of us. I might need to recall experiences of compassion offered to me or from me. I might need to stabilize my attention so that I have the capacity to meet the emotional overwhelm. I might need to immerse myself in a life-affirming activity.

At the height of my hospice work, many people died in the course of a week. At times when the grief was overwhelming, I did three things: I made a point of getting regular bodywork, often spending the better part of a session crying on the massage table; I regularly returned to my meditation cushion and the practices that stabilized my attention, regulated my emotional states, and cultivated pro-social qualities like loving kindness; and I would visit my nurse friends who worked in the unit at the general hospital caring for babies who have been born to addicted mothers. I'd sit in a rocking chair, hold these babies, and rock them to sleep. There was something about the innocence of the babies and the satisfaction of being able to soothe them that enabled me to reconnect with my compassion and meet the daily suffering that was part of the hospice experience.

When speaking about compassion, I always feel like I should put a warning label on the bottle. It's important for caregivers or those working with suffering to understand something about the presence of compassion. When compassion is truly present in the room, a great deal of pain and suffering is likely to show up in response. That is because the pain wants to expose itself to the healing agent of loving kindness.

Years ago, I was invited by the Zen teacher Bernie Glassman Roshi to help lead a multi-faith "bearing witness" retreat at the former Nazi death camps of Auschwitz-Birkenau. The idea was to immerse ourselves in an environment so unsettling that we had no choice but to drop our habitual ways of thinking. Bernie wrote:

> When you bear witness to Auschwitz, at that moment there is no separation between us and the people who killed. We ourselves, as individuals, with our identities and ego structure, disappear and we become the terrified people getting off the trains, the indifferent or brutal guards, the snarling dogs, the doctor who points right or left, the smoke and ash belching from the chimneys. When we bear witness to Auschwitz, we are nothing but all the elements of Auschwitz. It is not an act of will, it is an act of letting go. What we let go of is the concept of the person we think we are.

Every day, we sat along the train tracks at Birkenau, meditating, praying, and chanting the names of the dead. We also met daily in small groups to talk about what we were experiencing. The group I facilitated included a woman who told me she had been a child in the camps, as well as the sons and daughters of former prisoners and Nazi soldiers.

Feeling restless one night, I decided to go into the camp at Birkenau and meditate in one of the children's barracks. It was a long, grim building that had once been a horse barn. Shortly after I sat down, I heard someone enter the other end of the building. It was the woman from my group who said she had been a child prisoner in the camp. She began to cry and scream in the darkness.

I got up and sat beside her. And she kept wailing. I'd never heard such sounds. They were primitive, almost animal-like. The wailing went on for most of the night. No words were spoken. There isn't anything you can say when someone is experiencing such anguish. All you can do is bear witness. As light began to break, we returned to the hostel and silently hugged good-bye.

Later that day, I flew to Berlin to teach a workshop on grief and forgiveness. I didn't mention my experience at Birkenau; it can still be difficult to speak of such things in Germany. As the workshop was ending a day or two later, however, a woman in the very back of the room stood up and said, "I've been listening to you talking about forgiveness, but my father was a prisoner in the concentration camps, and I can't forgive his killers. My heart is like ice."

The whole room went silent. Again, the only appropriate response was to bear witness.

Then a woman on the other side of the room raised her hand to speak. I thought to myself, *Now the stories of the camps and the grief of those losses will come.*

She stood and said, "My heart is like ice, too. It feels like a stone. My father was a Nazi officer who was a guard in the camps. I know that he killed people. I can't forgive him."

Silence.

Then these two women did the bravest thing I have ever seen. They made their way across the large conference hall of 200 people and embraced. They didn't say a word. They didn't have to. They just held each other. Their actions were a clear recognition that they were no longer alone in their pain. For that moment, their suffering was all of our suffering.

It's easy to imagine that compassion requires some heroic strength that we do not possess. We may believe that we are not up to the task of meeting the suffering of the world. It can be helpful to consider the possibility that compassion is not a quality that we possess, but rather one that we access, inherent in the nature of reality. Love has been here all along. It is absolute because everything and everyone always has been held in love.

The later schools of Buddhism rest on the foundation of compassion. They include rich descriptions of different types of compassion tied to the development of *Bodhicitta*, which refers to the impulse of the "heart-mind" to awaken. At our Metta Institute trainings, my friend and colleague the Zen teacher Norman Fischer spoke of "radical connectedness" and how the wisdom of non-separation is the source of compassion. He said, "*Bodhicitta* is the feeling of love based on the deep recognition that what we have called 'self' and what we call 'others' are destinations, concepts, habits of mind not realities of the world. Real altruism isn't self-sacrifice for the benefit of others . . . arising from some guilt-driven sense that we should be good, we *should* be nice, we *should* be kind or helpful. It is a profound recognition that self and other are not *fundamentally different* only *apparently different*."

There are said to be two levels of *Bodhicitta*. They are Absolute and Relative. Through *Bodhicitta*, we transcend narrow self-interest and embrace all beings in compassion. In a more secular way, we might speak of *universal* and *everyday* compassion.

All spiritual traditions point to *universal* compassion as an innate and essential aspect of existence. In Buddhist thought, it is vast and boundless, the dynamic quality of reality that contributes to harmony. As a facet of love, it is open-ended and unlimited. Universal compassion is the foundation of all healing, an underlying source of benevolence and caring. Its nature is impersonal, yet it is always embracing us, even if we didn't know it. Even if our conditioning has obscured our ability to see it as integral to all activity.

Then there is *everyday* compassion. This is the compassion that gets expressed in daily life, when we help someone, feed the hungry, stand against injustice, change soiled sheets, give a foot rub, listen generously to a friend's broken heart, or contribute to an earthquake recovery fund. We may be effective or ineffectual in our efforts, but we do the best we can.

These two facets of compassion rely on each other. Everyday compassion can be exhausting. We get weary and worn out from our repeated efforts to care for our families, help others, or reduce the world's suffering.

This is why everyday compassion must be sourced in the abundance of universal compassion. But it's a two-way street. Universal compassion also needs everyday compassion. Without everyday compassion, universal compassion is just an abstract idea, a big prayer. And if prayers alone were enough to heal the world, we could have ended suffering a long time ago.

With this understanding, we see that compassion doesn't come from our individual efforts. It emerges from our basic nature, it is a dynamic expression that arises from reality itself. Universal compassion needs our arms and legs and strong backs. We are its vehicle. We are how it manifests in the everyday world. It uses our commitment, bright minds, and kind hearts. Meanwhile, everyday compassion is constantly refreshed because it arises from universal compassion. Gradually, we learn to trust that while there is endless suffering in this world, there is also endless compassion to respond.

Sometimes the presence of compassion seems to heal a particular pain right away. But sometimes the presence of compassion and loving kindness allows us to stay with suffering that might otherwise prove too difficult for us to tolerate. But by staying with pain and suffering, compassion allows a deeper truth to be revealed.

My friend Michael lived with multiple sclerosis for almost twenty-five years. He and I worked together for fifteen of those years, preparing for his dying. Yes, for fifteen years we talked. Once after he came home from a bad bout of pneumonia in the ICU, he said, "Frank, I'm not going back."

I said, "You're not going back to the hospital?"

"No, I'm not going back."

"How come, Michael?" I asked.

"I got really scared," he said. "All the work we've done, and I'm still scared!"

There was a long pause while we both took in the depths of Michael's suffering. Then in a moment of clarity that came from compassion more than expertise, I said, "Oh, Michael, that fear will never go away. The part of you that is scared will always be scared."

At first Michael looked a bit stunned. But after letting the words touch his heart, he said, "Wow, that's the most comforting thing anybody has told me about this whole situation."

It wasn't resignation; it was an understanding that while the fear was there, he was aware of the fear, and he could access that dimension of himself that was not scared. Awareness could be with the fear. Fear was no longer the only thing in the room. Now compassion was also present. It provided the necessary breathing space to see that the fear was workable. For a moment, Michael was the one who was not sick.

Compassion requires that we get in touch with what hurts. It's the pain, the suffering itself, that invites compassion to manifest. The intelligence of compassion brings forward a kindness that is not trying to get rid of suffering. This goes counter to the ego's wishes. Ego only wants to be protected from pain. Compassion opens to pain.

We have a closetful of strategies that we can employ to keep the unpleasant at bay, to keep suffering at arm's length. Our defenses render us blind and can mislead us about the true sources of our suffering. Fear, anger, guilt, worry, resentment, shame—these are all painful, reactive symptoms. Our psychological defenses can mask deeper dynamics in our psyches, keeping us from understanding the more fundamental causes of our suffering. In this way, our often unconscious defenses serve to recycle our suffering.

When compassion is present, our defensiveness can relax. When our defenses are down, we can look objectively at our situations and see the true origins of our suffering. Then we can intervene skillfully to address the real causes and not just the symptoms. So another aspect of compassion is the capacity to be with suffering as a means of coming to, and experiencing, more truth and greater freedom.

Once during a talk in Germany, Bernie Glassman Roshi referenced Avalokiteśvara, the bodhisattva of compassion. The deity is pictured with a thousand arms. In each hand, there is an ear to hear the cries of the world. A thousand arms are there to respond. Bernie was suggesting that compassion is a natural and appropriate response to suffering.

A man stood up and said, "This is all well and good, but I don't have a thousand arms. I have only two arms. What am I supposed to do to alleviate all that suffering?"

Bernie paused, then very beautifully said, "You're wrong."

The man insisted, "No, I am quite sure I have only these two arms."

Bernie asked everyone in the room to raise their hands up in the air. There were over five hundred people in attendance. "Look," he said. "A thousand arms."

His point was that it's an illusion to think we are doing this work all by ourselves. In truth, everything is intimately connected, related in a vast network of interdependence. All our thoughts, feelings, and actions affect everything else in that network. The great naturalist John Muir once said, "When we try to pick out anything by itself, we find it hitched to everything else in the Universe."

Which brings us back to the ocean, in which each of us are individual waves, unique yet inseparable from the whole.

When we look at reality from the vantage point of the separate self, we're constantly searching for what distinguishes us from others. All we see are things falling apart. All we see is suffering. But if we shift to the vantage point of connectedness, we can feel the harmony. We don't completely abandon our personalities, but we adopt more inclusive points of view.

Compassion is what enables us to come close to suffering, to know through intimacy. When we get that close, the illusion of "I and other" falls away. We know ourselves to be part of this web of mutuality. Wisdom shows us that the small, bounded sense of separate self we have taken ourselves to be is no more than a limiting story. When separation falls away, we recognize that we are everything. Being everything, compassion is simply an appropriate response, the natural way to serve and love what is really our whole selves, and to express its freedom.

THE FOURTH INVITATION

Find a Place of Rest in the Middle of Things

Rest is the conversation between what
we love to do and how we love to be.

—DAVID WHYTE

Adele was a tenacious, no-nonsense, eighty-six-year-old Russian Jewish lady. I had the honor of being with her at Zen Hospice the night she died. She sat on the edge of the bed, breathing with great difficulty; her every in- and out-breath was a struggle.

As I sat on the couch in the corner a kind and well-meaning nurse's aide sat beside Adele and tried to reassure her, saying, "You don't have to be frightened. I'm right here with you."

Adele snapped, "Believe me, honey, if this was happening to you, you'd be frightened."

The attendant began stroking Adele's back. "You're a little cold. Would you like a blanket?" she asked.

Adele shot back, "Of course I'm cold. I'm almost dead!"

I stayed in the corner.

Laughing to myself at her raw honesty, two things became clear to me. One, Adele wanted straight talk and authentic relationship. She didn't want to process her dying or talk about moving into the light. She had no interest in sentimental ideas. Second, despite having been given all the appropriate interventions, Adele was still struggling. There is a labor to dying as there is a labor to giving birth.

I pulled up a chair close to Adele, and our eyes locked. I asked, "Adele, would you like to struggle a bit less?"

"Yes." She nodded.

"I noticed that at the end of your exhale, there is a little pause. Can you put your attention there on that pause for a little while?" I suggested. Now Adele didn't care beans about Buddhism and had never meditated in her life. But she was highly motivated in the moment to be free of suffering. So she agreed to try. "I'll breathe with you," I said.

After a while, Adele was able to place her attention on that small gap between exhale and inhale. As she did, the fear gradually drained from her face. We continued to breathe together for some time.

Eventually, Adele put her head back on the pillow. A short while later, she died quite peacefully.

We often think of rest as something that will come to us when everything else in our lives is complete: at the end of the day, when we take a bath; once we go on holiday or get through all our to-do lists. We imagine that we can only find rest by changing our circumstances.

The Fourth Invitation teaches us that, like Adele, we can find a place of rest within us, without having to alter the conditions of our lives. After all, the conditions of Adele's life remained the same—her breathing didn't change; she was still dying. Nevertheless, she found a place of rest.

This place of rest is always available to us. We need only turn toward it. It is experienced when we bring our full attention, without distraction, to this moment, to this activity. With sincere practice, after some time, we can come to know this spaciousness as a regular part of our lives. It manifests as an aspect of us that is never sick, is not born, and does not die.

[12]

THE CALM IN THE STORM

Rest in natural great peace this exhausted mind,
Beaten helpless by karma and neurotic thoughts
Like the relentless fury of the pounding waves
In the infinite ocean of samsara.

—NYOSHUL KHEN RINPOCHE

There is a Zen story about a monk who is vigorously sweeping the temple grounds. Another monk walks by and snips, "Too busy."

The first monk replies, "You should know there is one who is not too busy."

The moral of the story is that while the sweeping monk may have outwardly appeared to the casual observer as "too busy," actively performing his daily monastic duties, inwardly he was not busy. He could recognize the quietness of his state of mind, the part of himself that was at rest in the middle of things.

Most of us think we are too busy. Probably we are, but also the way we think about the topic matters. When I was in third grade, the minute hand on the large, round school clock moved incredibly slowly as I awaited the two o'clock dismissal bell. Summer vacations seemed to last forever. Now time flies by, and vacations are never quite long enough. What happened? There are still the same twenty-four hours in every day, which means the feeling of "not having enough time" doesn't align with my objective reality.

What happens is that when I am caught in a time-driven, scarcity mentality or tumbling unconsciously from one moment to the next, I become a prisoner of my thoughts. I get trapped in a jail of my own construction. And I don't even realize that the cell door is not locked. I have only to choose to open it.

Finding a place of rest isn't about adding another task to your already too-long to-do list. Nor does it mean napping more during your workday (though this may prove helpful). It is a choice—a choice to be alert, to bring your attention to this moment. Multitasking is a myth that only serves to seize our attention and exhaust us. At the end of the day, it is neither enjoyable nor productive. Let's face it: none of us have that superpower; we can only live in one moment at a time.

Mahatma Gandhi once said, "I do not want to see the future. I am concerned with taking care of the present moment. God has given me no control over the moment following." This idea frustrates us. We want to spin plates, juggle balls, and live two dreams at once. Anything else sounds boring. "I'll sleep when I'm dead," we say.

As a result, we end up addicted to busy. We confuse rest with non-productivity and laziness. "No time to waste!" we chide ourselves as we race from one activity to the next. Yet we do it all in a continuous state of partial attention, imagining we're accomplishing more, when in reality we are living less.

The smartphone, our most constant companion, is a shining example of this mentality. A recent survey of San Francisco residents found that on any given day, most people interact with their smartphones more than they do with other human beings. Half of the people surveyed admitted to using their phones to escape social interaction, and nearly a third said they felt anxious when they didn't have access to their phones.

Remember when computers were sold to us based on the idea that they would create *more* leisure time and *greater* human connectivity? I want my money back.

In truth, many of us fear rest. Doctors and nurses often speak to me of how exhaustion is a central part of their training and how they continue to drive themselves ruthlessly at work. They fear that if they were to stop racing around, the enormous suffering they have witnessed would crash through their defenses. Tears would flow, and they would be unable to stop crying.

The armor we build around our hearts may lock out our pain, but it also prevents tenderness from entering. We are afraid that we will be forgotten, that if we stop going all the time, the loneliness and emptiness we fear will surface. So we build a false sense of security, warding off uncertainty by making a fetish of constant activity.

In this way, we become invested in our own exhaustion. During seminars with health care professionals, I like to ask them to explore the counter-intuitive question, "What's right about being exhausted?" At first they deny any benefits. With time, however, honest answers emerge. Some say, "People believe I am working hard. I get credit for being dedicated." Others respond, "Being overworked and worn out means I matter." One or two acknowledge, "People feel sorry for me, and that makes me feel loved." Often our exhaustion doesn't come from doing too much, but rather from a lack of full engagement or wholeheartedness.

There is a common phenomenon among those newly diagnosed with cancer. My friend Ange Stephens, a longtime therapist to people with life-threatening illness, calls it "a secret gratitude." After the initial shock subsides, many of her clients quietly express relief. "Now I can say 'no' whereas I always had felt obliged to say 'yes,'" they tell her. "Now I can finally rest."

Do we need to die before we can rest in peace?

Rest is found when we are present instead of letting our minds wander aimlessly through the hallways of fear, worry, and anxiousness. Rest comes when we become more by doing less, when we don't allow the urgent to crowd out the important. It is the result of a decluttering of the mind and decoupling from fixed views. Rest is a Sabbath, when we stop and turn to worship the possibilities of the ever-fresh moment.

Idleness is not an indulgence or a vice so much as it is indispensable. Nearly all plants go dormant in winter. Certain mammals hibernate, slowing their metabolisms dramatically. All are guided by inner clocks to emerge again in the fullness of time, when conditions are right. This period of rest is crucial to their survival.

We, too, need to heed our instincts and find a place of rest. My friend and Metta Institute faculty member, the late Angeles Arrien, was fond of saying, "Nature's rhythm is medium to slow. Many of us live in the fast lane, out of nature's rhythm. There are two things we can never do in the fast lane: we can neither deepen our experience nor integrate it." She would often encourage our students to spend an hour outdoors each day and at least a half an hour in silence every day. She said, "When we lose touch with the rhythms of nature, we become unbalanced. To be fully present within our nature, we must be in balance with the land around us."

Living out of touch with the primal rhythms of life takes a toll on us.

I like to scuba dive. It's one of the ways I get in touch with what nature has to teach. My favorite thing to do while diving is to sink slowly to the bottom and sit on the ocean floor. Most guides move too fast for me. They want to show you this coral reef and that wreck and the other thing. But I love to stay still, watching the underwater life pass me by and listening to my breath as it regulates in the infinite silence of the sea.

Once, while in Indonesia, I went for a night dive. It was breathtakingly beautiful that evening. We left at sunset, the sky ablaze with streaks of burnt orange, the clouds radiating a pink and purple peace. We traveled in rustic wooden longboats painted in vermillion reds, saturated yellows, and the turquoise of the sea. The calm ocean mirrored the sky, and the thin horizon line gave the impression of two worlds merging.

All we had to light our way once we got into the water were simple flashlights wrapped in duct tape, no special night-diving lights. As I traveled down into the darkness with my diving partner, I felt an urge to turn my flashlight off. And when I did, I quickly realized how truly dark it was; a kind of pitch blackness I had never experienced. I couldn't tell which way was up, down, or sideways, and I had no idea if anyone or anything was nearby. I could feel a physical contraction in my chest as I experienced a wave of anxiety, but the feeling soon passed, like a child's nightmare.

When I turned on my flashlight, my buddy and I swam around a huge coral reef. In time, we settled on the very bottom. It was even more still than usual at night. Even the fish seemed to be at rest. As the ocean enveloped us, I felt an imperturbable sense of peacefulness as spacious as the night sky.

At the end of the dive, when our time was up and our oxygen was running low, we began to ascend to the surface. When you come up from a dive, you have to move slowly, pausing at points to avoid getting sick. Midway to the top, we could feel the powerful ocean currents, like rivers coming from far away that move through the ocean, threatening to carry us away. When we surfaced, we realized that a huge storm was raging with torrential rains, thunder, and massive ocean swells. It was wild.

It's not the safest place to be—out at sea during a storm. But I howled at the top of my lungs in sheer glee. The turbulence wasn't frightening me. Contentment had traveled right up from the ocean floor with me. It wasn't something special. No hocus-pocus. I was just there, fully present with what was so, grounded in my own inner peace.

Fortunately, I could make out our boat a short distance away. My buddy and I were able to get on board along with all the other divers that night. We made it home safely—and I will never forget the thrill of the experience.

In teaching meditation practice, I often turn to the metaphor of the ocean to describe the layers of mind. On the surface, there is generally a fair amount of turbulence in our thoughts. We are affected by whatever winds are blowing at the time, the conditions of daily life, the busyness of the day, the stress, the anxiety. Most people live at this level, with a fair amount of mental agitation, with emotional storms threatening to drown us. It can feel like it is all about us. We see ourselves as the center of the universe. This painfully narcissistic mind-set, driven by our survival instinct, can lead to expectations that the world owes us or an inflated belief that we are responsible for much of what is happening.

Settle the mind a bit more through meditation, and we can begin to sense the more universal currents, those underwater rivers that help to produce the disturbances on the surface. We contact the deeper human tendencies, the instinctual drives, the primal forces, the ancestral conditioning that everyone is subject to and that are not limited to our individual circumstances. These ingrained patterns of mind attempt to construct a fixed sense of self and a stable world from a flow of continuous change. They shape our behaviors, create our habits, and distort our beliefs—all of which lead to suffering.

With mindfulness, we start to see, "Oh, there are these currents moving through my mind, pushing me around. They show up as reactivity, fear, anger, a desire for control. But they are not particular to me. They are moving through all of us. This is the human condition."

Moreover, we realize that these impersonal human conditions predate our births. They are not our fault. I didn't choose to be born into an alcoholic family. My unborn soul wasn't waiting up in heaven looking for a chance to jump into a body that would be sexually abused when I was just thirteen. But I did have to learn to deal with what happened to me. The critical point here is that while we need to be responsible *to* the impact these conditions have on our lives, we are not responsible *for* their appearance.

This is the beginning of our release from self-consciousness into a more expanded appreciation of life, this realization that we are all subject to conditions beyond our control. The recognition of previously unconscious currents gives rise to more empathy, compassion, and acceptance, not only of ourselves, but also of others.

If we drop still further beneath the surface of our minds, we encounter a vast, serene calmness. We recognize that while this human condition is always moving through us, we do not have to get caught up in it. We do not have to be swept away by these universal currents. In so doing, we are not escaping from the vicissitudes of life. We are simply finding a natural place of rest, as if sitting at the bottom of the sea, observing the movements of our minds and hearts like fish darting through coral.

Resting in this open awareness, we release ourselves from the habits of managing our circumstances and striving for control as ways to avoid pain and gain pleasure. We have more space, more freedom from reactivity. We are not denying, justifying, or rationalizing; we are allowing. When it is *this way*, we know that it is this way. When it is *that way*, we know that it is that way. This is a gentle yet committed and courageous way of appreciating the deeper truth of what it means to be human.

It may sound complicated, but it starts with basic awareness and putting into practice simple routines. I once worked with an executive at a billion-dollar technology company. He was experiencing dramatic symptoms of stress: skin irritations, bowel problems, and sleepless nights. He spent most of his day in a windowless conference room, meeting with various work teams charged with the development and rollout of new devices. Teams would come and go, but he rarely left the room.

We began with the very straightforward agreement that he would take a break each hour to use the bathroom. Gradually, we added a few conscious deep breaths during meetings and a mindful walk down the hallway to the toilet. Over time, the bathroom stall became his temporary meditation hut. There, he would reconnect with his own calm center and then, often quite serenely, return to his business meetings.

If we hope to find true rest, we need to see clearly the currents that disturb us. Yet recognition is only the beginning. To make real change, we have to dive deeper to understand the specific ways that we have been conditioned throughout our lives. Then we can address the underlying causes of our internal distress or lack of restfulness.

In the Buddhist tradition, there is an image known as the wheel of samsara. *Samsara* means the cycle of death and rebirth to which the material world is inextricably bound. The wheel as metaphor illustrates the continuous cycle of conditions that cause us to spin round and round. The engine that drives the wheel is sometimes referred to as *the three poisons*. These are the root causes of our suffering: craving (greed), aversion (hatred), and ignorance (delusion). At first, *poison* may seem like a strong word—until we begin to recognize the toxicity of these afflictive states and the ways they contaminate our minds, obscuring our natural openness. Still, I prefer a more contemporary and visceral way of naming these universal obstacles, which Martin Aylward, the resident Buddhist teacher at Moulin de Chaves retreat center in France, shared with me in a conversation. He called them *demand*, *defense*, and *distract*.

Craving, the first poison, is a *demand* that the objects of our desire provide us with lasting satisfaction so that we feel fulfilled, whole, and complete. It is the tendency to cling to someone, something, some idea, and become rigidly attached to it. Greed creates an inner hunger, which has us always striving for an unattainable goal: a new job, a new partner or child, a new car or home, a new body, a new attitude. We mistakenly believe our happiness is dependent upon reaching our goal, getting what we want. But the problem is that even if we do attain it, we find that we can get no lasting satisfaction from our accomplishment or possession because everything in life is subject to the law of impermanence. Circumstances will change, or we'll become accustomed to the new role or thing or person in our lives, and our pleasure inevitably will fade.

Tragically, inherent in *demand* is the notion that what is here now, what we have now, isn't good enough. We can sense this drive for more in our bodies as an energetic pull, the desperate wanting for something to fill up our underlying sense of deficiency.

The second poison, the *defense* of aversion, can show up as anger, hatred, bullying, loneliness, intolerance, or fear. We habitually resist, deny, and avoid unpleasant feelings, circumstances, and people—whatever we do not like or want. Defense traps us in a vicious cycle of finding conflict and enemies everywhere. It reinforces our mistaken perceptions that we are separate from everything and everyone. Energetically, we know this drive in our bodies as the opposite of pull. It is a pushing away. The irony is that whatever we push away usually pushes back even harder.

The ignorance of *distraction* is the third poison. It blinds us to the way reality works, giving rise to the tendency to pull (demand) and push (defend) against life. We misperceive the nature of things, which is that they are both interdependent and impermanent. Instead, we get lost in a loop of distractions as a way of disconnecting from our pain. Alcohol, shopping, eating, gambling, sex, social media and video games, even meditation—all can serve as habits and strategies for distracting ourselves, all can go unquestioned. We lose ourselves, get confused, and hold unhelpful views. We go about our lives in a kind of fog, unable to see clearly that there is a way through our pain, which requires us to turn toward it. By trying to ignore it, we continually trip and fall further into our suffering. Energetically, we feel spaced out, dull, or vaguely unconscious.

These are the three underlying, impersonal poisons that lurk below the surface of our awareness, impacting our everyday behaviors and preventing us from ever feeling at rest. Some people like to think of them playfully as Buddhist versions of the Myers-Briggs personality types. Imagine going to a party. The demand (craving) type heads straight for the buffet table. The defense (aversion) type complains about the décor, the food, and the music. The distraction (ignorance) type wonders if he's actually at the right party. It's a lighthearted way of recognizing these impersonal conditions that shape our personalities.

Generally speaking, we sense the presence of these conditions, but we prefer not to acknowledge just how strong of a hold they have on us. They are the universal currents batting our minds about like tiny ships at sea.

The antidote to all three poisons is mindfulness. Healing occurs through learning about these afflictive states of demand, defense, and distraction and realizing that they impact *all* moments of *all* experiences. Suffering is not random, nor is it a punishment for our personal failings or a sign of moral weakness. Suffering is the natural consequence of ignoring the truth of life's ever-changing causes and conditions. And our natural inclinations to crave, avoid, or distract ourselves won't go away by pretending they don't exist. On the contrary, they need to be seen and understood. When we realize how much pain they cause, we are less inclined to follow their commands.

In the Buddhist tradition, we say, "The obstacles become the path." The missteps we make as we demand, defend, and distract are also gateways to the innate beauty of our inner being. When we allow ourselves to rest in our natural openness, we can come to know these poisons clearly and recognize their detrimental impact on our lives. Once the blinders come off, we are no longer fooled. We see our conditioning, our identification with the poisons, with clear awareness. Then we wake up to the fact that our suffering was fueled by a drive to ignore the truth all along.

This is a moment of liberation. The truth that was obscured, yet was always present, now sets us free. It's a bit like the way our eyesight can change almost imperceptibly over time, blurring our perceptions of beauty. We get fitted for glasses and suddenly we see without distortion. The magnificence of the world becomes more apparent to us.

In addition to recognizing the three poisons, it also is helpful to cultivate balancing factors to temper their strong forces and transform them into something more positive. For example, we can nurture our innate generosity and equanimity to balance our demand urges, and discover contentment. When we do, we find that we enjoy far more the beauty and pleasure that already exist in our lives. Furthermore, we begin to think of ourselves as the temporary caretakers rather than the owners of what we have been given, and so we share our gifts openhandedly.

Loving kindness, gratitude, and compassionate action can soften our demands and relax our tendencies to defend. Tapping into a concern for others and a commitment to healing and connection, we utilize these capacities to challenge inequality, environmental devastation, and social injustice.

Wisdom cuts through distraction, and clear comprehension replaces delusion. When we use insight to loosen the grip of our self-centeredness, we come to appreciate that all of our actions have consequences. Then we feel compelled to act to reduce the suffering of the world and increase the happiness of all living beings.

Today, after spilling water on my laptop, I panicked. I raced to the computer store, where the technicians told me my device was beyond repair. I had to buy a new computer and reinstall all of my files.

During the first hour, I felt highly stressed. My primary reaction was defense: I wanted to push this experience away. Feeling myself to be a victim of the little blue line that signaled how long the installation would require, I thought, *Five hours? That seems like a long time.* Then later, *Wait, what? Fourteen hours remaining? What's going on here?*

That little blue line was maddening. For a while, it sucked me into an alternate reality where technology was my enemy. I blamed the computer malfunction for my anxiety and frustration, because it triggered the growing fear that I wouldn't be able to meet my promised deadlines.

Then I stopped, took a few deep breaths, and found a place of rest in the middle of things. I realized that I was telling myself a story based on my preferences, pointlessly fighting what was going on. With a simple shift of mind-set, I could counterbalance my instinctive defense reaction with gratitude. I recognized how fortunate I was, actually. I had remembered to back up my old computer the night before, so I hadn't lost that much work. Not only that, but I had the financial resources to purchase a new computer right away. It wasn't always that way, and who knows if it ever will be again in the future? I reminded myself to appreciate my gifts now, in this moment.

Everything was okay. Gratefulness filled my heart. I felt present again. I had rediscovered my peace of mind.

Taming our riotously active minds is a bit like training a wild horse—not easy, but not impossible. Gradually, the tamed horse calms down and can be put to useful work. Then we can enjoy some degree of balance and rest.

When you're able to do this in a relationship—whether with someone who is dying, or your boss, spouse, or child—you will find that you have a capacity to experience life in an entirely different way. You can see the causes and conditions of the situation and skillfully interact with them in order to alleviate your own and others' suffering. You can be the calm in the storm.

It may be necessary—skillful, even—to shift some of the causes and conditions of your life deliberately, rather than just floating along as a hapless passenger. I'm not saying you shouldn't take action. You may need to leave the job with the abusive boss, or get help for an addiction. But when you're on the surface of your mind, all you can do is react. You're at the total mercy of the storm, being tossed about like a tiny rowboat in a wild sea. When you travel into the calm depths, you can act from a place of wisdom and compassion.

The philosopher Blaise Pascal wrote, "I have often said that the sole cause of man's unhappiness is that he does not know how to stay quietly in his room." The deeper we go within ourselves, the more expansive we become. We allow everything to show itself, even what is buried in the unconscious. There is no need to repress the unwanted parts of our situations, ourselves, or others. We realize that everything is a product of our dynamics, our histories, and our reactivity—and that it's all part of the human condition. We can allow thoughts, feelings, ideas to come and go without being swept away by any of them.

When I am withfamily and friends or at the bedside I try to create a warm, open, and nonjudgmental space in which whatever needs to happen, can happen. This is best done if I can first become a refuge to myself. I can pause and call on the better part of my nature as a shelter from my habitual defensiveness, reactivity, or neurotic tendencies that cause me to be overwhelmed by the chaos surrounding me. We cannot always eliminate difficult conditions, but we can use our acquired skills to transform obstacles into opportunities. We can be that one calm person in the room.

In doing so, we can be a true refuge to others.

Samuel was a guest in our hospice. He had AIDS and was frail as a bird. At twenty-eight years old, he weighed just eighty-nine pounds. His friends decided to throw him a birthday party. They brought champagne and truffles and strawberries, balloons and music, and lots of good cheer. They were having a grand old time. Samuel was not. He seemed to be shrinking into the bed, his already tiny frame almost disappearing. His friends meant well, but Samuel appeared to be drowning in the stimulus.

Just then, Ray, a volunteer massage therapist, entered the room. Ray pulled a chair up to the foot of the bed, grounded himself with a few deep breaths, and nodded to Samuel with a slight smile. The gesture was something between "Nice to see you again" and a bow of respect, conveying Ray's attention and asking permission to touch.

None of Samuel's friends seemed to notice Ray's presence. The massage therapist's hands found their way under the covers to Samuel's foot. I couldn't see his movements; they must have been slight. I don't know if Ray was pressing on some special points or doing reflexology, but there was no mystery to this foot rub. What mattered was the deep contact made through touch itself. The connection between the two men was undeniable.

For half an hour Ray "listened," reassuring, exploring, responding to Samuel without a word being said. The hubbub in the room went on, but now Samuel was floating instead of drowning. Ray removed his hands slowly and deliberately. He sat back and paused. Samuel blew him a kiss, closed his eyes, and sank back into the pillow, at rest.

The conditions remained unchanged. The party was still going on. People continued to eat truffles and drink champagne. Ray and Samuel didn't even speak. Yet Ray helped Samuel turn down the volume of his emotionally charged state and his body's resulting agitation through caring touch. We often underestimate the comfort of silence and the value of simple human presence.

Similarly, while I was recovering from my heart surgery, my old friend Martha deBarros, the co-founder of Zen Hospice Project, often would come to my home to support me in the practice of meditation. She would end our sessions with a lovely ritual, one which she had been teaching for years to people in prison. She invited me to place my right hand on my heart and my left on my belly and repeat the phrases, "I am here now. We are here now."

Here and now is the only place of rest.

One night after my heart surgery, I awoke at two o'clock in the morning from a painful, fitful sleep and a difficult dream. I felt frightened and resistant to my suffering. Then I heard a voice. A voice from my soul. It was giving me guidance. Offering me my own words. "Find a place of rest in the middle of things," it said.

I thought, *Okay, Frank, just try to rest.*

Then I smiled.

The thing is, trying to rest is not resting; it's just more trying. Effort is necessary in life. You can't lift your bag into the trunk of a car if you don't extend effort. Yet when we apply this same sort of effort to resting, it backfires. We can't seek the deepest rest through striving to change the way things are. We can only relax the activity that obstructs our contact with rest.

When we look closely, we see that desire is almost continuous. It's a fire that is always burning within us, and it ignites and fuels our seeking. Being a *seeker*—an identity I myself have been proud to adopt at times—is an inevitable step on the spiritual path. It can easily become a hindrance. Energetically, seeking feels agitated, restless. It implies that I am deficient, disconnected from something essential in my life. I think something is missing, and that belief perpetuates my seeking.

Agitated looking won't ever connect us to our true nature. And trying to get rid of our desires, to stop seeking, doesn't work either. That's just more seeking, more effort, and more trying.

This is the real paradox of the spiritual life: that which can save us also can drive us mad. Don't get me wrong. Seeking has a place in this world. It isn't all bad. In order to begin our spiritual journeys, we must be motivated by seeking a better life—deeper connections with ourselves and others; explanations for our existential questions; relief from our pain and suffering. Yet too often our quests for peace and fulfillment get entangled with striving. We read books, seek out teachers, and go looking for our tribes. We accumulate practices, beliefs, and strategies as we seek solutions. We continuously search for answers outside of ourselves when in fact we already have everything we need, here, within us.

There is one form of seeking that I find useful. I call it *wholesome desire*. This is the desire to be free, to know what is true and be completely ourselves.

Wholesome desire does not feel agitated. In fact, it removes the restlessness because we stop looking outside ourselves for approval or satisfaction. It feels more like love. We love our true nature, we love presence, and because we so love it, we want to be close to it, to get intimate with it. It's a kind of love affair with truth. It's like when we are with our partners, we long to see them with as few clothes on as possible. We want them as they are, naked. Just so in spiritual life, we long to see the naked truth, unobstructed by preferences or the clothing of our treasured beliefs.

"I am here now. We are here now."

One of the qualities of a truly open mind is deep restfulness. We come to this restfulness by accepting and understanding our desires, not by rejecting them. We surrender our strategies and resistance.

Lying in my bed that morning, the desire machine churning and belching out all sorts of preferences, I felt discouraged, caught up in my effort to find rest when it eluded me. Then I remembered a lesson from my many thousands of visits with dying patients. How I always pause at the threshold of the room, because that pause breaks the momentum of habit. It gives us a choice.

That choice, the only choice we have really, is to be open or closed. Open to what is unfolding or selective in our acceptance of it. Actually, I don't even like the word *acceptance*—it has too many moral overtones.

The word *allow* is better suited to what I am describing. It's a softer word, a word that takes us beyond the concepts of accepting and rejecting altogether. It releases us from the whole idea of comparison, preference for or against, hope and fear. It is a true resting place.

And so I found myself resting in allowing. And in that moment, there was no disconnection, nothing missing, and therefore nothing left to seek. Lying in my bed, I dropped like a stone falling through thick liquid until I came to lie at the bottom of the dark, silent ocean. I gave myself completely to rest. Body at rest. Heart at rest. Mind at rest. Consciousness at rest.

Seeking doesn't end by finding. Seeking just ends. It ends when our awareness comes to rest in the peaceful depths of our essential nature. Then, like the sweeping monk, we can go about our daily activities while still functioning from a place of inner calm.

13

MIND THE GAP

In my end is my beginning.
—T. S. ELIOT

Want to know some of what death has to teach? Begin to look at endings. The end of an exhale, the end of a day, the end of a meal, the end of this sentence.

How do you meet endings in life? Do you go unconscious around them? Do you leave, either emotionally or mentally, before an event is over? Or are you the last one in the parking lot, watching as the final participants depart? Do you feel sad and get teary-eyed about endings? Or anxious? Or are you indifferent, isolating yourself and withdrawing into a protective cocoon? Do you stop talking to others before the end arrives? When leaving work for the evening, do you say farewell to colleagues and clients? Do you wait for others to acknowledge the end, or do you jump the gun? Do you visit friends who are dying? Do you think it doesn't matter if you don't say good-bye?

During an intensive retreat focused on impermanence, a student noticed the endings of each and every experience. A faded rose along the walking path reminded her of how beautiful the new bloom had been just days before. When she met with me in an interview, she complained, "Everything dies! It is so sad."

I replied, "It's true all things change. 'Sad' is the story you tell yourself."

The way we end one experience shapes the way the next one arises. Clinging to the old makes it difficult for something new to emerge.

Breath offers us an opportunity to study our relationship with endings in an intimate way. Breathing is a living process, constantly changing and moving in cycles—*inhale, pause, exhale, pause.* Every breath has a beginning, middle, and end. Every breath goes through a process of birth, growth, and death. Breathing is a microcosm of life itself.

We sense the journey of the breath from the tip of the nose all the way down the throat and into the pit of the belly. There we observe the subtle moment of transformation when the inhale becomes the exhale. Then we notice the breath beginning its long journey up and out of the body. At the very end of the exhale, there is a gap, a pause. It can be a moment of fear or faith: breath has left the body, and we don't know for certain if it will return. Do you trust that the next in-breath will emerge on its own? Can you rest your mind in the gap?

After a six-hour triple bypass surgery, nurses wheeled me into the coronary care unit (CCU) of the hospital. This high-tech zone was straight out of a science-fiction movie, replete with multiple electronic monitors and the incessant sound of beeping. My heartbeat was tracked by wires attached to pads on my chest. Clot-busting medications dripped stealthily into the veins in one arm, while morphine flowed into the other arm. A catheter traveled up into my bladder, and another plastic tube drained the fluids from my neck. A long intubation tube connected my lungs to the ventilator that was breathing for me. All the while, the staff quietly bustled in and out.

My mind sluggishly emerged from the thickness of anesthesia. I felt like I was driving down a foggy road. Details of the room and the faces of family and friends would appear in a dusty haze, then fade or mix with dream images. I was in suspended animation, existing in a liminal, in-between state for several hours.

At one point late in the evening, as my son Gabe and my dear friend Eugene sat by my bedside, a respiratory therapist abruptly entered the room. With great enthusiasm, he announced, "Let's take out that tube and see if you can breathe on your own." It gave me quite a start. I wasn't sure if I could breathe. I shuddered and waved him off, sensing that something was wrong with my left lung.

Since the breathing machine left me unable to talk, I scribbled on a notepad, "I'm scared."

Eugene is a smart, no-nonsense meditation teacher. He intuitively knew what to do. First, he instructed me to sense my body. But I couldn't do it. I got part of the way down my torso before giving up in frustration. Then he asked me to find my breath, and that was even worse. I had been meditating for years, but suddenly, I couldn't distinguish between my own breathing and what the machine was doing. I made a panicked motion, like I was drowning.

In that moment, a story I'd heard many times about Suzuki Roshi came to mind. This gentle Japanese man was one of the most revered Zen teachers in America. He was the founder of the San Francisco Zen Center, from which the Zen Hospice Project was born. He has been a central teacher in my life, even though we never met in person. He practiced and taught meditation for decades with wholehearted dedication. Nevertheless, the night before he died, his youngest son, Otohiro, was lowering him into the bathtub when the Zen master became terrified. He thought he might die right there in the bathwater. He started gasping for air and breathing fast.

Otohiro spoke quietly in his ear. "Father, calm down. Breathe slowly, breathe slowly." Otohiro himself began breathing loudly and deliberately.

Hearing his son's words and feeling the rhythm of his breath, Suzuki Roshi was able to ground himself and become calm once more.

If Suzuki Roshi can be scared, then I can be, too, I told myself. I let myself feel the fear in my bruised and battered heart. Having spent so much time sitting with my breath, I also trusted that ultimately I would be able to return to it again.

Gabe intuitively put his hand on my heart. It was like a conduit to the very source of love, and it stabilized me immensely.

I pulled Eugene toward me and put my ear next to his face. He understood, somehow, that I wanted to follow his breath.

"Just breathe," he said calmly. "Let the breath breathe you."

The sound of his breath and its steady, smooth rhythm became my lifeline. I borrowed Eugene's breath until I could find my own. Gradually, I grew more peaceful, more relaxed. After some time, I motioned for the respiratory therapist to do his work and detach me from the breathing machine.

With love and breath, I found my way home.

In the Judeo-Christian creation story, as told in the book of Genesis, we learn that on the first day, God said, "Let there be light." And there was light. The metaphor continues, as on subsequent days, God speaks and he creates the great waters, the earth, abundant plants, and moving creatures. On the sixth day, God forms a human in his own image from clay and dust of the earth. Then God gives this person the *breath of life*—not through words, but by breathing into the brand-new human's nostrils.

Once during a teaching at the Metta Institute, my friend the late Rabbi Alan Lew suggested that one way to understand the meaning of this element of the narrative is that breath is the most intimate connection we humans have to the realm of God. He explained that breath is the vehicle for reaching the transcendent. The breath takes us to that experience that is deeper than words, deeper than thought, deeper than form.

Breath animates human life and sustains it. Breath comes before thought and words. It is non-conceptual, wordless. It can't be described; it can only be experienced. We can breathe without speaking, but we cannot speak without breathing.

In meditation, we use breath to focus our attention on the present.

Breathing only happens in real time. It always occurs in the here and now. This is what makes it such a powerful vehicle for direct insight. Often, we think of the present moment only as a stepping-stone on our way to some future goal. But actually, life can only be lived in the present, not in the past or in the future. And this present moment is the only place where we can rest.

Normally, breathing is an involuntary process, proceeding without our conscious awareness, going along at its own pace, minding its own business. When we walk, we breathe. When we sleep, we breathe. The breath is always there, functioning without our interference. This is probably a good thing. Imagine if we were in charge and had to remember to breathe? Most of us wouldn't last very long.

Curiously, though, when we sit to meditate, we often start by trying to shape the breath. We make it deeper, quieter, as if there were such a thing as a "perfect breath." In Buddhist practice, a long breath isn't any better than a short breath. What's important is noticing that you are breathing.

The breath invites us into the body. John O'Donohue, the wonderful, wild Irish poet, once wrote, "We need to come home to the temple of our senses. Our bodies know that they belong . . . it is our minds that make us homeless." We come home as we sense the breath's texture, rhythm, and pace, the differing length of each inhale and exhale. With time and practice, we learn to align with the breath and move with it, to allow the breath its own natural depth and flow. Every breath takes us to where we belong. As we relinquish command of it, we gradually feel the breath breathing us. This is good training for releasing control of and understanding how to cooperate with life.

While we might believe otherwise, there is nothing boring about being with breath. When we open to the miracle of the breath and sense directly the process of oxygenation, we appreciate how, through a creative collaboration with our blood, air reaches every cell of our bodies. Every moment is totally new. Each breath is unique, purposeful, and essential to life. I liken it to being with a lover. Breathing consciously, we engage in an exploration, a tender discovery of life. Each breath is alive with wonder. Our minds can't help but become curious as our hearts fill with gratitude.

Our breath also serves as a window to how we operate in the world. With the in-breath, we may take in the world and claim it as "me" or "mine," constructing an image of a separate sense of self. Or with a simple out-breath, we can recognize our place in a complex web of interconnection with all life. We can appreciate how everything we think, say, or do ripples through that web, affecting everything else—whether it is obvious to us or not.

The breath invites us to rest, restore, and be revitalized. We unhook ourselves from the daily frenzy and bring into balance the instinctive tendency to fight, flight, or freeze. The book of Genesis reminds us that God "blessed and sanctified the seventh day" and rested from all work. When we gather our attention fully and completely into the present moment—whether on a meditation cushion, along a trail in nature, or lying down absorbed in a great novel—we discover the ease that emerges when we are not striving, scattered, or struggling.

Jeffrey, a meditation student of mine, described how his mind was consumed with confusion. He recently had lost his job, and his boyfriend had cheated on him with his best friend. His once familiar world was now in chaos. His mind was trapped in a bedlam of constant strategizing, which failed to deliver any relief.

I suggested he take a breath.

A few days later, he reported that by placing his mind completely on the breath, he could find rest. He said, "I realized that when my total focus was on the breath, my external world could keep spinning. I didn't need to stop it or resolve anything. The stories repeated over and over, a tape loop in my mind. It reminded me of the cyclone in *The Wizard of Oz*—houses, wagons, and tumbleweeds circling round and round. But there was nothing I needed to do about any of it. Breathing and sitting in the center of it all gave me a fresh perspective on the chaos. The breath became my resting place, a safe harbor."

Awareness of breath is one of the most straightforward and easiest ways to come into the present moment. Placing our warm attention on the breath connects body and mind: the breath calms the body, and the body in turn calms the mind.

With mindfulness, the mind becomes saturated with sensitivity and a balanced acceptance, opening and receiving the present moment just as it is, without clinging to or rejecting anything. We pause, we relax, and we allow. Our thoughts may wander, troubling feelings may unfold, but for once we are not trying to control, change, approve, or reject them.

When we gather our attention onto a particular object or experience and stay with it as it changes, we develop concentration and a certain mental pliancy. The growing stability of mindfulness predisposes us to move beyond superficiality, to penetrate experience and investigate it in order to have a deeper understanding. Gradually, we begin to have insights into why these thoughts, feelings, and emotions arose in the first place. But mindfulness is not just inward looking. It can guide our outward actions.

Clear comprehension illuminates how our relationship to our experience can either cause suffering or cultivate wisdom. This enables us to nurture a different, more helpful response the next time we encounter a challenging situation, person, or thought. It helps us to remain calm and grounded when in the midst of an argument with a child, neighbor, boss, or partner; when we confront illness; when we face loss. We can draw on our cultivated tranquility and access a wiser inner guidance.

One of my students, Liang, was a VP at a huge tech company and a new mother. She had to wake several times in the middle of the night to feed her baby, even though she was back at work in a high-pressure environment. She felt exhausted and stressed out. Every time her baby screamed in the wee hours, she felt instantly irritated. Breast-feeding, she found herself counting down the minutes until she could get back to sleep.

Then Liang started practicing mindful breathing while breast-feeding, and her experience shifted entirely. Instead of wishing the nursing session would just end, she instead began to consciously focus on her breath, noticing the sensations that arose in her body. This enabled her to deepen her connection with her baby. Liang felt happy and at peace, grateful for the opportunity to just be in the moment with her precious daughter. Back at work, she reported, she was still physically tired, but she no longer felt so worn out. She had a renewed enthusiasm for life.

These days, you can find mindfulness being promoted on TV, marketed on podcasts, sold as an app, and featured on the covers of popular magazines. In the cult of productivity, workplace mindfulness has become the latest and hottest hack promising good returns on investment. The current explosion of interest in the application of mindfulness to business, medicine, education, neuroscience, addiction, and social justice issues might have us believe it is a new discovery. But mindfulness is older than religion, older than magic.

Some people seem to think that mindfulness is the "new black"—a suitable solution for all problems on every occasion. There have been thousands of research papers published reporting the positive impact of mindfulness on stress reduction, pain management, heart rate variability, anxiety, gene expression, smoking cessation, disease progression, relapse of depression, personality disorders, grief, and even existential death anxiety. The future of mindfulness seems bright. However, research into mindfulness and neuroscience is still in an adolescent stage. It seems prudent to question popular treatment modalities to assure safety and avoid over-simplification of expectations.

It's easy to misunderstand the teachings from faith traditions and even such secular mindfulness practices and apply them in a way that skews their original intention. We hear an expert encouraging compassionate action and discouraging negative emotions, and we take that to mean that we should never get angry. That goal is not only unlikely, but also potentially cuts us off from discovering an inner strength we might need to survive difficult events. Pretty soon, we start to reject parts of ourselves in an effort to create a new "spiritual identity." I've done it, and most everyone I know has done it at some point.

The thing is, mindfulness isn't just about mental fitness, productivity, or achieving a specific outcome. It certainly can lead to healthy and positive changes in our lives. Yet the solitary pursuit of those ends can eclipse our appreciation of the deeper beauty of being fully human.

We are always messing with ourselves. We tell ourselves what we should be experiencing and what we shouldn't. We work hard to define ourselves, hoping that we are doing it in the right way. This constant activity is totally exhausting. Personal development easily becomes endless and effortful. We try—in fact, we can't seem to stop trying—to be better, to be someone special. There is a certain aggression in all this so-called self-improvement. Better to return to the true intention of meditation, which is to let go of the striving, to embrace things as they are, and, with equanimity, to discover freedom.

One of my students, a physician named Kandice, wrote to me after participating in our weeklong mindfulness meditation retreat:

> I used to view mindfulness as something to achieve. The degree to which I could focus on my breath equaled success. I would often critique the time I spent in meditation, such as, "Well, that session sucked. My mind wandered way too much. I got too fidgety." I also found myself labeling almost everything that entered my mind during meditation as "good" or "bad." I believed that keeping a scorecard would motivate me to "be better" at meditation, making my sessions more productive and efficient. I wondered if anyone else felt this way, but when I looked around the room, they all seemed so good at meditating. Sometimes I wondered why I had signed up for the course. I never liked practicing (just ask my mom about piano lessons), but I wanted results, so I kept hanging in there.
>
> Then one day, some of your words got my attention: "Mindfulness results in a non-judgmental way of being." This sentence was a catalyst

for change in my world. The utter relief I felt at not having to spend so much energy judging everything (including myself) was freeing, wide, and expansive. My whole body chilled out. My shoulders dropped, my neck stopped hurting, and I stopped cracking my elbow all the time. I began to develop true mindfulness, understanding that it begins and ends with a simple choice to pay attention to what is so. Period. No scorecard. No grade. No labels. No pressure.

Now when I am being mindful, I feel open to things without assigning them a value: pain, joy, sorrow, anxiety. Past, present, and future all become the same. It can all be there, and that's okay. There is room for everything to exist. I am here to notice and learn, not to run away from my most challenging emotions or to crave one state over the other. In fact, when I do run away, crave, or attach value, I suffer greatly because I want things to be different than they are. Yuck!

The practice of mindfulness as I now know it continues to be pretty difficult at times. But more and more often, when I am sitting in silence, I know I am there. Literally, I know I am there. I sense my body. This is so important: I really feel my feet on the floor, the air moving in and out of my nostrils, the little goings-on internally, like my pulse, my growling stomach, my aching back.

Slowly over the course of the week, I felt grief surfacing—grief for all the years I had spent living in my head, judging, critiquing, and analyzing. There are still times when I meditate that I cry about this, but I can breathe through it and later, the tightness is gone. Mindfulness is, and always will be, about getting back to my breath. It feels like a very safe place to land, a home, a loving embrace.

I no longer feel as compelled to grade myself on performance. I have learned that mindfulness is not about achieving some perfect state or being the best at something. It is about me being authentic, imperfect, vulnerable, and, well, human.

Meditation is not a cure-all. Even when we practice mindfulness regularly, we can be insightful about certain aspects of our lives and blind to others. I know experienced meditators who are highly attuned to their bodies, but out of touch with their emotional lives. I know others who understand the mind, but completely ignore their bodies. I can think of longtime practitioners who are able to sit in silence for days, but have limited interpersonal skills. Still others have a universal love for all beings, but are unable to love themselves or others in a personal way.

My friend John Welwood, the psychologist who first coined the term *spiritual bypassing*, once said, "We often use the goal of awakening or liberation to rationalize premature transcendence: trying to rise above the raw and messy side of our humanness before we have fully faced and made peace with it."

Initially, I'll admit, I also used meditation to escape the tangle of relational pain in my past. Meditation proved to be as effective a way for me to bypass my difficult history as alcohol was for my parents and drug use was for my brother Alan.

My meditation sessions were full of striving. I developed enormous powers of concentration, which gave rise during intensive retreats to states of incredible rapture and peace. I felt proud of my accomplishments. But when the retreats were over, I'd quickly realize that I wasn't any happier. I was disappointed to discover that the unhealed wounds, the unexplored traumas, and the conflicts of my life were still there waiting for me when I came home.

Focus, even intense focus, does not produce insight in and of itself. In Buddhist teachings, we use concentration to calm the mind and body so that we can harness them for the development of wisdom. But an attachment to tranquility can cause us to ignore, bury, or deny big swaths of our life experiences.

Idealism is one of the occupational hazards of the spiritual path. It can be the death of any practice. When we create a spiritual ideal, we hold tight to some vision of where we think we should be, but then we use that idea to not be where we are. For instance, we promise ourselves that we will meditate every morning for an hour. But then, after a week, we miss a few days, and we give up meditating altogether.

This is a tricky way for the personality to hijack our spiritual practices for its own ends. If I have a tendency toward narcissism, I may flaunt my meditation habits to feel important and special. If I have a tendency to withdraw from inner difficulties, I may be drawn to teachings on non-attachment and renunciation. If strong feelings scare me, I may subscribe to the belief that a spiritual person isn't supposed to get visibly upset, and I may talk about "getting beyond our emotions." By distracting us from our immediate and direct experiences, these defense mechanisms disconnect us from our inner resources.

During retreats, I enjoy the individual meetings with students in which they share their experiences with meditation. It's a bit like having my own crazy mind walk through the door, only in different costumes. Margie's personality judges her meditation practice harshly, insisting that she is the worst meditator ever born. Barry has a clear sense of superiority and tries to do everything a bit more mindfully than everyone else on the retreat. Jason fills his journals with brilliant ideas, humorous and onerous anecdotes, and a "golden chain" of insights in place of doing walking meditation. Jeanette gets lost in procrastination, in all-or-nothing thinking. Charlotte admits to slipping out of the retreat to go for ice cream, her personality insisting she deserves a break. Jeremiah complains that meditation is not helping solve his relationship difficulties with his wife.

All of them are me.

Even when you teach this stuff, the mind's habits continue. I was sitting at a meditation retreat with a good friend who is also a meditation teacher. We can be a bit competitive at times. In an interview with our teacher, my friend reported, "Frank beat me in slow walking meditation, but I was much better at mindful eating." It's amazing how the mind reacts to the simple instruction to sit quietly. The personality believes we have to make something happen. There are problems to be solved.

In Buddhist circles, we often say, "Meditation doesn't solve your problems; it dissolves them." Our minds are wild. We don't tame them by trying to stop our thoughts, by repressing our emotions, or even by resolving our problems. We have a lot less control over life than we imagined. To paraphrase Suzuki Roshi's very kind meditation instruction, which he recited often at the Zen Center, "To give your cow a large, spacious meadow is the best way to control him."

Your mind didn't become wild when you started to practice meditation. The mindfulness simply made you aware of what had been happening in the background all along—what your personality is reacting to and trying to manage.

Here is a counter-intuitive suggestion: allow it all. The thoughts, the strong emotions, and the associated energetic patterns—don't be bothered by them. Let it all stop by itself. Your cow will be much happier.

We're "still crazy after all these years." The object of meditation isn't to change ourselves, to throw out the old and bring in the new. It's about making friends with ourselves, meeting each and every part of our lives with curiosity and compassion. This doesn't mean simply that we must tolerate the difficult stuff that comes up in meditation. It means that we have to explore it in order to become deeply familiar with our inner world.

Darlene Cohen, a Zen teacher who lived for many years with rheumatoid arthritis and cancer, said:

> People sometimes ask me where my own healing energy comes from. How, in the midst of this pain, this implacable slow crippling, can I encourage myself and other people? My answer is that my healing comes from my bitterness itself, my despair, my terror. It comes from the shadow. I dip down into that muck again and again and then am flooded with its healing energy. Despite the renewal and vitality it gives me to face my deepest fears, I don't go willingly when they call.
>
> I've been around that wheel a million times: first I feel the despair, but I deny it for a few days; then its tugs become more insistent in proportion to my resistance; finally, it overwhelms me and pulls me down,

kicking and screaming all the way. It's clear I am caught, so at last I give up to this reunion with the dark aspect of my adjustment to pain and loss.

Becoming liberated in this human experience means including the personal, psychological, and emotional aspects of life, and also going beyond the personality toward a fuller awakening. We have to be willing to meet our suffering, to uncover the hidden shadows, to acknowledge our neurotic patterns, to heal childhood wounds, and to embrace what we have rejected. I've needed to balance spiritual practice with good psychotherapy, somatic work, grief counseling, and other methods of inquiry. Those wise therapeutic relationships have been invaluable in helping me integrate what I first discovered in silence.

These days, I speak of my mindfulness practice as "a practice of intimacy." We can't know ourselves, each other, or death from a distance. This work is up close and personal. Meditation is all about learning to be intimate with ourselves, with others, and with all aspects of this worldly life, bringing the healing power of loving awareness forward so that we can meet what is scary, sad, and raw.

When we see through the mind's conditioning and our habitual behaviors, we come to understand the ways in which we cause ourselves unnecessary suffering. This is where the real freedom of the practice lies. It doesn't help us to escape from life or transcend our pain. Instead, we become intimate with everything, and know ourselves as not separate from any of it.

The American Buddhist teacher and bestselling author Jack Kornfield popularized the expression "After the ecstasy, the laundry" in a book by the same name. What this means is that even after a deeply insightful transcendent experience, we still have to deal with the nuts and bolts of life, the everyday activities like cooking and cleaning and caring for our children and elders. I've often wondered why we don't use doing the laundry as a method to discover the ecstasy in the first place. Is this idea too far-fetched?

A meditation student had several small children at home. She found that, as a single mother, she simply could not do her formal practice sitting on a cushion. She would be interrupted too many times. This brought up for her a sense of despair.

When her teacher came to visit, the mother asked, "What shall I do?"

"What do you spend most of your time doing?" he inquired.

"Washing clothes and dishes," she replied.

So he stood next to her as she washed the clothes and cleaned the dishes, and he coached her in being mindful the whole time. That became her practice, at least until her children grew up and she could return to more formal seated meditation sessions.

Everything we do can be used in the cultivation of mindfulness: driving to work, eating, raising our children, being with our beloveds. We can roll it all into what we call "our spiritual practice" and seamlessly integrate it into every aspect of our everyday lives. Waking to a new day is a holy moment—doorways offer themselves as thresholds to new possibilities, trees are utterly themselves. All things are a potential source of support and awakening. When we attempt to separate the sacred from the ordinary, we create a false dichotomy.

For many years, I have appreciated the teaching of the Indian guru of non-dualism Sri Nisargadatta, who famously said, "The mind creates the abyss, the heart crosses it." This statement is often understood as highlighting the division between the thinking mind and the emotional heart, and how love is the bridge between the two.

Over the years, I have come to a deeper understanding of what Nisargadatta might have meant. In the Buddhist tradition, *mind-heart* is one thing. The abyss is formed when we split mind and heart into two. As when we split off the ordinary from the sacred, they appear as two sides separated by a gap. Nisargadatta is reminding us about the vast, limitless space of awareness that is beyond thought and emotion. This space doesn't separate. When the mind and heart are awake, you see everything in its unique detail, even your problems, and it all comes to rest in love and wisdom.

It's what Rumi is referring to in his famous lines:

Out beyond ideas of wrongdoing and rightdoing
there is a field. I'll meet you there.
When the soul lies down in that grass,
the world is too full to talk about.
Ideas, language, even the phrase "each other" doesn't make any sense.

Yes, there is space between each breath, each thought, but it actually connects them. It's a bit like experiments in perception that use the picture of the old woman who, if we look carefully, we can also see as a young woman. Heart and mind, ordinary and sacred—all are in fact a unified whole.

When the mind is attentive, focused, we notice the space. Here is where we discover a place of rest. Claude Debussy is credited with saying, "Music is the space between the notes." The white space on this page allows your eyes to rest on the words. In art, negative space is just as important as the image itself, helping to bring balance to a composition. No matter how much activity, no matter how many forms exist in our lives, there are pauses and spaces everywhere, inviting us to rest.

These days, I allow myself to slip into the gaps. The gaps are not the enemy. The transitions, the in-between places in life, are where I find peace and tranquility, the refreshment of pure awareness, the still point, the perspective that recognizes the holiness in all things.

Mind the gap. The sacred can be found in the ordinary. Rest can be found in the middle of things.

14

COURAGEOUS PRESENCE

*I realize that if I wait until I am no longer afraid to act, write,
speak, be, I'll be sending messages on a Ouija board, cryptic
complaints from the other side.*

—AUDRE LORDE

For Charles, courageous presence is accompanying his father to Sloan
Kettering to discuss his inoperable cancer. For Steve, it's leading a memorial service for his best friend's young daughter, who fell to her death
off an ocean cliff. For Tracy, it is being torn apart by both grief and love
as she sits at the bedside of her dying mother while holding her newborn
son. For Jackson, it is going to a maximum-security prison to sit face-to-
face with the man who murdered his mother. For Terry, it is allowing
his body to tremble and shake for three days while the contractions of
old sexual traumas are released during a meditation retreat. For Joanna,
it is embracing a new lesbian lover at age seventy-five, when she had
imagined that she would never have another relationship.

When fear speaks, courage is the heart's answer.

I have known Janet for twenty years. She is a student, friend, and living reminder of the basic goodness in humans.

Years ago, Janet was enjoying a backyard BBQ with her husband, their
good friend Albert, and their families. Looking around, she couldn't see

her three-and-a-half-year-old son, Jack, or Albert's son, Daniel, in the yard. Concerned, she said that she was going to check on the boys. But her husband and Albert called her back, saying, "You're always jumping up. Sit down with us. Relax." They assured her that the kids were fine, likely playing inside the house.

Moments later, they all heard a crash and a scream. Young Daniel came running up to the adults. Janet ran past him to the front of the house, where she found Jack lying near-lifeless in the middle of their normally peaceful neighborhood street. The car that had hit her child had driven off.

Janet scooped up Jack, and they all piled into the truck, heading to the emergency room as quickly as possible Albert was a physician, so he worked heroically throughout the ride to restore Jack's breathing. Janet felt overwhelmed by guilt and shame, though her primary concern was for Jack's obviously broken leg. How could she have allowed this to happen? she wondered as they drove.

It turned out that Jack had suffered injuries far worse than a broken leg. The doctors at the hospital did their best to save the boy, but they explained that his head wounds and the resulting brain damage were too severe. Janet's son would not survive. She and her husband eventually made the decision to unhook little Jack from life support. He died almost immediately.

Everyone was in shock, frozen in time and disbelief. Janet held her baby close, rocking him as she had so many nights as she settled him to sleep with a sweet lullaby. There would be no waking from this dream.

Full of fear and sheer horror, the parents drove back home shortly before dawn. The country road hugged the nearby river. Janet noticed the rising full moon reflected in the water. This contact with something outside herself helped her sense a deep, clear part of her being, a calm awareness that, for a moment, could cut through the guilt, grief, and disbelief. An inner guidance spoke to her, saying, "If I am going to honor Jack's life, I cannot let this accident destroy me."

Still, the next day, when the police phoned to confirm the hit-and-run, her whole being filled again with the heat of rage. Then, at 11:00 A.M., another shift occurred. There was a knock on the screen door. An older man, a stranger, appeared on the other side. Instinctively, Janet knew he was the driver of the car. The anguish on his face temporarily washed away her rage, and the grieving mother invited the stranger into her home.

The poet Henry Wadsworth Longfellow once wrote, "If we could read the secret history of our enemies, we should find in each man's life sorrow and suffering enough to disarm all hostility."

The driver apologized, admitted his liability, and explained that he did not know that his car had hit anyone. Once again, Janet's guidance spoke to her with an inner strength reminiscent of the drive along the river. She looked compassionately at the man and, without any false sympathy, spoke honestly. "Jack's death is a responsibility that we four adults all share," she said.

Janet and the man who had accidentally killed her son talked awhile longer. Janet cried as she spoke of how she, her husband, and their friend had been preoccupied and hadn't kept a close enough eye on the young boy. The driver explained how his daughter was getting married and that he had been rushing to the wedding rehearsal. In Janet's mind, it was a moment of distraction on all their parts that had led to this disastrous outcome. A brief moment of inattention, nothing more.

We tend to like simple causes: they tidy up life's uncertainties. We want such accidents to be brought under human control. We want someone to be held accountable. We want the outrageous and impossible to be understood, so as to alleviate our sense of helplessness. But life does not always present itself in ways that are right or reasonable. The truth is, we are rarely in control of such catastrophes, of the twists and turns of fate, and most especially not of our deaths.

In her humility, Janet understood that she could only be saved from this inexplicable horror by accepting it. She said to herself, *I need to take my share of responsibility in order not to live a life full of shame and blame.* She found a middle ground, one without unnecessary internalizing ("It's all my fault") or externalizing ("It's all his fault").

There were still years of grief work to be done, pain to be felt, anger toward the driver, herself, and even Jack for dying. It all had to be reckoned with, and it took courage to face it directly. But Janet recognized the importance of meeting her suffering if she ever was to have a good life again. Her small rural community of Mormons, Mennonites, old-timers, and hippies helped her to heal. A bouquet of flowers would appear on her doorstep one day, a basket of fresh eggs the next.

Janet told me later that being with her grief opened her to a new level of love. For a while, she lived with the fear of the absolute precariousness of life, warning other young mothers of dangers to their children that they might not recognize. In time and with attention, however, her heart cracked wide open. Her relationship to the precariousness of life transformed, giving rise to gratitude and a sense of being fully alive. Now she would not turn away from any part of life.

Her marriage didn't survive the trauma of Jack's death, but Janet did. She went on to become one of the most amazing hospice professionals I know. She has taught hundreds of volunteers and family caregivers how to live with grief and accompany death. She is the person her community calls to stand beside parents when there are sudden or traumatic deaths of children. Jack made all that possible. What a powerful little guy to have made such a difference in so many lives.

The old Buddhist texts refer to "the great and courageous bodhisattvas." These are beings who, like Janet, have the fortitude to stand with suffering that might bring the rest of us to our knees. It's not that such people have no fear. Rather, they are able to maintain a courageous presence while they are afraid. They open to fear and are willing to hold it, learn from it, and be transformed by it. In this way, fear serves as a catalyst, a doorway to compassion, and a pathway to transformation for all beings who are afraid.

Janet's actions in the face of unimaginable grief and pain show us that courageous presence is not only for the rare bodhisattvas, brave soldiers, and Mother Teresas of our world. Ordinary people put courageous presence into practice in small, beautiful ways every single day.

I know a brave man named Julio. Julio is a nursing assistant in a major metropolitan hospital, whose job it is to clean up the emergency room. After the pandemonium of a "code," during which the medical team has tried and failed to resuscitate a trauma patient in cardiac arrest with shock paddles and chest compressions, the adrenaline stops pumping, and the team walks away. This is when Julio enters the room.

There, he finds the patient lying motionless on the stretcher, dressed in nothing but a hospital gown. An intubation tube awkwardly protrudes from the body's mouth. The floor is speckled with puddles of blood and the gauze pads thrown aside during the procedure. The red crash cart drawers dangle open like a mechanic's neglected toolbox in an auto shop. The room still hums with residual activity. The walls seem to hold the lingering voices of the emergency room team shouting their instructions and reports just minutes before.

Julio enters silently. He spends a moment taking in the chaos, letting his eyes and ears move over the room, establishing what needs to be done. Then his gaze falls gracefully on the now-dead patient, whose name he does not know. He approaches, leans over respectfully, as if bowing to the person's nobility, and whispers softly in the ear, "You have died. It's okay now. I will do my best to wash away all dust and confusion."

Once Julio has straightened up the room, closed the crash cart drawers, picked up the bloodstained gauze, and mopped the floor, he washes his hands. Then he begins to bathe the patient. A recently hired nursing supervisor sticks her head in the door. "We need the room as soon as possible," she barks. Julio pays her no mind. Others on staff at the hospital know of and respect his work—they will protect this sacred moment. Julio takes the time he needs to honor the dead.

The willingness to sit with fear is an act of courage.

Fear is both a psychological construct and an irrefutable biological function of stimulus/response involving the release of adrenaline and cortisol into the bloodstream, increased heart rate, tightening of certain muscles, the formation of goose bumps, and the dilation of the pupils. Fear is a normal human reaction, sometimes a necessary survival response to a perceived threat, which generates a specific pattern of behavior.

We speak about rational and irrational fears. But all fear is subjective. What makes me only nervous, such as the possibility of a huge earthquake hitting California, can generate full-blown panic in another person. What makes you cringe in terror, like a spider, might not cause me any apprehension at all. Fear can arise from an accurate perception of a situation, or from a completely distorted view.

The fear of saber-toothed tigers is real—or at least it was when saber-toothed tigers roamed the earth. Now that fear is a story, an old story that lives inside our imaginations. Still, we can scare ourselves with the thought that we always are being hunted or that we must hide away after dark to stay safe. We can even get anxious about the possible return of actual saber-toothed tigers in the future.

Fear doesn't require a basis in reality in order to have an impact on us. No matter what its cause, the fear still feels real. That said, it's best not to treat fear as the absolute truth.

Living from a place of fear can narrow our vision, shrinking our lives down to what is comfortable and familiar. We easily become consumed with safety precautions and the dread of uncertainty, constantly looking over our shoulders. It is reasonable to want to protect ourselves and those we love. But being driven by fear alone, we stop using our common sense and make unwise decisions. We grow less willing to take risks and face conflict or disapproval and may even slip into compliance to gain the security promised by authorities.

For some, fear manifests in counter-phobic tendencies. We engage in dangerous, high-risk activities, continually testing our own limits or others' loyalty. We become aggressive, even bullying, to mask our fear or deny its impact on our lives. When we place all our emphasis on overcoming fear, there is no rest.

Either way, compliance or rebellion, in the end, unaddressed fear is a self-imposed exile, a prison of our own making.

There will always be things that frighten us. It's foolish to imagine otherwise. I have a lot of fear. My fear shows up as second-guessing myself, procrastinating, difficulty trusting, and looking for reassurance from others. The goal is not to one day get rid of all fear. It is rather to free ourselves from fear's choke hold around our lives, to learn to face our fear with courageous presence.

When Gabe was five years old, he developed a typical childhood fear of monsters in the closet. One night when he couldn't get to sleep, I climbed into bed with him and pulled the covers up over our heads so that we could hide from the monsters.

"Do you think they're out there now?" I asked with utmost sincerity.

"Yeah, Dad. They're in the closet," Gabe replied, eyes wide as saucers.

"You think so? You want to go see?"

"No!" he said, pulling the covers up even higher.

I let a playful, comfortable atmosphere sink in as we lay there under the covers giggling for some time. Then I suggested, "You sure you don't want to go see? We could bring the pillows with us for protection."

"Okay," he said.

So we scooped up the pillows, got down on the floor, and crawled very slowly toward the closet. I opened the door just a little bit, and then shut it quickly. Over and over I did this, making a big show of peeking inside to look for monsters, then crawling back to safety. It made Gabe laugh.

After a time, I swung the door open wide and chucked all our pillows into the closet. A few items came tumbling out onto the floor—a pair of sneakers, a soccer ball, an empty box—but no monsters. Gabe began laughing hysterically. The more he laughed, the more relaxed the atmosphere became, and the more curious he got, until he was climbing into the closet to explore what was inside. Slowly but surely, his fear drifted away.

Gabe didn't get scared of monsters anymore after that. He didn't have to be afraid of them because he had gone and looked for them himself.

He had faced his fear directly. If I had only told him, "No, don't be silly. There aren't any monsters in your closet. Now go to bed," and shut off the lights, then he would have had to take my word for it. This way, he realized that the monsters didn't exist. They were only stories inside his head.

It turns out it's not so different for us grown-ups. The monsters we face may feel bigger and uglier and more challenging than the ones who lived in our childhood closets, but just like Gabe's, our fears boil down to the stories we tell ourselves.

Taking fear as our teacher and learning to work skillfully with it can lead us to some degree of inner freedom. We quickly see that operating from a place of fear means we have little trust in reality. We are separated from others, from the possibility of unity. This is our default position. In Buddhist circles, the small, cut-off sense of self is sometimes called "the body of fear." It takes physical form as a shell of tension around us, a stiffening of our bodies, a thickening of our defenses against the fear. Then the mind becomes rigid and confused. The heart closes.

A separation does need to occur, but not the one we might have imagined. In coping with fear, it is helpful to distinguish our emotional states from the object of which we are afraid. When we obsess about the objects we fear—insects, identity theft, rejection, terrorism, speaking in public—we avoid contact with the emotion itself. Like the monsters in the closet, the thing we fear may not even exist, but all of our attention to it turns the illusion into reality.

When we discern the difference between the emotion and the object, we can see the part we play in the process. Then we can begin to unhook ourselves from the overwhelm. We relax and temporarily hold the fear in the container of the body, supported by steady breathing, so that we can examine the mind's operations—the beliefs, assumptions, memories, and stories that underpin the fear. In this way, we can begin to reduce our reactivity.

When I was a boy, I would get called into the principal's office fairly often. At my school, this usually meant one thing: you were in big trouble. In my case, however, I knew I wasn't being summoned due to misbehavior. My mother regularly would call the school asking for me to come home.

Usually, she wanted my help because she was having trouble breathing due to her emphysema. I would arrive to find her on the back porch gasping for air. I would get her inhalers, have her practice pursed-lip breathing to increase air flow, and put her at ease while I set up the nebulizer. When her breathing was especially difficult, I would help her use the portable oxygen tank. I was surprisingly unafraid of her poor health condition or assisting her with these medical procedures.

At other times, when my parents had been drinking heavily, my house would become a place of fear. My mother would speak of suicide, and my father could get violent. I wasn't sure what kind of situation I might encounter when I walked through the front door. I vividly recall the feel of the cold brass doorknob as I turned my wrist slowly, the creaking sound of the hinges, the effort required to push the door open, and the courage it took to step through to the other side. I moved apprehensively through the many rooms of the house. I might find the kitchen stove left on. I might find my mother passed out on the basement floor. My mind was hypervigilant, my body tense as I crossed multiple doorways.

Many years later, when I took up meditation, a teacher gave us instructions on being mindful in all activities. The idea was to reduce our automatic behaviors and increase our capacity to be present. One exercise emphasized careful attention to the way we opened and closed a door when entering a new space. I was surprisingly adept at this particular exercise. I found myself keenly aware of the approach, sensing the temperature of the door handle, feeling the door's weight, opening it with purpose. But emotionally, I was absent.

So I started to practice sensing my body as well as the door handle when pausing at the threshold. I felt a clenching in my belly and noticed an uneasiness that seemed unrelated to the task at hand. Suddenly, I began to cry so hard that I couldn't get through the door.

The teacher was a great support in helping me make the connection with the fear I had experienced earlier in life. He explained that it was no big surprise I was having such a reaction to the exercise given my up-bringing.

Opening doors became a central practice in my life for a time. Gradually, with practice, mindfulness replaced my learned hyper-vigilance and contributed significantly to a process of healing my old wounds. One way we express courageous presence is through the mindful practice of touching with mercy and tenderness that which we previously touched only with fear.

There are three types of courage needed to live fully, face death directly, and discover true freedom: the courage of the warrior, the courage of a strong heart, and the courage of vulnerability.

Our most common image of warrior courage is related to bravery in emergencies or dangerous situations. We might think of soldiers who demonstrate vigor and persistence, and whose training, beliefs, and pure adrenaline allow them to take risks, override fear, or at least learn not to be stopped by their fear. Physicians and health care professionals receive a similar type of training in pushing past exhaustion. For some people, simply getting out of bed in the morning requires warrior courage. For others, it is summoned to bear emotional turmoil, start a new job, or live with chronic illness, depression, and despair. For most of us, everyday life takes some degree of courage. Courage may be the choice to do what we believe is right.

A healthy warrior courage is motivated by honor, loyalty to comrades, service, or commitment, and is balanced with intelligence in its application. However, there is a shadow side to this type of warrior courage. It can be aroused by shame, coercion, a need to control, or a desire to gain approval, leading to defensiveness and a false sense of invulnerability.

When I was coming up in Buddhist practice, I heard a lot of talk about "spiritual warriors," illustrated with stories carried over from the Asian traditions. Buddhist texts are replete with battlefield imagery. One suggested the meditator imagine being surrounded by an army of ten thousand soldiers. It was said that conquering this army would be easier than taming one's mind. These teachings never resonated with me. I found that such images encouraged a great deal of striving and rejection. They were of limited value and little service to people with wounds of self-hatred and self-judgment.

Nevertheless, there is a place in our lives and meditation practice for warrior courage. It helps us to stay steadfast in the face of difficulty, to turn toward suffering, to risk the known for the unknown, and to confront ignorance. It keeps us from being seduced by the habit of complacency and the pull of uncertanity. We may feel the ground of this courage in our bellies.

This story of a samurai and a monk illustrates the unshakeable warrior courage and integrity needed to release our attachments and face fear directly.

A samurai climbed a mountain to reach a small temple. There, the warrior found a monk calmly sitting in meditation. "Monk," the samurai barked in a voice accustomed to obedience. "Teach me about heaven and hell!"

The monk looked up at the warrior and replied with utter disdain, "Teach you about heaven and hell? I couldn't teach you about anything. You are ignorant, dirty, a disgrace to the samurai class. Get out of my sight."

The samurai grew furious. Overcome with rage, he pulled out his sword and prepared to slay the monk.

Looking straight into the samurai's eyes, the monk said, "That is hell."

The samurai froze, recognizing the compassion of the monk who had risked his life to show him this lesson. The warrior put down his sword and bowed in respect and gratitude.

The monk said softly, "And that is heaven."

Fearlessness is not about eliminating, ignoring, or pushing fear away; it is about developing a capacity to be courageously present with our powerful states of mind and heart even when facing terror.

Courage of the heart asks us to be undefended. It is the courage to feel, to allow both beauty and horror to touch us. It calls for a different kind of fearlessness, which requires as much, if not more, passion than the courage of the warrior. We find this type of courage when we are lionhearted in our dedication to staying with the truth of our experience, when we don't reject our experience and instead face what is right here, right now.

The courage of a strong heart activates a fearless receptivity to what is happening, which creates space for us to recognize, explore, and integrate our fear. Then, we can include whatever it is that we had wanted to avoid. Not only that, but this type of courage opens us to a deep compassion for the suffering of all beings. We realize that we all have fears, and, like bodhisattvas, we stand with others in their fear.

With so much mass violence in the news these days, it is easy to miss the underreported stories of courage of the strong heart. Jencie Fagan, a Nevada gym teacher, risked her own life to stop a fourteen-year-old boy who came to school one day with a handgun. He walked into the schoolyard and fired three shots. The first bullet struck another boy in the upper arm. A girl was hurt when the second bullet ricocheted off the floor, burying itself in her knee. The third shot thankfully did not hit anyone.

Jencie calmly approached the boy, walking right up to face him and his gun. After talking with him for a while, she persuaded him to drop his gun. This is where the courage of the warrior would have stopped—with an undeniably brave act, and one that almost certainly saved lives.

But Jencie demonstrated the courage of the strong heart when she then surprised everyone by hugging the shooter. She reassured the young boy that she would not leave him alone. She would accompany him to the station and throughout his legal process to make sure that he was safe and to ensure that the police didn't hurt him.

Later, when asked why she had acted so compassionately toward the shooter, Jencie, who is a mother herself, replied, "I think anybody else would have done it. I look at the students as if they're my own."

Vulnerability, the third type of courage, is the doorway to the deepest dimensions of our inner nature. Mostly we associate vulnerability with weakness, emotional exposure, and being susceptible to harm. Getting hurt. Being wounded. We are therefore terrified of vulnerability and want to avoid it at all costs. But our vulnerability is not just a curse; it is a blessing.

The courage of vulnerability enables us to sit with a friend whose child died in a car accident, to sense her pain and listen openly without preconceived bias. With vulnerability, we can acknowledge our fear of starting a new venture, share news of a divorce, respond to the yearning to get pregnant again after a miscarriage.

Vulnerability is not weakness; it is non-defensiveness. The absence of defense allows us to be wide open to our experience. Less defended, we are less opaque and more transparent. We become sensitive to the ten thousand sorrows and the ten thousand joys of this life. If we are not willing to be vulnerable to pain, loss, and sadness, we'll become insensitive to compassion, joy, love, and basic goodness.

The courage to love requires vulnerability. Is there a more vulnerable state than love? It is full of risk, uncertainty, intensity, intimacy, conflict, and truth-telling. Being vulnerable means we are sensitive, impressionable, more receptive to others and to our own inner guidance. We recognize the illusion of control, the reality that suffering is inevitable, and we are invited to release our grips and let go into the inexplicable and unpredictable.

The courage of vulnerability opens the doorway to the invulnerability of our essential nature. This invulnerability is not stoicism or an immunity to the ups and downs of life. In our culture, invulnerability usually implies a stance against emotion, a false sense of being impenetrable, that this body cannot be hurt or will not die. But the invulnerability of our essential nature is a pure openness, an undefended spaciousness in which we step back and allow the winds of fear to blow right through us. There is no place for our fear to stick, no ground on which it can land. We can drop the struggle, relax our unnecessary efforts, and rest in a state of defenselessness. We recognize that we are not separate from anything or anyone. Fear subsides as we realize that the basic essence of who we are is never damaged, never gets sick, and never dies.

The night before my open-heart surgery, I was in an agitated state, with fears of disability, doubts about the need for the procedure, and endless questions spinning in my mind.

My friend Sharda, a Buddhist meditation teacher, arrived with no answers.

She sat beside me, held my hand, and barely spoke. We stayed in silence together for quite a long time, just the two of us in the hospital room. Every once in a while, I would say, "You know, I'm scared about this surgery. I'm scared I might die."

She would nod and say, "Yeah," and go back to being silent. She exuded love and served as a clear mirror for the deepest part of me, a part bigger than my fear. In her face, I could see a reflection of my own loving nature.

There's a dynamism that happens between two people. After an argument, you can feel the negativity and tense energy in the room. The same is true under the opposite circumstances. You can feel when there has been a courageous presence in the room.

Sharda didn't stay very long, half an hour maybe. Then she stood up calmly and said, "I've got to go home."

I said, "Yeah, I know."

She said, "I love you."

And I said, "Yeah, I know." And then she left.

After her visit, I felt calm, my confidence in the procedure, myself, and the world restored. Gratitude nourished a sense of well-being. I felt a connection with others who might be suffering that night and moved beyond the fear that had plagued me.

I slept well that night. Early in the morning, when they came to fetch me as they do in the hospitals at some gray and lonely hour, I was relaxed. My son Gabe and my wife, Vanda, walked my gurney to the doors of the surgical room. Equanimity took me the rest of the way.

Entering into a state of vulnerability makes us sensitive to experiencing the pleasures and pains of our bodies, to feeling our emotions, and to noticing our thoughts. It's not easy to feel all of this or to face the root of our suffering, which is believing in our tightly constructed selves. But our capacity to be vulnerable also makes it possible for us to experience all levels of reality. We feel how permeable we actually are—how our identities are not fixed, nothing in existence is permanent. We see the emptiness of our compulsions and fixations. Undefended, vulnerable, we are open to all of it, to all the possibilities of human existence, including the subtler, deeper dimensions of our being. Hence, paradoxically, the courage of vulnerability brings us to rest in the openness of our ultimate invulnerability.

In getting to know our fear, a dry fact-finding tour of the mind will not prove sufficient. To transform fear into courageous presence, we need love. One of my foremost teachers, grief specialist Elisabeth Kübler-Ross, used to claim that there were only two primary emotions: love and fear. I'm not sure it's that simple, but certainly, we could say that love and fear are two sides of the same coin. Fear is the contraction side; love the expansive side.

Can we befriend fear? Can we meet it with mindfulness, touch the suffering it causes with deep compassion and cultivate the loving equanimity that will allow us to stay with it? If so, then we can find a place of rest even with fear.

Ram Dass once said, "After many years of undergoing psychoanalysis, teaching psychology, working as a psychotherapist, taking drugs, being in India, being a yogi, having a guru, and meditating for decades, as far as I can see I haven't gotten rid of one neurosis. Not one. The only thing that changed is that they don't define me anymore. There is less energy invested in my personality, so it is easier to change. My neuroses are not huge monsters anymore. Now they are like little shmoos that I invite over for tea."

It is possible for us to learn to love our fear. Choosing love over fear speaks to a trust in benevolence, in the basic goodness of reality, in something larger than the fear. But to embrace our fear, we need to feel safe.

Donald Winnicott, a preeminent English pediatrician and psychologist, developed the concept of the "holding environment," which is foundational to attachment theory in contemporary psychoanalysis. He saw the mother's holding as a prerequisite for a child's healthy development—loving the baby in such a way that she feels cared for, safe, understood, and continuously adored. When a child is held like this, she develops a sense of trust in her mother, which she then extends out to others and the world. If the holding is less than optimal, the child is likely to be more reactive, seeing the environment as untrustworthy.

Watch an infant with relatively healthy attachment to her primary caregiver interacting with the world. When there is "good enough" holding in her life, the child ventures off to try new things. Maybe she tries walking and takes a spill. The mother figure holds her baby, filling her up with love so that the infant has the courage to try again. Each time, the little one gains the courage to venture further beyond her previous boundaries.

I experienced the power of the holding environment a few days after Gabe was born. Out of the blue, it seemed, he started crying uncontrollably. After trying everything to bring Gabe comfort, his mother was exhausted. The midwife and a friend who had raised her own four children, when called upon to help, couldn't console Gabe, either.

Finally, I said, "I know I'm a guy, but let me try something." I scooped Gabe up, put him right against my chest, and brought him outside into the open air. I breathed deeply and whispered, "I love you, you know. I will always love you." Then I sang to him the song I had sung while he was still in his mother's pregnant belly.

It was a simple but remarkably intimate contact with my child. As deep as any experience in meditation. In a way, I loaned him my nervous system. I wasn't worried. I didn't feel upset about his state of distress. I didn't judge how he was feeling, either. I just held him within the safe container of my arms and chest, letting his upset spill out of him and evaporate into the spacious sky, until he calmed down and drifted off to sleep.

Suppose that we thought of awareness itself as this holding environment? Imagine if when we meditated, we first established ourselves in the posture, paying attention to the body and breath, and then evoked our loving attention as a way to foster trust. Sometimes when I sit, I like to imagine that I am my own "good mother." I evoke the warm presence of an archetypal mother or grandmother. Occasionally, I repeat a phrase from the Buddhist teachings on loving kindness, the Metta Sutta: "Even as a mother at the risk of her life watches over and protects her only child, so with a boundless heart should one cherish all living things, suffusing love over the entire world."

I believe that when we feel the safe holding environment of awareness embracing us, it allows our fear, pain, and ugliness to come out and show themselves and to be gently held without judgment so that they can be healed. We feel the support and courage to go beyond our previously limiting beliefs. This enables us to face a seemingly impossible situation, such as our own death or that of a child, with grace. Awareness itself is the ultimate resting place.

THE FIFTH INVITATION

Cultivate Don't Know Mind

A mind is like a parachute. It doesn't work if it is not open.
—THOMAS ROBERT DEWAR, REPEATED BY FRANK ZAPPA

Zen koans are stories, dialogues, or phrases meant to help us deal with our very human problems. Koans often appear contradictory, but they are not intended as riddles or puzzles to be solved. Rather, they are meant to help us gain insight, freeing us up from our ordinary ways of seeing and knowing the world by propelling us toward our direct experience.

The koan "Cultivate don't know mind" may seem confusing at first. Why should we seek to be ignorant? But this is not an encouragement to avoid knowledge. Don't know mind is one characterized by curiosity, surprise, and wonder. It is receptive, ready to meet whatever shows up as it is.

Before I had open-heart surgery, my son Gabe, who was in his late twenties at the time, visited me in the cardiac care unit of the hospital. We fell into a tender conversation, reminiscing about our relationship. Our sharing was filled with love, kindness, and laughter.

At one point, Gabe stopped talking and became quite serious. "Dad, are you going to live through this surgery?" he asked.

Now, I love my son beyond words, and so like any father, I wanted to reassure him that of course I would live, I would be just fine. But I paused for a moment, searching for the right response. I felt into my experience before answering. Then I heard myself say, "I'm not taking sides."

My answer surprised us both. What I meant was that I wasn't taking sides with life or death. Either way, I trusted that everything would be okay. I don't know where the words came from; they spilled from me without censorship. I wasn't trying to appear sage or to be a good Buddhist. Yet we both were reassured by my response. I think it was because we knew we were in the presence of the truth spoken with love.

We hugged, and Gabe went home with a promise to return in the morning.

As we go about our day-to-day lives, we rely on our knowledge. We have confidence in our ability to think through problems, to figure things out. We are educated; we have training in specific subjects that permits us to do our jobs well. We accumulate information through experience, learning as we go. All this is helpful and necessary in moving through our lives smoothly.

Ignorance is usually thought of as the absence of information, being unaware. Sadly, it is more than just "not knowing." It means that we know something, but it is the wrong thing. Ignorance is misperception.

Don't know mind represents something else entirely. It is beyond knowing and not knowing. It is off the charts of our conventional ideas about knowledge and ignorance. It is the "beginner's mind" Zen master Suzuki Roshi spoke of when he famously said, "In the beginner's mind there are many possibilities, but in the expert's there are few."

Don't know mind is not limited by agendas, roles, and expectations. It is free to discover. When we are filled with knowing, when our minds are made up, it narrows our vision, obscures our ability to see the whole picture, and limits our capacity to act. We only see what our knowing allows us to see. The wise person is both compassionate and humble and knows that she does not know.

This moment right here before us, this problem we are tackling, this person who is dying, this task we are completing, this relationship we are building, this pain and beauty we are facing—we have never experienced it before. When we enter a situation with don't know mind, we have a pure willingness to do so, without attachment to a particular view or outcome. We don't throw our knowledge away—it is always there in the background, ready to come to our aid should we need it—but we let go of fixed ideas. We let go of control.

Don't know mind is an invitation to enter life with fresh eyes, to empty our minds and open our hearts.

15

THE STORY OF FORGETFULNESS

A memory is a complicated thing,
a relative to truth,
but not its twin.

—BARBARA KINGSOLVER

Leroy was in his mid-seventies when we met. He had been a workingman throughout his adult life, mostly in steel mills. Big, black, and imposing, Leroy was accustomed to having his way. Now he had lung cancer with brain metastasis. Often confused, he lived in and out of time.

One night, I was feeding him mashed potatoes in his hospital room when he bellowed, "Lucinda, can't I get more gravy? You know I love your gravy, woman. Love to pour it on and lap it up." It took me a minute to realize he wasn't talking to the nurse, but to another woman, his dead wife.

The next moment, we were in his '53 Pontiac, cruising down a country road, headed to his favorite juice joint. Leroy was driving like a bat out of hell and shouting at me to turn up the volume on the radio.

Joining Leroy on his imagined journey was fun at first, but then I found myself feeling scared. It could have been that Leroy's disorientation triggered my own fear of dementia. But it seemed more basic than that. I believe it had something to do with my not being recognized. Not knowing where I fit in had a disruptive impact on my sense of reality. I began thinking that I should remind Leroy that he was a patient in the hospital and we were not in his Pontiac. I felt lost as Leroy kept hurtling down that country road in his beloved car. I just wanted to get out.

On the overhead speaker came an announcement: "Dr. Jeffrey, your car is blocking the entrance. Please report to the loading zone immediately."

I turned to Leroy and lied. I flat-out lied to this man. "Leroy," I said, "I'm sorry, but they are paging me. I have to move my car right away. I'm afraid I can't stay." I was out the door in a flash.

I was already standing in the parking lot under the stars before I realized how ridiculous my behavior had been. I had allowed my discomfort to consume me.

It's confusing to be around people who are confused. Their apparent irrationality and the absence of customary social patterns disturb us. We expect people to make sense.

We are so strongly identified with our rational-thinking minds that the idea of losing control is frightening to most of us. We are not nearly as concerned about the functioning of our spleens as we are about the ability of our brains to form understandable sentences. We say to our friends and family, "Anything but that, being demented or unable to think clearly. I would hate that." And it is this aversion to being out of control that leads us to distance ourselves from people who are confused. In our fear, we are the ones who withdraw, even from those we love.

In our reactivity to our own helplessness, we may get frustrated with our parents with Alzheimer's when they forget to take their medicine. We can't understand the garbled words of people who have suffered a stroke, and so we dismiss their concerns as ramblings. We stop trying to reach Grandma, who is curled up in her hospital bed in a fetal position, because we easily make the assumption that "no one is home."

My aunt Mimi was eighty years old when I visited her in a nursing home. A series of small strokes and the growing effects of age-related dementia had left her quite disoriented. Slouched in her wheelchair, she muttered to herself constantly, occasionally tossing her dress over her head. She called me by a variety of names, imagining I was different people from her past—a brother, a teacher, a colleague. It was impossible to have a real conversation.

I got curious. I wondered aloud why Aunt Mimi had never married. "Did you have a secret sweetheart?" I asked.

At that, Aunt Mimi gave me a commanding stare. Sitting straight up in her chair, she folded her arms defensively across her chest and, enunciating the words perfectly, said, "Some questions are too personal to ask!"

Surprised by her sudden moment of clarity, I simply nodded in agreement. We sat quietly together after that, holding hands throughout the afternoon.

To understand another's disorientation or confusion, we must start with our own. Feeling how difficult it is to be unable to make contact with another person is an excellent place to begin. What is it like to be lost in the moment, to not know what is happening, to be unable to connect?

Meeting this experience with kindness and acceptance enables us to imagine how isolating it can be for those who can't make themselves understood. We can feel empathy for their sense of loneliness, how frightened they might be. We can sense the shame of not being able to function "normally," and the tendency to want to conceal an illness from others. We can appreciate how we might lash out in anger or resist caregivers' efforts out of the desire to regain control over our own lives.

People with Alzheimer's or dementia are often unable to control their own behavior, even when they are trying as hard as they can. This means that neither you nor they can prevent problems from arising. However, the attitude that you bring to the encounter can impact their behavior. Their well-being often depends upon your well-being. If you are in a hurry or if you are irritable, people with dementia are likely to sense these feelings. Frequently, like small children, they become anxious and resistant. Your calm presence, accompanied by compassionate touch, can often provide a sense of order in the midst of chaos, a replacement for the internal structure they are missing. It's almost always reassuring to just sit quietly with people in this state.

Not long after bringing her demented mother home to live with her, Gillian walked into the living room to find her beloved books, including sacred Buddhist texts, scattered across the floor. Her mother announced, "I'm tired of all these dusty old books. I'm going to give them to my dentist."

Gillian was momentarily trapped by her anger. She scolded her mother's attendant. "How could you let this happen?"

The attendant, who was not caught up in the drama, replied, "Ma'am, today I pack the books up, and tomorrow I will unpack them. If this gives a sense of control to a woman who has lost so much, well, then, it's okay with me. It doesn't matter so much. I just like being with her."

Gillian suddenly saw her own powerful need to be in control of the situation, and this gave rise to compassion for her mother's experience of helplessness. The daughter sat down on the living room carpet and enjoyed spending time with her mother that afternoon, right there in the middle of the mess.

The next day, Gillian entered the living room to discover that the attendant had indeed returned the books to the shelves.

When I spend time with people who are living with dementia or Alzheimer's, I make an effort to look past the surface and see the whole individual. I sit without doing, making space to simply be present without the customary busyness or setting of agendas. I strive to meet people with acceptance, listening from the heart, withholding any judgments about their mannerisms or confusion. I cultivate don't know mind. From that place, I find that I can enjoy the often playful exchanges of language without worrying about logic, literal interpretations, or if what is being said is correct. For a little while, the gods of reason and rationality do not rule our interaction, and I find that quite relaxing. I also embrace the intense underlying emotions that often arise, as torrid and unpredictable as the fierce winds of a hurricane.

This allows me to see the entire nature of relationships in a fresh way. I realize how false our notions of autonomy and separateness are; I again recognize our inseparability and interdependence. I feel myself becoming more human.

And if, like me, you sometimes mess up and find yourself out in a parking lot overcome with anxiety, please be kind to yourself. We are only human, and we all make mistakes. Take a few deep breaths. Feel your body again. In caring for someone who is confused, we face our deepest fears. This can prove emotionally draining and physically exhausting. It is a time for mercy. Cultivating forgiveness and acceptance of ourselves is what allows us to extend the same to others.

The fear of losing our memories is a common one. I find it useful and even reassuring to recognize that, actually, we have been losing our memories all along.

I remember growing radishes in the garden at age five. I remember cracking a rib the next year after jumping off the chicken coop roof. I remember the vaulted ceilings of the ceramic studio above the garage where my father washed cars and the way I delighted in the colorful pots of glaze. I remember my mother's white seersucker dress, but wish I could remember her smell. Then, of course, there are the memories I wish I could forget, but can't.

In our rational world, we have an unquestioning faith in the efficacy of reason. We connect clear thinking with competency and worth. We associate memory with accuracy, and accuracy with truth, and truth with righteousness. How many times have you argued with a partner over whose memory of an incident is correct?

Husband: "You wore a red dress on our first date. You looked beautiful."

Wife: "Thank you, but my dress was purple. I know because I wrote about purple being my favorite color in my journal."

Husband: "Well, I remember those heels. I didn't know how you could walk in them."

Wife: "I am sure I wore sandals. You must be thinking of another girl-friend."

In reality, forgetfulness happens to us all. We don't need to be suffering from dementia or Alzheimer's in order to forget things, although this does naturally occur with greater frequency as we age. We absentmindedly walk into a room, then struggle to remember why we entered. A brief lapse in memory causes us to arrive late for an appointment. The car keys, a joke we heard the other day, the Spanish word for *dreams*—we begin to lose track of small bits of knowledge. And then even what used to be so important to us starts slipping away—memories we cherished, names of people we love. We forget more and more details as we move through life. Perhaps that is what scares us so much when confronted with other people's forgetfulness: we recognize that not only our memories, but even our lives will soon be forgotten.

Our brains are not computer hard drives. Human memory is not a simple matter of "accurate data in, accurate data out." It is a far more complicated, subtle, and beautiful process. Forgetfulness is actually built into the system. Memory has a "use it or lose it" quality. Brain scientists speak of memory transience—the way the brain gets rid of unused memories to make room for new ones. Often, people with severe amnesia cannot form short-term memories, forgetting information almost immediately. But we all are cleaning out the closets of our brains on a regular basis.

This means that memory is not objective, truthful, exact, or by any means permanent. Our memories are malleable constructs. One study demonstrated that every time we remember something, our brain networks change in ways that alter our recall of the original event. Like the old game of "telephone" we used to play as kids, small inaccuracies arise each time we remember something. These "errors" then become part of our experience. Eventually, the memory of an event can grow so imprecise that it becomes totally false.

After my heart surgery, I experienced significant cognitive deficits and memory loss. I would forget simple facts, confuse names, and transpose calendar dates. My nurse friends told me this is a common side effect for people who have been on heart bypass machines or endured long periods of time under anesthesia.

At first I found my memory loss embarrassing. I would tap my head with my fingers, hoping this would bring some bit of knowledge to the top of mind. I tried to hide my mistakes, and I was full of self-criticism when I got things wrong.

Eventually, however, I came to a place of acceptance about my forgetfulness. I felt more at ease when I told the truth about my memory loss without shame or blame. I accepted the fact that I probably would never be quite as mentally sharp as I had been before the procedure.

Truthfully, others are not always so tender with me. Some friends and colleagues get annoyed at my memory loss, my inability to understand a scholarly reference they make, or my need to use notes when giving a talk. They want the old reliable Frank back.

But I remind them that we all have always been forgetting. Our memories are constantly being rewritten. Memory fails. This is part of the process of being alive. Best, then, to focus on remembering what matters most. Not the details of dates or conversations, but that we are loved and that we are capable of loving others. When there is full acceptance of our not knowing, instead of fear, when we stop insisting that reality should be otherwise, then we can relax with things as they are.

When memories are taken as truth, they go unquestioned. That frequently leads to fixed assumptions, all-or-nothing thinking, which may have unintended consequences on future decisions. Bringing a sense of curiosity and open-ended inquiry to these assumptions may help us discover new ways of understanding old stories.

A very sweet old Italian woman named Rose stayed with us at the Zen Hospice Project. She checked in with a prognosis of seven weeks left to live. Seven months later, she was still with us.

Day after day, volunteers kept describing the same conversation with Rose. They would walk into her room and say, "Rose, how are you doing today?"

And she would say with a tone of resignation, "I just want to die." Always the same response.

This became a sort of running gag in the house until I told the volunteers, "We're not taking Rose seriously. We're laughing at her when we need to listen to exactly what she is saying."

The next morning, I walked up to her bed and said, "Rose, how are you doing today?"

And again she said, "I just want to die."

So I asked, "What makes you think that dying is going to be so much better?"

She looked at me as if to say, "What kind of a question is that to ask an eighty-year-old woman?"

But I pushed on. "You know, Rose, there are no guarantees that it's any better on the other side."

"Well, at least I'd get out," she replied.

"Out of what?" I asked.

And that question opened the floodgates. Rose began to tell me the story of her relationship with her husband. It became clear that, for as long as she could remember during their fifty years of marriage, Rose had always taken care of her husband—shopping for and cooking his meals, balancing his checkbook, buying and cleaning his clothes, and accommodating his moods. Now that she was sick, Rose couldn't imagine how her husband could possibly take care of her. She didn't want to be a burden. Better to go to strangers to be cared for, she thought. So she moved into the hospice.

After she shared her story, Rose and I spent some time talking. I suggested that she might consider sharing her feelings with her husband.

I wasn't there for their conversation. But three days later, Rose moved out of the hospice and returned home. She lived there for another six months before she died, her husband serving as her devoted caregiver.

I didn't provide Rose with a solution. I simply inquired about her experience, and that inquiry helped her question her assumptions. Rose then came to a new understanding of her life circumstances. She realized how wedded she had been to the notion that she had to care for her husband. By letting go of her attachment to this idea and cultivating don't know mind, a new option emerged, one she hadn't allowed herself to consider before—that she could ask her husband to care for her.

There is an old Yiddish saying: "Sometimes we need a story more than food." Telling our stories, and having others listen, is a powerful way to gain new understandings of and fresh perspectives on our lives.

Once we realize that we don't recall our memories with any reliable accuracy, then we can free ourselves to tell the stories we need to tell. Sharing our stories is not about nailing down the facts of an event or the exact recall of circumstances. Rather, the point of stories is to take the separated, isolated, broken pieces of our lives and, in the telling of them, produce moments of wholeness.

When we share our stories, we relax our need to interpret life events in a particular way. We open ourselves to don't know mind and allow a deeper part of ourselves to come forward and speak. In a way, what emerges is our souls' stories.

We cannot change an originating event that may have caused us pain, but we can absolutely change our reaction to what happened. We realize that when we dwell on and retell a story, this unquestioned recirculating of memories can lodge old suffering even more deeply in our minds, causing the present to be defined by our pasts. When we observe our present reactions with compassion, we are able to release ourselves from the grip of old wounds. We can impact how we think about events now by looking at our interpretations, shifting our perceptions, and discovering new meanings. We can become aware of the memories that were holding us back, and then we can let go.

Telling our stories allows us to pull back and see the big picture. We remember things differently and become more aware of certain details, the ones that we might not have noticed before. Often buried in an old story is the strength we need to accept our current situations. Healing requires more than just a change in story line, but the telling of a story can start a process. When we tell our stories, we heal. When someone listens to our stories, we heal.

Michael, a Zen Hospice Project volunteer, was an English teacher who understood the power of story. He loved to spend time with patients, encouraging them to share moments from their lives. They would tell Michael stories of their childhoods or speak to him of their dead relatives and express love. They spoke of regrets and shared hidden secrets, and they talked about how they might have done things differently if given a second chance. Some had imaginary conversations with God.

Michael would tape-record these exchanges. Later, at home, he would transcribe the tapes. Then he would craft beautiful, handmade storybooks, binding them with a leather cover that featured a photograph or image that highlighted an element from the story. He would gift wrap the books, tie the box up with a red ribbon, and give people back their stories in their own words.

These were such tremendous gifts. The books became legacies that patients left to their families and friends. Sometimes, if they had no family or friends, people would ask that their books be returned to Michael when they died, since he understood the importance of gracefully receiving another person's story.

One day, a teenager with green-and-purple hair, tattoos on his arms and legs, and piercings through his nose, ears, and cheeks showed up at Laguna Honda Hospital. He told the volunteer office that he had come to this predominantly geriatric hospital in the hopes of "helping old people."

The conservative volunteer coordinator took one look at him, handed him a long form to fill out, and said, discouragingly, "We'll call you if we have an assignment we think is right for you."

The young man hung his head low in rejection and turned to leave, when he bumped into our hospice doctor. The doctor asked where the boy was headed. The kid said, "Well, I wanted to volunteer to help old people, but they don't want me here."

The doctor got curious. He asked the young man what he might like to do with the "old people."

The teen pulled a small video camera from his backpack and said, "I like to make movies." So the doctor decided to invite him to visit our hospice unit.

It just goes to show that you never really do know, because it turned out that this punk kid was incredibly warmhearted, and he created one of the most amazing therapeutic interventions I've ever witnessed (even though I'm pretty sure he didn't have a clue what he was doing).

The young man asked each of the thirty-eight residents on our ward a simple question: "If you could leave the hospital for the day and go anywhere, where would you go?"

Grace said, "I would go to the beach. I love the sandpipers."

Sally said, "I'd go to Tiki Bob's piano bar, where I used to sing and see my old gang."

Chester said, "I'd go back to the house I grew up in."

So the kid went to all those places with his little video camera. At Ocean Beach, he filmed the waves burying his toes in the sand and the birds running along the water's edge. At Tiki Bob's, he asked if anybody remembered Sally. Then he filmed her old gang of salty sea dogs as they broke into a rendition of "Friends in Low Places." He went to Chester's boyhood home and somehow talked his way into the house. The current owners, cautious at first of this odd-looking young man, let him film their living room, Chester's old bedroom, and the treehouse that still stood in the backyard.

A few weeks later, we had a film festival at the hospital. Everybody got to watch the seven-minute videos this young guy had produced. They weren't very good films, technically speaking. The sound quality was poor, the colors were off, and sometimes people's heads were cut off by the way he framed the shots. But it didn't matter. All our residents got to see their films, and afterward, we invited them to share their stories while we all listened. We found threads of our own stories in everybody else's.

The kid disappeared the next day, and we never saw him again. Bodhisattvas are like that. They come, do their work, and move on.

Stories are a way we find meaning, but rarely a single meaning. Usually, there are layers of meaning. Maybe things are this way. But maybe they are not. This is where *don't know* can help us understand ourselves and each other better. When we are not so fixed in our views, stories can take us on a journey past plotlines or even facts to reveal a truth that we may have missed when we were only looking with our ordinary minds. Most real-life stories don't have clear beginnings and endings. But they do help us make sense of life and embrace its mystery. Through stories, we knit ourselves together as a family, a community, and a culture, joining ourselves with the larger human story.

Many spiritual traditions and most transpersonal psychologists point to dimensions of the mind that reach beyond conventional views of memory, past neural networks and synapses and the limiting idea that we are only thinking machines. Ancient Buddhist texts speak of a moment-to-moment continuum of our very subtle minds that has no beginning and no end, which is called *Mind Stream*. But even contemporary scientists agree that there is something more to the human mind, something subtler and more complex, which we often refer to as *consciousness*.

Harrison Hoblitzelle, or Hob as he was affectionately known, was a comparative literature professor, psychotherapist, and Buddhist teacher. A man of great kindness and good humor, he took immense pleasure in the life of the mind.

Even after being diagnosed with Alzheimer's, Hob continued to teach Buddhist practices. Sometimes while teaching, his memory would fail.

Jack Kornfield tells the story of a particular evening when Hob was giving a Buddhist dharma talk.

One evening, however, he found himself standing before a meditation group having forgotten who he was and why he was there. So he simply began to mindfully acknowledge out loud his experiences: "blank mind . . . curiosity, nervousness, calming, blank mind, loving feelings, warmer, less trembling, still uncertainty," and so on for several minutes. It was all he could do. He stopped, resting quietly, and bowed to the audience. They stood up and applauded in honor of his presence and his courage. It was, as several said, "among the finest teachings I have ever received." For a moment, Hob had transformed even Alzheimer's into freedom.

Hob's illness had made him confused. He lost certain cognitive capacities. But in that moment, he found a place of repose in consciousness. Thanks in no small part to his decades of training in mindfulness meditation, he could rest comfortably in don't know mind. He didn't actually have to know who he was, where he was, or what he was doing in order to sit back in awareness and observe the emotions and experiences at play. He was able to touch his present experience with curiosity and wonder.

When we cultivate don't know mind, we are not throwing out our knowledge. Hob's lifetime of experience allowed him to be in an intense state of not knowing; he was using his knowledge, but was not limited by the ignorance or the knowing.

Consciousness seems so familiar, yet it is at once challenging to describe, impossible to locate in the brain, and the subject of much debate. If I were to ask, "Are you aware now?" you would, likely without a thought, answer, "Yes." Even if we were experiencing dementia or suffering from Alzheimer's, still when asked, "Are you aware?" we would answer, "Yes."

So what do we mean?

Our resounding *yes* is based on our direct, intimate, and immediate experiences. We are not just what we think, what we say, or what we do and certainly not just what we remember. Those experiences don't define all that we are. Who we are is bigger than that. Awareness, our capacity to witness experience, is not just a cognitive function. Awareness is beyond thought, beyond feeling, beyond action. Our stories about who we are and what we know are only a contraction of consciousness. Witnessing or awareness is always present. We can take a stance within our experience, as with an emotional state or a judgment, or we can take a stance in non-reactive awareness.

Remember this, if you can: *everything* comes and goes in awareness. That is the ground of who we are. The rest is just smoke and mirrors.

16

NOT KNOWING IS MOST INTIMATE

Wisdom tells me I am nothing.
Love tells me I am everything.
Between the two, my life flows.

—NISARGADATTA MAHARAJ

The idea of don't know mind originates in a story about two Buddhist monks in ancient China: Fayan, a young wanderer, and Dizang, his teacher.

Dizang saw Fayan dressed in his traveling clothes and embarking on a journey.

Dizang asked, "Where are you going?"

Fayan responded, "On a pilgrimage."

Dizang asked, "What is the purpose of your pilgrimage?"

Fayan answered, "I don't know."

Dizang said, "Not knowing is most intimate."

Being a koan, this story is about more than just a pilgrimage in ancient China. The pilgrimage is a metaphor for daily life. It says something about our journeys, the way we can either wander around aimlessly, or get fixated on a certain destination. We could easily reframe Dizang's questions as, "Where are you going in your life? Why do you think being someplace else will be better than where you are now? What is the purpose of all this searching?"

Since we were children, people have asked us a similar question: "What do you want to be when you grow up?" As adults, when we first meet someone, usually one of the first questions they ask is, "What do you do for a living?" When we respond, we want to sound like we have it together. We want to be perceived as intelligent and focused. So we have our answers all lined up, perhaps even an elevator pitch about what we have done and what it is that we plan to achieve. The point is that we know things. And in our culture, knowing is power.

Now Fayan was a pretty smart guy, a mature student who had studied a lot of spiritual texts and practiced meditation for years. Surely he could have offered a more virtuous or impressive response to his teacher than "I don't know." But what is delightful about this story is that Fayan answered in an undefended way, with a kind of childlike innocence, saying, "I wish I knew, but honestly I can't tell you." Maybe he hoped his teacher had the answer. Maybe, like many of us, he imagined he had a destiny to fulfill and that a wise person could point him to the right path. But a good teacher doesn't tell you what to know, he or she shows you how to see.

This teacher, in a disarming way, replied, "That's fantastic, Fayan. It's great that you don't know. Not knowing is most intimate."

In Zen, the word *intimate* is synonymous with awakening, realization, or enlightenment. But all those words seem to imply a far-off, special state of mind or a supernatural, metaphysical, transcendent experience that somehow transports us to another dimension beyond life's day-to-day problems.

I prefer the word *intimacy* because it is an invitation to come closer, to fully embrace and lovingly engage with your life right where you are, rather than trying to move beyond it. It is a recognition that we already belong. To me, intimacy better expresses what I imagine enlightenment might actually feel like. It's relaxed, receptive, ordinary even. It is not found elsewhere, apart from life, but in the middle of it. As another Zen teaching says, "The path is right beneath your feet." Intimacy offers an encouragement to connect to the sound of the birds, the spring breeze, each other, and this very life, here and now.

We've all had moments when we discovered solutions to our problems without needing to "figure them out." We've said things like, "All of a sudden, it became clear," or "The answer just came to me," or "There was no question in my mind what I had to do." When we slow down enough to listen carefully, we can hear what the Quakers call "the still, small voice within," what we often refer to as our intuition. It is a quality of mind that senses what is needed without relying solely on rational processes.

When we don't know where we are going, we have to remain fully present, carefully feeling our way inch by inch, moment by moment. We have to stay close to our actual experiences. When we don't know, anything is possible because we are not limited by old habits of thinking or others' points of view. We see the bigger picture. Not knowing leaves room for wisdom to arise, for the situation itself to inform us.

At the deepest level of intimacy, subject and object fall away. There are no longer any hard and fixed boundaries. "I" am not intimate with "you." Our separateness dissolves. We experience undefended openness, complete union. This is the real heart and beauty of don't know mind.

In the days before his death, my friend John was in a kind of waking coma. His face was full of tension, his head thrust back, the muscles in his throat tight and constricted. Every breath was a struggle.

As I sat at John's bedside one night, I worried, wondering what to do.

A well-known Buddhist teacher with experience in such matters told me that John's spirit was trying to leave his body and that I should touch the top of his head to show it the way. So I did this, but nothing changed.

John's doctor phoned to say that I should increase the morphine a bit to relax John's breathing. So I did this, but nothing changed.

Later that evening, a bodyworker came by. He encouraged me to hold two special points on John's feet. The acupressure would relieve his tension. So I did this, but nothing changed.

All this knowing wasn't helping. So I turned inward. I let go of every-one's advice and my own fear, and I took a few deep breaths.

I began to sense an urge arising within me. Instinctively, I realized, I just wanted to wrap myself around this suffering man. Not something I would normally do. But I trusted my gut. I climbed into bed and cra-dled John in the curve of my arm. Rocking him back and forth, quite spontaneously, I started singing John sweet lullabies. Not the nursery rhyme variety, but the kind you make up as you go along. Words and sounds mixed together randomly, not making any sense at all. Love sounds, I call them. Every parent has done this for a sick or frightened child. And as I sang softly in John's ear and kissed his forehead, my hands knew what to do, although I had no goal in mind. My fingers gently ca-ressed his throat and stroked his face. My hands circled around his heart, very softly.

We lost all sense of time. I could feel John sink into me, my body cush-ioning what was left of his bony form. Eventually, his throat relaxed and his head came forward. His eyes opened for a moment. He looked relieved. Then he fell asleep.

Later, I wondered briefly if I had done the right thing. Had I pulled John back from a near-death state, stopped a spiritual process of release too soon? I don't know. But I do know that the heart has to be soft before any of us can be free.

In retrospect, I realized the problem underlying all the expert strate-gies I had employed prior to simply holding John: they all stemmed from the idea that what was happening to John was not okay. Those methods were aimed primarily at alleviating his symptoms. Along the way, John, the person, seemed to get lost. It wasn't until I became exhausted by the inefficacy of all of these strategies that I was willing to surrender, to let go of my preconceived ideas about what was supposed to happen. Then my mind relaxed, and my heart started to lead the way. I could see pos-sibilities that I hadn't recognized before. I could allow myself to move naturally, without any interference from my knowing mind. All I needed to do was listen and get out of my own way. And in doing that, I was able to honor and connect to John, who he really was and what he really needed in that moment. Not knowing is most intimate.

A willingness to not know is, at times, our greatest asset. The degree to which we are able to live in this ever-fresh moment—that's the measure of our ability to be of real service.

When Tom, a sweet young Zen Hospice volunteer, attempted to move JD, a resident, from the bed to the commode, Tom failed miserably. JD's toothpick legs collapsed from under him, and he tumbled to the ground. There he lay on the cold tile floor, his pajama pants down around his ankles, his diaper partway off, his arms tangled. Physically, JD was fine, but everything was a terrible mess. Tom was an absolute wreck. He phoned me, embarrassed and full of self-criticism, asking me to review the nursing procedures for positioning a frail person. Tom wanted to arm himself with more information so that he wouldn't "screw up the next time around."

Now, having trained Tom myself, I was quite certain he knew the procedures. What's more, I had a sense that more information would not settle the fear and doubt that were running rampant through his mind. Instead, I tried to address the heart of his concerns with a simple instruction. "Next time, before you move JD, check your belly. Notice if it is tight or contracted. Don't do anything until it is soft."

Tom responded with impatience. "Yeah, yeah, I know all that stuff, but how do I cross his legs? Are you supposed to move the lower body first, or the upper?"

I persisted. "Just check your belly. Feel the breath there and let it soften before you take action." Then I told him to phone me at the end of his shift.

Later that evening, Tom called back, enthusiastically saying, "I went to position JD, and the most amazing thing happened. As I leaned over the bed, I thought of what you said. I noticed that my belly was hard as a rock. I saw that I was scared. For a few moments, the fear seemed to course through my body. Then, with an inhale and exhale, it began to dissipate, and my belly softened. The next thing I knew, I was cradling

JD in my arms like he was a lover or a small child. Moving him to the commode was effortless. Everything happened so gracefully. I instinctively understood what to do. It was really lovely."

Not knowing is a gateway to a deeper appreciation of the potency of our basic nature, which cannot be known by the conceptual mind alone. It takes us beyond our ordinary way of thinking and seeing things, and into intimacy with this very moment.

One characteristic of all humans that death illuminates is our desire for security in an ever-changing world. We believe who we are and how things are for us should remain fixed and permanent. We want to know what the future will bring. Most of all, we don't want who we think we are to die.

When we take our personalities, our separate sense of self, to be all that we are, death becomes "the external other" that we fear. It threatens our long-held belief in the primacy of a bounded and unique identity. Who will "I" be without my familiar story of self? It's no wonder we are afraid of letting go. We don't know anything else but this all-powerful "me." We cling to the known, and we fear entering into the unknown.

Watch children in a playground swinging from the monkey bars. They move freely, letting go of one rung and reaching for the next in a fluid motion. Have you ever noticed adults on the same structure? Rarely happens. But when it does, you'll see that they maintain a tight grip on one bar and won't let go until they have a good hold on the next.

Even with superficial reflection, we can see that our attempts to make ourselves solid, separate things opposes the way reality works. When we mistakenly attempt to pull ourselves out of the river of change, we wind up feeling increasingly alone, isolated, and afraid. This causes a great deal of suffering at the time of our dying, but also right now in the middle of our lives today. In the end, pursuing security leaves us feeling even more insecure.

We are in a fight against nature.

Reality cannot be mapped. It is beyond description or any one view. It is not a single static truth, but rather an endless, unfolding mystery. It is alive, dynamic, and constantly being expressed through form and formlessness.

The Heart Sutra is one of Buddhism's most renowned, beautiful, and confounding teachings. Its most central lines read:

> Form is emptiness; emptiness itself is form;
> Emptiness is no other than form;
> Form is no other than emptiness.

The words are almost incomprehensible upon first reading. The first time my son encountered this teaching, he said, "Dad, is this gobbledygook what you talk to people about on your meditation retreats? This is what you do for a living?" It made me laugh.

But if we stick with it, we can see that the sutra describes the nature of our minds and of reality quite accurately. Just as we cannot pull life and death apart, neither can we separate form and emptiness. They are a package deal, always arising together.

Emptiness is a difficult word for most Westerners. We normally associate empty with deficiency, sterility, a void. Most of us relate more easily to the words openness, spaciousness, or better still, boundlessness. I like to think of emptiness as an open expanse, a field with no edges that is not limited by any concepts.

Think of how, upon walking into a large room, we first notice the objects in it: the tables, chairs, sofa, artwork, and lamps. But with a bit more attention, we might observe how the light is shifting from moment to moment. We become aware of the space that surrounds and holds the objects as they abide in it.

Similarly, when we look at our minds, first we see the objects in it— our thoughts, feelings, memories, daydreams, plans, as well as the sensations coming to us from our bodies, our perceptions of the events that are happening to us. A little bit more reflection reveals that we are cognizant of these activities in our minds because they are occurring in the open space of awareness. This awareness is always there; we just don't normally pay attention to it because we're preoccupied with the objects, our perceptions, and emotions—just as when we walk into the furnished room, our attention went to the tables and chairs, not the empty space. So we could say that the open space of our boundless awareness, which contains the "forms" of our thoughts and perceptions, is "empty."

The funny thing is we usually think of forms as permanent. They are what we turn to in our search for security. Yet upon closer examination, we discover that even the forms themselves are empty, impermanent. Our ideas, fantasies, and physical sensations—we may think of these as solid things, but they are more like bubbles. They appear for a while, then dissolve. They come, they go. Just like us. Just like everything in the universe. We exist, and then we don't. Each life, each occurrence, each feeling, every lovemaking, every breakfast, every atom, every planet, every solar system is fleeting. Every form takes its turn on the wheel of living and dying.

Emptiness, on the other hand, is never ending. Emptiness, in fact, gives birth to form. Emptiness makes everything possible.

Jennifer Welwood, a psychotherapist, author, and dedicated Buddhist practitioner, writes about the "poetic beauty" of form and emptiness in an insightful essay. She states:

> In both the inner and outer worlds, whenever we look deeply into emptiness, we discover form; and whenever we look deeply into form, we discover emptiness. This is the sense in which form and emptiness are inseparable, indivisible, and nondual. In tantric language, we could say that they are lovers joined in eternal embrace—distinct yet not separate; not one, not two . . .
>
> Taking ourselves to be some kind of solid form, we see emptiness as something that could undermine or annihilate us. Rather than recogniz-

ing emptiness as our own nature, we see it as an enemy that we have to
avoid or defeat. And we see form as something that we have to fabricate
or defend or promote. So when we fail to recognize the non-duality of
form and emptiness, they become divided, and rather than being insepa-
rable from one another as lovers, they become opposed to one another as
antagonists. We have to avoid emptiness and we have to fabricate form.

When we take ourselves to be separate, solid forms, death becomes
the enemy. Death is the emptiness that threatens our forms. We can relax some when we realize that our true nature is open, spacious, and
boundless and that flowing through that huge valley of emptiness is a
river of constant change.

Emptiness need not scare us because it doesn't mean complete noth-
ingness, that we don't exist or that we don't have any value or that we
are not each unique, beautiful individuals. We are all of that. It's just that
we don't exist apart from everything else. We are a tentative expression
of the great field of seamless emptiness. Emptiness is not some kind of
heaven or absolute reality apart from us. It is a fertile boundlessness
from which all form perpetually arises. But no individual or thing has a
separate independent existence; emptiness is woven through the fabric
of all life. Without emptiness we would never have arrived here in the
first place.

The great Tibetan master Kalu Rinpoche famously wrote, "We live
in the illusion and appearance of things. There is a reality. You are that
reality. When you understand this, you will see that you are nothing.
And being nothing, you are everything. That is all."

The story of Tommy and his mother, Ethel, is a good illustration of
form and emptiness at play in the world. Ethel had brain cancer. She came
to live with us at the Zen Hospice Project when caring for her at home
became more than her family could manage. Her son, Tommy, had Down
syndrome. Although he was in his young teens, his emotional and psychological development were similar to those of a six-year-old child.

He visited his mother frequently, and we came to enjoy each other's company. Over the months, we developed a certain level of trust.

The morning Ethel died, I called her husband, Peter, Tommy's father, and asked if he would like to bring the family to be with Ethel's body.

"What should I do about Tommy?" Peter asked. I suggested that he bring Tommy along. Peter hesitated, explaining that first he wanted to talk with Tommy's therapist about it.

A while later, Peter called back. "The therapist doesn't think it's a good idea. She told me that when she was a little girl, she went to a family funeral and was forced to kiss her dead grandfather. She thinks exposing a child to a dead body might be too traumatic." He paused for a moment, then added, "I don't know what to do because Tommy is asking to see his mother."

"Why don't you bring Tommy and invite his therapist to come, too?" I suggested.

An hour later, the hospice doorbell rang. There stood Peter, Tommy, his therapist, and a few other family members. Tommy had a small Instamatic camera dangling from around his neck.

"Hi, Tommy," I said. "I see you have your camera. What do you want to take pictures of today?"

He smiled. "You, Mr. Buddha, and my mom." So we went to the living room, where Tommy took photos of me and the big Buddha statue. Then we went upstairs to Ethel's room.

Everyone was quite apprehensive. How would Tommy react to seeing his dead mother? He and I walked hand in hand to her bedside. He spontaneously reached over the bed rail and kissed his mother on the forehead, as he had done on most every visit. Then Tommy turned and looked at me, not with fear, but with innocent curiosity, and asked, "Where has all that gone?"

Form and emptiness. What was animated and full of life before was now empty. Tommy could sense the absence of Ethel, even though her body was still present. A silence fell over the room. Most of the adults squirmed nervously, trying to imagine how to respond.

I said what I usually do. "I don't know, Tommy," I said. "What do you think?"

Tommy thought about it for a minute before launching into an animated description born from his imagination. The story of what might have happened to his mother included images of a butterfly emerging from a cocoon and scenes from the popular movie *Terminator 2*, in which human forms morph from one shape into another.

The adults exhaled and relaxed. They could see that Tommy was not frightened. In fact, he was incredibly curious about what was absent. We drank tea and Coca-Cola as we visited in a natural way.

Before the family left, I asked if Tommy and I could spend a few minutes alone with Ethel. I sensed his need to be with his mother one last time. Since we had built up so much trust over time, Peter agreed.

Once the room had cleared, Tommy moved to his mother's bedside again and asked a few more questions.

"When you are dead, can you feel?" he asked.

"I don't know if dead people can feel, Tommy, but can you feel your mom?"

"Yes, I can," he responded. "But she's not moving."

"Yeah, when people die, they don't breathe or eat or talk anymore," I said. My simple, matter-of-fact answers seemed to satisfy him for the moment. Then I said, "Tommy, if there's anything you want to say to your mom or do for your mom, now would be a really good time."

I watched as Tommy gently touched his mother's arm, feeling its texture and changing temperature. After a moment, he did the sweetest and most remarkable thing. Leaning over his mother's body, he smelled her from head to toe. It reminded me of watching a whitetail deer fawn once on a country road. The fawn's mother had been hit by a car. The young deer moved tenderly, sniffing her mother's body with curiosity. Tommy's movements had a similar, almost primitive feel. They were completely uncensored.

Of course, Tommy would still need to grieve and take time to understand the loss of his mother. But in this moment, there was nothing more that needed to be done or said. Tommy's way of knowing was visceral and palpable. I doubt many grown-ups would ever allow themselves that sort of intimacy with death.

I wondered, what if death could be as natural for adults in our culture as it was for Tommy?

Suppose we became more intimate with form and emptiness in everyday life?

17

SURRENDER TO THE SACRED

Now is the season to know that
everything you do is sacred.

—HAFIZ

The sacred makes surprise appearances.

Walking the gauntlet of thirty beds on the long single hospice ward at Laguna Honda Hospital, I noticed Isaiah out of the corner of my eye. An African-American man raised in Mississippi, Isaiah was actively dying. His breathing was labored, and he was sweating up a storm. I sat down next to him.

"You look like you're working really hard," I said.

Isaiah raised his arm, pointed to the distance, and said, "Just gotta get there."

"I forgot my glasses. I can't see that far in the distance. Tell me what you see."

Isaiah described a bright green pasture and a long hill leading to a grassy plateau.

I asked, "If I promise to keep up, can I come?"

He grabbed my hand tight, and Isaiah and I started climbing together. His breathing got shorter, and he perspired more with every step. It was a long walk. Not an easy one.

"What else do you see?" I asked.

He described a one-room red schoolhouse with three steps leading up to a door.

My training informed me that Isaiah was disoriented to time and location. I could have told the old man that his visions were likely being caused by brain metastasis and morphine. I could have reminded him that we were in a ward at Laguna Honda Hospital. But that was only true on the most superficial level.

The deeper truth was that we were walking to a little red schoolhouse.

I asked, "Do you want to go in?"

Isaiah sighed. "Yeah. I've been waitin'."

"Can I go with you?" I asked.

"Nope."

"Okay, then, you go," I said.

A few minutes later, Isaiah died quite peacefully.

To know the sacred is not to see new things, but rather to see things in a new way. The sacred is not separate or different from all things; it is hidden in all things. And dying is an opportunity to uncover what is hidden.

The beloved Zen master Thich Nhat Hanh uses a simple exercise to illustrate this point. He holds up a blank sheet of white paper and asks the audience to name what they see.

Most respond, "White paper."

Children and poets answer more creatively. They say, "Clouds, rain, and trees."

Because as Thich Nhat Hanh says, "Without clouds, there will be no rain; without rain, trees cannot grow; and without trees, we cannot make paper. And if we continue to look, we can see the logger who cut the tree and brought it to the mill to be transformed into paper. And we see the wheat. We know that the logger cannot exist without his daily bread, and therefore the wheat that became his bread is also in this sheet of paper. And the logger's father and mother are in it, too. When we look in this way, we see that without all of these things, this sheet of paper cannot exist. Looking even more deeply, we can see we are in it, too."

This is a way of expressing our deep belonging and interdependence with everyone and everything. This is a way of understanding that the sacred is not something apart from us. It is here with us in every moment.

The sacred has always existed. Everything is saturated with it. It is the nature of reality. Yet most of the time, we walk around in the sacred world with ordinary vision. It is as though we are color-blind, unable to clearly distinguish the different hues of the spectrum; we don't always perceive or distinguish the sacred. We don't appreciate the full breadth of its beauty. We see in a conditioned way, staying on the surface of life. When we pay attention, however, we realize that the sacred reveals itself continuously.

The word *sacred* is a symbol that points to the unnamable. The sacred cannot be fully described. All we can do is speak of certain qualities that characterize its presence, its influence on consciousness, and the ways in which we can access it.

Literally, *sacred* means "to make holy." The root, *sacra*, also means "to set apart what is highly valued or important." In the Jewish tradition, the room known as the Holy of Holies was the innermost and most sacred area of the tabernacle of Moses. It housed the golden Ark of the Covenant, which contained the holy tablets etched with the Ten Commandments. No ordinary person could enter. Only the holiest person, the high priest, could enter this holiest place on earth, and then only once a year, on the holiest day of the year. In the Catholic church where I served as an altar boy, the tabernacle had two golden doors. It was located on the highest altar and housed the Holy Eucharist, said to be the dwelling place of Christ. Only an ordained priest could open those golden doors.

If we were not taught the deeper meaning of these traditions, practices, and metaphors, we might erroneously assume that we lack the qualifications to know the sacred. We might believe that the sacred can

only be accessed by special people with special training at special times. But ordinary people, like you and me, can and do regularly experience the sacred in myriad ways and forms, including visions of little red schoolhouses.

Uluru, also known as Ayers Rock, is a massive sandstone formation in central Australia. It is a stone unlike any other, emerging majestically out of a flat plain. The aborigines of the area don't worship the stone, for the stone is more than a stone to them. They recognize it as a manifestation of the sacred. When we stand in reverence before Uluru, at Chartres Cathedral, atop the Inca citadel of Machu Picchu, or in the stillness of a redwood grove, we may feel that we are standing on sacred ground.

I cannot explain why human beings have made pilgrimages to such sites for thousands of years. Perhaps we need to attribute the power of the sacred to a place, an object, or a person in order to make it more real, more accessible. Perhaps these places are doorways, portals that somehow aid our perceptions. Who can say? The most important questions frequently remind us to live with them, not reaching too early for conclusions.

Regardless, it is clear that we all go to certain places to still our busy minds, such as the seashore, mountaintops, and monasteries. Sometimes we find stillness in a brief, uninterrupted moment on the couch. Intention and attention increase our chances of contacting the sacred. But recognition that the sacred is present may also arise suddenly and spontaneously, as it did with Jacob when, according to the biblical tale, he awoke from a deep sleep and said, "Surely the Lord is in this place, and I did not know it."

Our response to the sacred might include joy, ecstasy, inspiration, inclusiveness, expansiveness, and a feeling of reverence, as if we have encountered what is holy in life. It is evident and unmistakable. Sometimes the experience has an intensity or density that is palpable. We may sense an inner stillness, as if the momentum we have counted on to keep us moving through life is no longer needed. The urge to do, fight, or control is released into non-doing. We come to a recognition that who we are is inseparable from stillness and the silence it introduces.

Zoe worked as a packer for a clothing manufacturer prior to moving into the Zen Hospice residence. Her favorite pastime was watching staged wrestling on TV. Advanced liver disease had caused jaundice, turning her skin yellow. The buildup of fluids made her belly swell, and due to the discomfort, she lost her appetite and stopped eating.

Yet despite feeling pretty miserable, Zoe maintained a buoyant spirit. The disease caused severe drowsiness, and so she slept sixteen hours each day. In the final weeks of her life, she moved into still deeper states of sleep that often would last a day or two, making for what I called "practice runs at dying."

When Zoe returned to the surface of consciousness, she would share what had occurred on these dreamlike journeys. Once, she described a visit to a place of utter peacefulness, remarking, "If I had known silence was that beautiful, I would have spent a lot more time in quiet during my life."

Deep silence is not merely a pause between sounds. It is an inner quietness felt in the heart, still as new-fallen snow on a mountain pass. This silence strips us of both belief and disbelief. It takes us beyond the known, beyond language, and into the sacred.

Silence is a natural response to the presence of the sacred no matter where it appears. Through silence, we become aware of the majesty in the ordinary; the beauty, the unity, and the depth of the sacred that is always around us and within us.

Birth is among the most real, honest, and unglamorous of human events, common to us all. Yet anyone who has witnessed a child being born cannot help but feel a reverent hush in the emerging presence of new life. In the midst of the mess of blood and tears, the pain, the emotional intensity, the shouts and chaos, there is beauty, unbounded joy, and an awesome power and authenticity expressed by the woman giving birth.

Childbirth is an invitation to enter the sacred. The key that unlocks its door is love, a love unlike any we may have known before. Ask any mother.

Death offers us the same invitation. In fact, birth and death come very close to one another. It's difficult for us to say precisely when life begins or ends. Both can be times of great aliveness. Both ask us to accept our vulnerability, to be open to the unexpected, and to let go of life as we have known it.

Both birth and death can serve as portals to the sacred. Or not.

For many, death is utterly mundane, a purely biological event, a matter of physical science devoid of any mystery. Some people's dying time is spent watching the *Wheel of Fortune* game show on TV. That's okay with me; I've become very good at the puzzles. For some, death is full of tragedy. But for others, dying is a time of spiritual transformation that takes them beyond personal identity, bringing forward a sense of absolute safety, fearlessness, and even perfection in the face of the unknown. In the dying process, many ordinary people come to know themselves as what I can only call "an undying love."

A Gallup survey showed that "people overwhelmingly want to reclaim and reassert the spiritual dimensions in dying." But this doesn't necessarily mean that they want more religion or beliefs thrown at them. It means that they are seeking more than the mastery of modern medicine.

Spiritual support is not a matter of esoteric practices and existential discussions. It can be as simple as offering our kind and reassuring presence or chicken soup made with affection. At Zen Hospice Project, we adopted the view that when people are dying, they need intensive care—intensive love, intensive compassion, and intensive presence. Ultimately, spiritual support is the fearless commitment to honor the individual's unique way of meeting death.

Early on in the dying process, people often need help discovering what has value and purpose in life. Without meaning, life becomes mechanical, empty, soulless, too small for human beings to exist. Victor Frankl identified self-transcendence as an indispensable human capacity for meaningful living when he wrote, "Man is not destroyed by suffering; he is destroyed by suffering without meaning."

Death comes to all. Whether we like that fact or not, it is certain to happen. Instead of avoiding this truth, it is useful to understand its meaning. Facing our own mortality can shift our priorities and values, and profoundly change our views of reality. Sometimes adversity is what helps us to discover our strengths, just as dying can help us discover the beauty in life. There is a commitment in the act of accepting death that can help us move from tragedy to transformation. Suffering is suffering. We can't always explain it, let alone control it. But we can meet it with compassion. We can meet it with presence, look at it directly, understand it, and perhaps find meaning in our relationship to it. Meaning isn't about assigning a cause. Meaning has a way of strengthening us; it builds resilience and enables us to confront suffering without running away.

Of course suffering isn't necessary in order for us to find meaning. Some people discover meaning through activities such as making art, listening to music, being in nature, journaling, and storytelling. Others find meaning through relationship—the joy of companionship, the legacy of gift giving, reminiscing with loved ones about old times, or healing estranged friendships with forgiveness. At some point, however, meaning loses its importance to people who are dying. They withdraw from the external world as they are pulled into a more inward journey. If we—their well-intentioned friends, family members, and caregivers— keep distracting them by pulling them back to the world of time, objects, and meaning, we may break their connection to the flow of the sacred. Grandma doesn't want to talk anymore about her first kiss on the Ferris wheel at the county fair. Playing your father's favorite song no longer sends him into a reverie about his wedding day. Auntie Ellen's heroic expedition to Antarctica, which was once the defining adventure of her life, fades in importance.

Remember the stillness and quiet I referenced that we feel at places that are doorways to the sacred, like Chartres Cathedral or a grove of redwoods? Now imagine several tour buses suddenly arrived and two hundred tourists disembarked with their cameras and loud voices, swarming through the place. Our attention would be sidetracked by the commotion. While the sacred would still be present, we might temporarily lose our connection with it. When caregivers and loved ones appear with their own agendas, memories, and needs, they become like the annoying tourists—an unpleasant distraction to those who are dying. But it need not be that way. As loved ones and caregivers, we can choose instead to act as quiet companions or trustworthy guides as the person who is dying journeys deeper into the sacred forest.

It is common for people at the time of dying to demonstrate distressing physical symptoms, mental agitation or grogginess, and emotional turmoil. In order to care for them, we must effectively address the pain, appropriately manage the symptoms, and attend to any disturbing issues. This requires mastery. However, if we bring only technology and medical expertise to the service of the dying, we will miss its holy significance. We may even interrupt an opportunity for growth and transformation.

Dying happens on two levels simultaneously—the physical and the spiritual. The body is closing down, while the consciousness is opening up. In order to compassionately companion the dying, ideally we attend to both processes at once. It can prove challenging for one person to manage all this. I find it difficult even with three decades of experience. That is why I often find it valuable to have more than one person in the room. One cares for the physical needs of the individual; the other accompanies the person on a spiritual journey.

Jennifer was dying after a long and difficult course of lung cancer. Laurie, a remarkable nurse, gave her undivided attention to Jennifer's body. Laurie breathed with Jennifer through her shortness of breath, dabbing her cracked lips with a moist sponge and attending to all of Jennifer's physical symptoms with skill and love.

Sitting at Jennifer's bedside, I settled into my own body and came closer to myself, to the unperturbed silent awareness that rested under the agitation. Quieting my mind, I evoked the compassion in my heart.

I attuned with presence to Jennifer's state of being, to her changing consciousness, allowing it to impress itself upon my own. I remained present, clear, and calm, attempting to meet whatever occurred with equanimity. Undistracted by the superficial, I sensed that Jennifer's essential self already had embarked on the journey. We traveled together, just as Isaiah and I did to the schoolhouse. I was honest with myself about my limitations. I knew that I could only accompany her so far. I offered her the spaciousness of my mind.

I did not know how Jennifer should die. Death is unknown and timeless. We discover it moment to moment. So I did my best not to interfere. I trusted in the wisdom of compassion, that our loving hearts would be our reliable guides. Just as two midwives had helped my son Gabe to take his first breath, Laurie and I helped Jennifer take her last.

Sitting next to Jennifer that day, I was reminded of a poem by Antonio Machado, which beautifully expresses for me how, while those who are dying might appear agitated on the surface, internally they can be quite still.

> *No my soul is not asleep.*
> *It is awake, wide awake.*
> *It neither sleeps nor dreams but watches,*
> *its clear eyes open,*
> *far off things, and listens*
> *at the shores of the great silence.*

It is not uncommon for people to emerge from a deep sleep or semi-coma state and tell me that they remember being with me at such times. Often, they thank me for being with them without interference. This nonverbal contact, being to being, is at the heart of healing. The felt sense of shared presence with another human helps us to appreciate that awareness is not ours alone, that it extends and continues beyond our separate selves. Objects, experiences, and even people come and go in awareness. Awareness is the background where there is no change. All change happens against it. Awareness is like a movie screen that knows what is being projected onto it.

Normally, we only see the suffering of impermanence, the coming and going of constant change, the coming together and falling apart, without realizing that all this appears and disappears on the background of perfect harmony. When we take what in Zen is called the "backward step," we can look from the vantage point of open awareness, we know ourselves to be this background, this pure, bare awareness, against which all personal and universal change occurs. This is what we surrender to.

I have witnessed an increasing radiance as ordinary people with no spiritual practice become transparent to their essential nature. It is similar to the process of transformation that occurs for meditation practitioners after decades of contemplative practice.

The potential these experiences have shown me is undeniable. Without a doubt, dying holds an unmatched possibility for transformation. It can be inspiring and awesomely beautiful. And it can also be intense, messy, and complicated. Even in dying, we are impacted by conditions beyond our control.

Medical technology has dramatically altered the dying experience. The idea of a "natural death" is slowly vanishing from our culture, having been replaced by a more antiseptic, institutionalized death managed by medical professionals. There are wonderful benefits to modern treatments and interventions. However, there are also serious drawbacks. Witness the advances in life support, where the line between who is alive and who is dead has become increasingly hazy.

It seems we can't resist meddling with the experience of death both technologically and philosophically. Idealized notions of a "good death" or a "dignified death" are equally troubling. They can blind us to what is actually happening, causing us to override the unpleasant and trample the sacred. Arbitrary standards about things "going according to plan" exert enormous pressure on dying people, adding guilt, shame, embarrassment, and a sense of failure to an already challenging process. Dignity is not an objective value. It is a subjective experience. Care with dignity promotes self-respect, honors individual differences, and supports people in the freedom to live their lives and their deaths according to their personal wishes.

When we interfere, we may miss out on or even interrupt the subtler dimensions of the dying experience. No matter how noble our intentions, we need to resist the temptation to act on our own biases or impose our well-meaning advice or spiritual beliefs on people who are dying.

Hannah was a Christian scientist with a deep and unwavering faith in God. At ninety-three, she had arrived at a place of acceptance of her death. She told me that her image of death was "to rest in the lap of Jesus."

Hannah's well-meaning granddaughter, Skye, came to visit. Skye shared that she had been reading a number of books on near-death experiences. According to these books, at the time of death, people are often greeted by their deceased relatives. Skye said, "Grandma, you don't have to worry, because when you die, everyone you know who died before you will be there to meet you."

When she heard this, Hannah became terrified of dying. The secret she had never shared with her family was that her husband, Edgar, had physically abused her for a good portion of their married life. He had died five years before. The idea of meeting Edgar again "on the other side" and spending eternity with him filled Hannah with desperation.

A contemplative approach to dying includes ways of being such as mindfulness, warmth, authenticity, stability, and generous listening. This allows us to enter the question of dying without so many answers. Being with dying calls for humility, acceptance, and a willingness to let go of control.

In the process of dying, a gradual awakening occurs. Almost imperceptibly, we begin a long, slow process of letting go, relinquishing what we know we can no longer hold on to or control.

Letting go is an entry into unknown territory. Grief is the toll that we pay. Tears are the fluids that ease the release.

In dying, we cannot hold on to our treasured possessions. One hospice resident, Brian, taught me this when he wept and then gracefully gave away his Gibson Les Paul guitar. "We are not what we have," he said. "And anyway, there are no storage units in heaven."

As we lose our ability to engage in our favorite activities, we must let go of traveling or cooking or making love, and then even simpler pleasures like swallowing without difficulty. We relinquish the roles we played in our families, workplaces, and communities and release the dreams we have carried with us for a lifetime but never achieved. In our dying, we must even let go of the future and everything and everyone that we loved.

Letting go is how we prepare for dying. Suzuki Roshi said that renunciation is not giving up the things of the world, but accepting that they go away. An acceptance of impermanence helps us learn how to die. It also reveals the flip side of loss, which is that letting go is an act of generosity. We let go of old grudges, and give ourselves peace. We let go of fixed views, and give ourselves to not knowing. We let go of self-sufficiency and give ourselves to the care of others. We let go of clinging and give ourselves to gratitude. We let go of control and give ourselves to surrender.

Surrender is not the same thing as letting go. Normally, we think of letting go as a release often accompanied by a sense of freedom from previous restraints. Surrender is more about expansion. There is a freedom in surrender, but it is not really about setting something down or distancing ourselves from an object, person, or experience, as it is with letting go. With surrender, we are free because we have expanded into a spaciousness, a boundless quality of being that can include but not be constrained by the previously limiting beliefs that once defined us, keeping us separate and apart. We release the fruitless habit of clinging to changing objects as a source of happiness. In surrender, we are reconstituted. We are no longer enslaved by our pasts. No longer imprisoned by our former identities. We become intimate with the inner truth of our essential nature. In surrender, we feel ourselves not gaining distance, but rather coming closer.

Surrender means moving into flow. I remember watching my father float in the Atlantic Ocean. He seemed to disappear into the sea. All I could see was his soft, white belly rising and falling on the waves. You cannot float if you hold on too tightly.

Surrender happens when we stop fighting. We stop fighting against ourselves. We stop fighting with life. We stop fighting with death. Surrender is a state in which resistance of any kind ceases to occur. We no longer put up any defense.

I'm not convinced that surrender is a choice. It seems involuntary. It feels to me like an inescapable undertow or karmic thread drawing us home. Qualities that engender surrender include faith, love, religious conviction, confidence in acquired wisdom, a sense of awe, and also something far more common—exhaustion.

Once, while river rafting on one of America's wildest rivers, I was thrown overboard into a whirlpool. I did all the wrong things. I tried to swim at the edge of the whirlpool, imagining that I could somehow hoist myself out of the water as I might on the side of a swimming pool. My companions threw me ropes and shouted instructions, but I kept fighting the force of the whirlpool, trying to escape. I quickly became exhausted. Eventually, I was defeated.

The whirlpool took me down into a watery chaos. I was tossed around by a power much larger than me. It was relentless. I did not experience a gentle letting go into the light. I was terrified, filled with despair, and fighting for survival. I felt like I was breaking apart.

At one point, I no longer had the energy to fight. This was the moment when surrender entered. I had an experience that many people describe just before they're in a car accident. Time stood still, and I could see clearly the distinct details of my surroundings, even in the turbulence of the muddy waters. Chaotic patterns shifted into a perceived order. I felt a growing sense of ease, some kind of mercy, and then a complete

release. Consciousness was no longer confined to form. The river sucked
me down, dragged me along the bottom, and spit me out in an eddy
downstream. When I emerged, I felt like I had a new set of eyes. I could
see my life in a fresh way, with pristine clarity.

I would not call this a near-death experience. However, my encounter with total surrender has helped me come closer to the reality experienced and described by patients who are dying. I have a sense of what
Barbara meant when she said, "I am no longer in charge." I could relate
to the ease in Ruth's voice when she told me, "Now I just fall back into
the breath, and it catches me." I recognized the smile in Joshua's eyes
when he almost sang, "Got no more worries. I'm just resting my head
in the hands of Jesus."

Surrender is infinitely deeper than letting go. Letting go is still a strategy of the mind occupied with the past. It is an activity of the personality,
and the personality is primarily concerned with perpetuating itself.
Letting go is still *me* making a choice. Ego cannot surrender. Surrender
is the effortless, easeful non-doing of our essential nature without interference. We are simply aware.

Surrender is more like an initiation, in which the dispensable is sacrificed to the essential. While we may resist, our fighting ultimately
proves ineffective. The dissolution of the false will naturally stimulates
a sense of fear, and the voices in our heads tell us to pull back. But the
sacred is so magnetizing, the surrender so compelling, that fear does not
stop us. In time, the struggle ceases. Our consciousness recognizes that
the power we feel, once so terrifying, is our own deep being. We surrender to the reality of non-separation.

Surrender is the end of two and the opening to the one.

Epilogue

DYING INTO LIFE

The breeze at dawn has secrets to tell you.
Don't go back to sleep.
You must ask for what you really want.
Don't go back to sleep.
People are going back and forth across the doorsill
Where the two worlds touch.
The door is round and open.
Don't go back to sleep.

—RUMI

Dying is a stripping-away process, a release, a surrender, a change that
holds profound possibilities. Change, like death, is inevitable. We have
seen that transience is in the nature of all experience. Yet change itself
does not guarantee transformation.

Transformation is a deep internal shift through which our basic
identities are reconstituted. It is a metamorphosis, as radical as the
caterpillar's movement from chrysalis to butterfly. In the process of
transformation, the scales fall from our eyes, and we see and experience
everything in a new way. We realize that we are more than our stories.
Limiting personal boundaries dissolve. A deep peacefulness and universal sense of belonging infuse our awareness. The expansive freedom of

being is beyond our current understanding and almost unrecognizable to our former selves.

The transformation of consciousness, which is possible for each of us in our day-to-day lives, requires our active engagement. We cannot think our way through it. It is not a strategic plan that we execute. Transformation requires an open-ended willingness to be fully vulnerable to the experience of the unknown.

Fundamentally, death is perhaps the greatest unknown. And our relationship to that unknown is worthy of our attention. I once asked a Chinese woman named Shu-Li, who was dying of a strange form of cancer, what she thought it might be like after she died.

Shu-Li answered, "When I was young and immigrating to America alone, I could see pictures of the cities, the countryside, the buildings. I could read books and watch movies about the people in America, their food and lifestyles. I had a sense of what it might be like here. But the reality was different than I imagined." Then she added, "I have no more images. Living with the uncertainty of my illness has prepared me for death. It seems to me that most people are afraid of death because they don't know how to be with the unknown."

We are aided in our journeys of transformation when we open to mystery, an intangible experience or force that we cannot predict, measure, or explain. The mystery I am speaking of is not like those Agatha Christie novels you might enjoy reading on a summer's beach. It is not about adding up the clues like the hero detective does and then declaring that the butler did it! The encounter with death is pervaded with mystery. It cannot be solved or even fully known by the conceptual mind. It cannot be captured, but, as when we listen to an extraordinary piece of music, we can give ourselves over to mystery completely. We don't just observe mystery; we realize that we *are* mystery. It lives through us.

In my experience and that of so many people I have accompanied, the encounter with mystery is often marked by awe and wonder, as when our jaws drop open at the sight of unimaginable beauty. The usual activity of the mind stops and our consciousness rests. We become absorbed in tranquility and humbly bear witness. In such moments, time no longer devours our lives. We enter the eternal now. The future doesn't exist; it hasn't happened yet. The past doesn't exist; it has already happened. Here in the place beyond the tyranny of time, there is no fear of death. And whenever there is an absence of fear, there is also a presence of love. Love is the lubricant that lets us slip out of the boundaries of the body. Love is the longing that calls us home.

In life-transforming moments such as dying, giving birth, meditating, making love, being immersed in the beauty of nature, connecting with a great work of art, or falling into the eyes of an infant, we have a sense of looking into the vast unnamable. Here, it feels utterly safe. There is no deficiency. Everything we need is present. Each taste of this experience expands our love and draws us further toward the endless, inexhaustible mystery of being.

The contemplation of life, death, and the inherent mystery in each moment is too important to be left to our final hours. Coming to terms with our fears and discovering what dying has to teach us about life are essential to our transformation. These Five Invitations are a call to that transformation. They can take you to the threshold, but it is up to you to walk on. As Rumi wrote, "The door is round and open. Don't go back to sleep."

Every wisdom tradition offers a path to harnessing the transformative power of death. Pick a path and start walking, or wander off the marked trails. There is no one right way. Ultimately, all paths lead to an open field. They ask us to release our holding on to habits of mind and preconceived notions, to meet life in a fresh and curious way. As a teacher once asked me, "Can you let go of your history and step into the mystery?"

In Buddhism, the reflection on death is an essential spiritual practice. It is not seen as an ideology to be adopted as a protection against death. Rather, it is an opportunity to become more intimate with death as an inevitable part of life. While such reflections may seem morbid to some, I have found the practice of cultivating a wise openness to death to be life affirming. The value of these reflections is that we see how our ideas and beliefs about death are affecting us *right here, right now.*

. . .

Sono lived alone, on the edge, surviving on a meager Social Security check. Now she was living out her final days at the Zen Hospice Project. She was a straightforward, no-nonsense woman, and I remember asking Sono a few days after her arrival how she thought it might be living there. She said, "I think it's going to be all right because in this place, I can die the way I need to die."

It was clear that Sono had come to us to face death directly. I knew we would get along well.

One day, we were sitting at the kitchen table together. Sono was writing in her journal, and I was reading the book *Japanese Death Poems*. There's an old tradition in Japan of Zen monks and others writing short verses in preparation for death. Myth suggests that these poems, composed on the day of one's death, express an essential truth discovered in one's life. In general, they are short, intense poems, sometimes profound, sometimes satirical, often expressing an immediate beauty and natural simplicity. They remind us that we are most alive when we are present at the edge of the unknown.

Sono asked me to read her a few. I chose some of my favorites.

This powerful one is attributed to the founder of the Soto Zen School in Japan, Dogen Zenji, who died in 1253.

> *Four and fifty years*
> *I've hung the sky with stars.*
> *Now I leap through—*
> *What shattering!*

Another entertaining poem, by Moriya Sen'an, who died in 1838, speculates on the afterlife.

Bury me when I die
beneath a wine barrel
in a tavern.
With luck
the cask will leak.

An unflinching poem by Sunao, who died in 1926, expresses the sometimes harsh reality of dying.

Spitting blood
clears up reality
and dream alike.

And Kozan Ichikyo, who died in 1360, offered this poem of elegant simplicity.

Empty-handed I entered the world,
Barefoot I leave it.
My coming, my going—
Two simple happenings
That got entangled.

After hearing these death poems read to her aloud, Sono became inspired to write her own. She asked me about form and length. I suggested that she not concern herself with such matters. I invited her to simply write what she believed to be true.

Sometime later, Sono called me to her room. "I've written my death poem," she announced.

"I would love to hear it," I responded.

"I want you to learn it by heart," she instructed. And then she went on to say, "When I die, I want you to pin it to my clothes. I want to be cremated with my poem."

"I promise, Sono," I said, my tears expressing the honor I felt in being given this gift.

Sono's poem was an invitation to be open-minded and openhearted, even in relationship to the great unknown of death. She read it to me several times. Then she had me recite it over and over, to be certain I had learned every word.

That is where it has lived ever since, in my heart. I've never written it down until today. I share it as a beautiful reminder of what is possible when we live fully in the light of death. Sono found her way. It is up to each of us to find ours.

SONO'S DEATH POEM

Don't just stand there with your hair turning gray,
soon enough the seas will sink your little island.
So while there is still the illusion of time,
set out for another shore.
No sense packing a bag.
You won't be able to lift it into your boat.
Give away all your collections.
Take only new seeds and an old stick.
Send out some prayers on the wind before you sail.
Don't be afraid.
Someone knows you're coming.
An extra fish has been salted.

—MONA (SONO) SANTACROCE (1928–1995)

ACKNOWLEDGMENTS

I bow in gratitude to the many visible and invisible beings and forces that have shaped my life and this book.

I bow to my beautiful bride, Vanda Marlow, as I did on our wedding day. You have been endlessly visible in your support and encouragement. This book is in print because of your fifteen years of love and persistence. My apologies for being so absent while writing and not writing. As I promised, I will always come back. Love you beyond words.

Thank you to my loving family, who has given and given up so much to encourage my being of service in the world. Gabe and Carin, your love inspires me daily. I leaned into your faith in the writing. Your giving birth to Nico, the embodiment of love, as I wrote about death, reminded me of the preciousness of life. My sweet daughter, Gina, passionate heart, the look in your eyes when I read you passages moved me to keep writing. Ours is a reliable love that you can always count on. My brother Mark, I am in awe of the way you embrace the challenges of illness with such grace. Vickie, my former wife, thank you for bringing Dominic, Nicolas, and Gina into my life and for the joy of raising our kids together.

Your love and selfless support during those early hospice days allowed me to give myself fully to those who were dying and my heart's call to service.

Rachel Naomi Remen, M.D., my soul friend of thirty years, thank you for writing the inspiring, insightful, and poetic foreword that is so central to this book, and for living wholeheartedly in the mystery.

MeiMei Fox has been my collaborator and the champion of my words in the writing and editing of this book. Thank you, dear friend, for midwifing this book from conception to birth. It took longer than either of us anticipated. Thanks for keeping the faith, for chiseling away the unnecessary and shining a light on the essential.

Deep thanks to the friends who engaged me in courageous conversations, read numerous unedited drafts, gave honest feedback, and held up a mirror to my best self. This book would have been a mess without the help of Barry Boyce, Jessica Britt, Susan Kennedy, Sharda Rogell, and Ange Stephens.

Big thanks to the whole team at Flatiron Books, especially to Bob Miller, president and publisher, who saw this book before it was written and patiently waited for its arrival. To Whitney Frick, executive editor, for the judicious use of your red pencil and for seeing the love in this book. And to Laura Yorke, my literary agent, who instinctively saw this book's potential and advocated with enthusiasm for its publication. Thanks also to Hugh Delehanty, whose early interviews evoked my stories and helped shape my intention for the book.

I've been inspired by many spiritual friends and teachers whose words have entered my heart and whose wisdom and compassion I have borrowed and at times paraphrased on these pages. Please forgive my errors and accept my thanks for your guidance. Special thanks to Hameed Ali, Ram Dass, Norman Zoketsu Fischer, Karen Johnson, Jack Kornfield, Elisabeth Kübler-Ross, Stephen Levine, Kathleen Dowling Singh, Brother David Steindl-Rast, and Shunryu Suzuki Roshi.

Thank you to the core faculty of the Metta Institute, my playgroup, whose friendship, conversations, and wisdom have been a deep well of inspiration. Ours has been a legacy project made of love. Bows to my co-teacher, kind and patient friend Ange Stephens and to the pioneering spirits of Angeles Arrien, Ram Dass, Norman Zoketsu Fischer, Charlie Garfield, Rabbi Alan Lew, Rachel Naomi Remen, M.D., and Frances Vaughan. A special thanks to Patty Winter for embodying selfless service, to Gregg Ruskusky for being a mountain of kindness, and to Suzanne Retzinger for assembling my talks with heart and hopefulness.

My dharma sister, Martha deBarros, gave birth to Zen Hospice Project. As co-founders, we worked side by side creating what Martha called "a peaceful revolution whose battle cry is as quiet and profound as two strangers holding hands before death." Thanks also to the thousand volunteers we trained at Zen Hospice Project. You were always the heart of the work.

Thank you to the many individuals who have participated in my retreats and seminars and studied with me over these past thirty years. Your trust and insights have informed me and made me a better student and teacher.

Thank you to those who gave me the permission to share your names and stories, and to the others whose names and details I have changed to protect their privacy. You all know who you are.

A bow of deep respect to the many individuals who invited me to walk with them through their loss and grief. And finally, to those who graciously allowed me to accompany them in their dying process, to the vulnerable crossroads of life and death. You are my true teachers.

AUTHOR RESOURCES

Frank Ostaseski has dedicated his life to service and introduced thousands to mindful and compassionate end-of-life care. He is a Buddhist teacher, founder of the Metta Institute, and cofounder of the Zen Hospice Project, the first Buddhist hospice in the United States. He teaches internationally, serves as a consultant to leading health-care organizations, and is a frequent speaker at conferences from Wisdom 2.0 to the American Academy of Hospice and Palliative Medicine. He has been featured on *The Oprah Winfrey Show,* Bill Moyers's groundbreaking TV series *On Our Own Terms,* and has been a guest lecturer at Harvard Medical School, the Mayo Clinic, and Heidelberg University, and a teacher at major spiritual centers around the globe.

Frank wants to support you in integrating the Five Invitations into your life and invites you to continue the exploration. To connect directly with Frank and learn more about his speaking engagements, retreats, and online programs, and to download free audio recordings and additional resources visit www.fiveinvitations.com.

NOTES

ix   *fly in silence*: Mark Nepo, *The Book of Awakening* (San Francisco: Conari Press, 2011), https://books.google.com/books?id=YvVJGfCD7UAC&pg=PA155&lpg=PA155#v=onepage&q&f=false.

1   *passed on unopened*: "Rainer Maria Rilke: Love and death are the great gifts that are given to us; mostly they are passed on unopened," Quoteur.com, http://quoteur.com/love-and-death-are-the-great-gifts-that-are-given-to-us-mostly-they-are-passed-on-unopened/.

3   *love, more possible*: Rollo May, *Love and Will* (New York: Dell, 1969), 98.

8   *diagnosed with HIV*: *HIV/AIDS Epidemiology Annual Report 2009* (San Francisco: San Francisco Department of Public Health, 2009).

10   *die at home*: John Cloud, "A Kinder, Gentler Death," *Time*, September 18, 2000, http://content.time.com/time/magazine/article/0,9171,997968,00.html.

10   *long-term-care facility*: "Worktable 309: Deaths by Place of Death, Age, Race, and Sex: United States, 2005," Centers for Disease Control, http://www.cdc.gov/nchs/data/dvs/Mortfinal2005_worktable_309.pdf.

15   *absolutely everything, counts*: Sogyal Rinpoche, *The Tibetan Book of Days* (Canada: HarperCollins, 1996).

16   *true moment after moment*: Jack Kornfield, *A Path with Heart* (New York: Bantam, 1993), 138.

17   *all is metamorphosis*: "Henry Miller on Art, War, and the Future of Humanity," Maria Popova, Brain Pickings, November 7, 2012, https://www.brainpickings.org/2012/11/07/henry-miller-of-art-and-the-future/.

18   *tonight in Samarra*: W. Somerset Maugham, *Sheppey* (London: W. Heinemann, 1933), 112.

20   *same river twice*: *Cratylus*, Plato, Internet Classics Archive, http://classics.mit.edu/Plato/cratylus.html.

21   *her with love and compassion*: "Creation and Destruction of Sand Mandalas," Dark Roasted Blend, February 2014, http://www.darkroastedblend.com/2014/02/creation-and-destruction-of-sand.html.

25   *a liberating opportunity*: "Living and Dying: A Buddhist Perspective," Carol Hyman, Dharma Haven, July 31, 2016, http://www.dharma-haven.org/tibetan/mom.htm.

27   *your own disappearance*: "David Whyte—On Belonging," Coach's Corner, http://coaching counsel.com/awareness/david-whyte-%E2%80%93-on-belonging/.

30   *Lucky me, lucky mud*: Kurt Vonnegut, *Cat's Cradle* (New York: Dial Press, 1963).

31   *entering the river*: Mark Nepo, *The Book of Awakening* (San Francisco: Conari Press, 2000), 175.

32   *only the dance*: T. S. Eliot, *Four Quartets* (New York: Houghton Mifflin, 1943), 3.

38   *when we exhale*: Shunryu Suzuki Roshi, *Zen Mind, Beginner's Mind* (Boston: Shambhala, 1987), 29.

41   *being moment after moment*: Shunryu Suzuki Roshi, San Francisco Zen Center transcriptions of dharma talks, March 23, 1967, http://suzukiroshi.sfzc.org/dharma-talks /tag/time/.

43   *to be surprised*: Russell Stannard, *Why?* (New York: Lion Hudson, 2003), 115.

44   *all of the darkness*: Deborah Solomon, "The Priest," *New York Times Magazine*, March 4, 2010, http://www.nytimes.com/2010/03/07/magazine/07fob-q4-t.html.

44   *orientation of the spirit*: "Hope: An Orientation of the Heart," Volunteacher, January 26, 2010, https://thevolunteacher.wordpress.com/2010/01/26/hope/.

46   *wisdom and objectivity*: Angeles Arrien, *The Four-Fold Way* (San Francisco: Harper San Francisco, 1993).

56   *a constant attitude*: "Quote by Martin Luther King Jr.," Goodreads, http://www .goodreads.com/quotes/57037-forgiveness-is-not-an-occasional-act-it-is-a-constant.

58   *healing to begin*: Rachel Naomi Remen, *Kitchen Table Wisdom* (New York: Riverhead, 1996).

65   *ancient and eternal law*: Dhammapada, verse 5.

73   *see the moon*: Lucien Stryk and Takashi Ikemoto, ed. and trans., *Zen Poetry* (New York: Grove Press, 1995).

77   *I can change*: Carl Rogers, *On Becoming a Person* (New York: Houghton Mifflin, 1961), 17.

80   *being petty, finicky*: Chogyam Trungpa, *The Collected Works of Chogyam Trungpa*, vol. 5 (Boston: Shambhala, 2004), 20.

86   *longer than I realized*: Henri Nouwen, *The Return of the Prodigal Son* (New York: Doubleday, 1994), 14.

96   *death as we get older*: "Heroes or Role Models," Dr. Laura Blog, August 11, 2011, http:// www.drlaura.com/b/Heroes-or-Role-Models/10003.html.

96   *it is precious*: "Freud and Buddha," Mark Epstein, Network of Spiritual Progressives, http://spiritualprogressives.org/newsite/?p=651.

97   *power to heal*: Carl Jung, *The Collected Works of C.G. Jung, Volume 16: The Practice of Psychotherapy*, trans. R. F. C. Hull (Princeton: Princeton University Press, 1966), 116.

99   *homosexuality and child molestation*: "Facts About Homosexuality and Child Molestation," UC–Davis, http://facultysites.dss.ucdavis.edu/~gmherek/rainbow/html/facts _molestation.html.

103 *ends with love*: "Tsoknyi Rinpoche quote: Life begins with love, is maintained with love, and ends . . . ," AZQuotes, http://www.azquotes.com/quote/1141464.

103 *thing its loveliness*: Galway Kinnell, "Saint Francis and the Sow," *New Selected Poems* (New York: Houghton Mifflin, 2000), 94.

104 *love discover us*: John O'Donohue, *Anam Cara: A Book of Celtic Wisdom* (New York: HarperCollins, 1998), 11.

115 *No part left out*: Ono no Komachi and Izumi Shikibu, *The Ink Dark Moon*, trans. Jane Hirshfield (New York: Vintage, 1990).

117 *peanuts for the monkeys*: Dorothy Salisbury Davis, *A Gentle Murderer* (New York: Open Road, 1951).

128 *work of the soul*: Rachel Naomi Remen, "Helping, Fixing, or Serving?," *Shambhala Sun*, September 1999.

132 *love them enough*: Glenn Clark, *The Man Who Talks with Flowers* (New York: Start Publishing, 2012).

134 *their inner voice*: "Peggy O'Mara Quotes (Author of Natural Family Living)," Goodreads, https://www.goodreads.com/author/quotes/30657.Peggy_O_Mara.

143 *aggression toward yourself*: Pema Chödrön, *The Wisdom of No Escape* (Boston: Shambhala, 1991), 17.

143 *dealing with basic anxiety*: Karen Horney, *Our Inner Conflicts* (New York: W. W. Norton, 1945).

144 *who you really are*: Matthew Burgess, *Enormous Smallness: A Story of E. E. Cummings* (New York: Enchanted Lion Books, 2015).

149 *must endure burning*: Viktor Frankl, *Man's Search for Meaning* (Boston: Beacon Press, 1959).

151 *space to be itself*: A. H. Almaas, *The Unfolding Now* (Boston: Shambhala, 2008), 36.

156 *much like fear*: C. S. Lewis, *A Grief Observed* (New York: HarperOne, 1961).

166 *be happy, practice compassion*: His Holiness the Dalai Lama and Howard Cutler, *The Art of Happiness* (New York: Riverhead, 1998).

169 *makes sense anymore*: Naomi Shihab Nye, "Kindness, in Words," *Words Under the Words: Selected Poems* (Portland, OR: Far Corner Books, 1995).

170 *of love and compassion*: His Holiness the Dalai Lama, *Ethics for the New Millennium* (New York: Riverhead, 1991).

171 *when they wish*: Carl Rogers, *A Way of Being* (New York: Houghton Mifflin, 1980).

174 *person we think we are*: "Bernie Glassman Dharma Talk: Bearing Witness," Bernie Glassman, Zen Peacemaker Order, 1996, http://zenpeacemakers.org/who-we-are/zen-peacemakers-sangha/dharma-talks/bernie-bearing-witness/.

176 *only* apparently different: Norman Fischer, *Training in Compassion: Zen Teachings on the Practice of Lojong* (Boulder, CO: Shambahala, 2013), 12.

179 *else in the Universe*: John Muir, *My First Summer in the Sierra* (Boston: Houghton Mifflin, 1911), 110.

181 *we love to be*: David Whyte, *Consolations* (Langley, WA: Many Rivers Press, 2015).

183 *ocean of samsara*: "Natural Great Peace," Sogyal Rinpoche, Rigpa.org, https://www.rigpa.org/index.php/en/teachings/extracts-of-articles-and-publications/242-natural-great-peace.html.

184 *the moment following*: Anthony J. Parel, *Gandhi, Freedom, and Self-Rule* (Lanham, MD: Lexington Books, 2000), 59.

184 *access to their phones*: Marissa Lang, "Smartphone Overuse Is Someone Else's Problem, Study Finds," *SF Gate*, June 22, 2016, http://www.sfgate.com/business/article/Smartphone-overuse-is-someone-else-s-problem-8316381.php.

186 *land around us*: Angeles Arrien, *The Second Half of Life: Opening the Eight Gates of Wisdom* (Boulder, CO: Sounds True, 2007), 140–1.

194 *quietly in his room*: Blaise Pascal, *Human Happiness*, trans. A. J. Krailsheimer (London: Penguin, 1966), 136.

199 *end is my beginning*: Eliot, *Four Quartets*.

202 *brand-new human's nostrils*: Gen. 1:3 (International Standard Version).

203 *make us homeless*: John O'Donohue, *Eternal Echoes* (New York: Cliff Street Books, 1999), 3.

204 *rested from all work*: Gen. 2:3 (International Standard Version).

209 *made peace with it*: "Human Nature, Buddha Nature," Tina Fossella, John Welwood's website, http://www.johnwelwood.com/articles/TRIC_interview_uncut.pdf.

210 *way to control him*: Shunryu Suzuki Roshi, *Zen Mind, Beginner's Mind* (Boulder, CO: Weatherhill Publishing 1991), 31.

211   *pain and loss*: "Quotes from Dharma Talks," Darlene Cohen, http://darlenecohen.net
      /quotes.html.

212   *the same name*: Jack Kornfield, *After the Ecstasy, the Laundry* (New York: Bantam Books,
      2000).

213   *heart crosses it*: Jack Kornfield, *The Wise Heart* (New York: Bantam Dell, 2008), 147.

214   *doesn't make any sense*: Czeslaw Milosz, ed., *A Book of Luminous Things* (Orlando: Harcourt,
      1996), 276.

214   *between the notes*: Léon Vallas, *Claude Debussy: His Life and Works* (London: Oxford Uni-
      versity Press, 1933), 551.

215   *no longer afraid*: Audre Lorde Quotes, quotehd.com

217   *disarm all hostility*: Henry Wadsworth Longfellow, *The Works of Henry Wadsworth
      Longfellow*, vol. 7 (Boston: Houghton, Mifflin, 1885), 405.

226   *they're my own*: "'Hero' Teacher Stopped Shooting with Hug," ABC News, March 16,
      2006, http://abcnews.go.com/GMA/story?id=1732518&page=1.

229   *over for tea*: "Ram Dass Quotes," Ram Dass's website, April 2, 2015, https://www.ramdass
      .org/ram-dass-quotes/.

230   *environment as untrustworthy*: D. W. Winnicott, *The Child, the Family, and the Outside
      World* (New York: Penguin, 1964).

231   *the entire world*: Danya Ruttenberg, *Nurture the Wow* (New York: Flatiron Books, 2016), 254.

233   *it is not open*: "Lord Thomas Dewar Quotes," Quotes.net, http://www.quotes.net/authors
      /Lord Thomas Dewar.

234   *there are few*: Shunryu Suzuki Roshi, *Zen Mind, Beginner's Mind* (Boston: Shambhala,
      1987), 12.

237   *there are no phones*: Billy Collins, "Forgetfulness," *Questions About Angels* (Pittsburgh:
      University of Pittsburgh Press, 1999).

243   *becomes totally false*: Maria Paul, "Your Memory Is Like the Telephone Game," North-
      western University, September 19, 2012, http://www.northwestern.edu/newscenter
      /stories/2012/09/your-memory-is-like-the-telephone-game.html.

249   *Alzheimer's into freedom*: Kornfield, *The Wise Heart*, 181–2.

251   *my life flows*: Dasarath Davidson, *Freedom Dreams* (San Diego: Book Tree, 2003), 78.

259   *to fabricate form*: "Dancing with Form and Emptiness in Intimate Relationship," Jennifer
      Welwood, jenniferwelwood.com/wp-content/jw-assets/DacingWithFormAndEmptiness1
      .pdf.

259   *That is all*: Larry Rosenberg, *Breath by Breath* (Boston: Shambhala, 1998), 18.

263   *you do is sacred*: Hafiz, *The Gift*, trans. Daniel Ladinsky (New York: Penguin Compass,
      1999), 161.

265   *we are in it, too*: Thich Nhat Hanh, "The Fullness of Emptiness," *Lion's Roar*, August 6,
      2012.

266   *did not know it*: Gen. 28:16 (International Standard Version).

268   *dimensions in dying*: George H. Gallup International Institute, "Spiritual Beliefs and the
      Dying Process: A Report on a National Survey," conducted for the Nathan Cummings
      Foundation and the Fetzer Institute, 1997.

269   *suffering without meaning*: Frankl, *Man's Search for Meaning*, 135.

271   *the great silence*: Antonio Machado, *Times Alone*, trans. Robert Bly (Middletown, CT:
      Wesleyan University Press, 1983), 14.

277   *back to sleep*: John Moyne and Coleman Barks, *Open Secret* (Boston: Shambhala, 1999).

280   *book* Japanese Death Poems: Yoel Hoffman, comp., *Japanese Death Poems* (Tokyo: Tuttle,
      1986).